DISMAL FREEDOM

DISMAL FREEDOM

A History of the Maroons
of the Great Dismal Swamp

J. Brent Morris

All The best !

Brent Morris

2·2023

THE UNIVERSITY OF NORTH CAROLINA PRESS

CHAPEL HILL

*This book was published with the assistance of the
Z. Smith Reynolds Fund of the University of North Carolina Press.*

Manufactured in the United States of America
Designed by April Leidig
Set in Caslon by Copperline Book Services, Inc.

The University of North Carolina Press has been a
member of the Green Press Initiative since 2003.

Cover illustration: Detail of Thomas Moran (American, 1837–1926),
Slave Hunt, Dismal Swamp, Virginia, 1861–62. Oil on canvas, 34 × 44 in.
Philbrook Museum of Art, Tulsa, Oklahoma. Gift of Laura A. Clubb, 1947.8.44.

Library of Congress Cataloging-in-Publication Data
Names: Morris, J. Brent, author.
Title: Dismal freedom : a history of the maroons of the
Great Dismal Swamp / J. Brent Morris.
Description: Chapel Hill : The University of North Carolina Press, [2022] |
Includes bibliographical references and index.
Identifiers: LCCN 2021054810 | ISBN 9781469668253 (cloth) |
ISBN 9781469668260 (ebook)
Subjects: LCSH: Maroons—Dismal Swamp (N.C. and Va.)—History. | Fugitive
slaves—Dismal Swamp (N.C. and Va.)—History. | Fugitive slave communities—
Dismal Swamp (N.C. and Va.)—History. | Free blacks—Dismal Swamp
(N.C. and Va.)—History. | Dismal Swamp (N.C. and Va.)—History.
Classification: LCC E450 .M775 2022 | DDC 975.5/523—dc23/eng/20211116
LC record available at https://lccn.loc.gov/2021054810

David Eagleman writes in his book *Sum* of what he calls the three deaths: "The first is when the body ceases to function. The second is when the body is consigned to the grave. The third is that moment, sometime in the future, when your name is spoken for the last time." *Dismal Freedom* is dedicated to the people whose names I have been able to recover who I reasonably believe marooned in the Great Dismal Swamp at some point in their lives. For most of them, the last mention of their name was in unfavorable newspaper coverage, "runaway" ads, or the like. Let their names be resurrected to live on in these pages alongside the stories of their brave, remarkable lives:

Aaron, Abraham Lester, Abraham Turner, Abram, Adeline Wiggins, Angola Peter, Auger, Benjamin Randolph, Bev, "Big Charles," Bob, Bob Ferebee, Bob Garry, Bob Ricks, Bonaparte, Bristol, Caesar, Charlie, Cox, Daniel, Daniel Carr, Dave, David, Davy, Dick, Dilworth (General Jackson), Diver, Drew, Edward Lewis, Eli, Elisha, Emmett Ruffin, Frank, "The General," "General Peter," George, George Dismal, George Langdon, George Upshur, Harry, Harry Grimes, Jack, Jack Dismal, Jack Stump, Jacob, Jerry, Jesse, Jim, Jim Hinton, Joe, John, John Hall, John Nichols, John Salley, Joseph Harris, King Brown, Larinda White, Lawrence, Lemon Shaw, Lewis, "Little Isaac," Lucy Wiggins, Mills, Mingo, Moses, Nancy Dismal, Ned Downs, "Old London," "Old Will," Osman, Paul Wiggins, Pompey, Pompey Little, Prince, "Runaway Jim," Salvadore, Sam, Scipio, Simon, Spence, Stephen, Suck, Sukey Dismal, Tobey Fisher, Tom, Tom Copper, Tom Shaw, Toney, Tony, Tony Nelson, Venus Dismal, Washington, Will, William Kinnegy, and Willis

CONTENTS

ILLUSTRATIONS

DISMAL FREEDOM

INTRODUCTION

"History," says Thierry, "has not understood these outlaws; it has passed
them over in silence, or else, adopting the legal acts of the time, it has branded
them with names which deprive them of all interest—such as 'rebels,' 'robbers,'
'banditti.' But let us not," continues the historian, "be misled by these odious titles;
in all countries, subjugated by foreigners, they have been given by the victors
to the brave men who took refuge in the mountains and forests, abandoning
the towns and cities to such as were content to live in slavery."
Such were our refugees in the Dismal Swamp.
—Augustine David Crake, *The Rival Heirs*, 1882

ABOLITIONIST EDMUND JACKSON was a busy antebellum investi-
gative journalist. He endeavored to lay bare the brutality of slavery,
and his extensive travels undercover in the South, his many essays
published in Boston's *The Liberty Bell*, and his close interactions
with self-emancipated people who had reached freedom in the North established him as somewhat of an authority on the South's "peculiar institution."[1]
Jackson was fascinated by the clear and undeniable evidence that, contrary to
enslavers' loud assertions, enslaved people were not content in their bondage
and frequently resisted their enslavers through means up to and including
escape and outright revolt. By 1852, he seems to have concluded that the legendary maroons of the Great Dismal Swamp perfectly paired "exodus" and
"insurrection," and therefore were of enormous symbolic importance in the
fight to end American slavery. Notebook in hand, he headed south to Virginia
on a fact-finding expedition.

The full details of the maroons' circumstances, however, eluded his discovery. The swamp, he came to understand, was "a city of refuge in the midst of
Slavery" and was home to "a large colony of negroes, who originally obtained
their freedom by the grace of God, and their own determined energy." Beyond
that, he could ascertain little else. "How long this colony has existed," he admitted, "what is its amount of population, what portion of the colonists are
now Fugitives, and what the descendants of Fugitives, are questions not easily
determined." Many of the inhabitants he understood had lived their entire
lives without seeing people or places outside of the swamp's depths. Many

formerly enslaved maroons would die in the Dismal after a long and full life of freedom in the swamp.[2]

Reliable knowledge of the Great Dismal Swamp and its maroon inhabitants was nearly impossible to come by for outsiders. Four years after Jackson wrote about the swamp, journalist David Hunter Strother went on assignment to the Dismal for *Harper's New Monthly Magazine* with the specific hope of catching a glimpse of one of these legendary "fugitives." When he did stumble upon a fierce-looking and legendary maroon leader named Osman, Strother's curiosities were quickly replaced by the terror of being himself discovered by the well-armed and notorious "protector of fugitive slaves."[3] Seconds seemed like an eternity, and the journalist could only shake off his paralysis once the "sable outlaw" had disappeared back into the swamp. All Strother took away from his experience was adrenaline and the image of Osman seared into his memory, from which he made a quick sketch afterward. He could not extract more intelligence than this maroon's first name from two enslaved men back at his camp, who both clearly knew much more than they let on but seemed terrified to have given away even that bit of information.[4]

For the swamp's inhabitants, secrecy was the point. Maroons—self-emancipators from enslavement who formed independent communities—set out to remain undetected, out of sight, and concealed as much as possible, and were remarkably successful in this goal. Their friends, families, and acquaintances outside the swamp—some free, most still enslaved—seldom gave up the secrets of the swamp either. Their fidelity was fervent, and they understood that its maintenance was a matter of life and death.

The immense swamp, too, guarded their secrets. The Dismal extends north and south fifty miles inland from the Atlantic on both sides of the Virginia–North Carolina border. Its area is about 1,000 square miles, the size of Rhode Island. Before drainage of swampland began in the nineteenth century, the area was at least double that, nearer the size of Delaware at 2,000 square miles, stretching from the James River to the north and the Albemarle Sound to the south. As colonial maps of the Virginia and North Carolina Tidewater region filled up from the early seventeenth century with detailed place-names, villages, towns, cities, and roads, the Dismal Swamp—or "Desert," as it was sometimes called—remained an enormous dark and daunting blank space.

Few whites of the colonial and antebellum plantation country had any reason to approach the Dismal Swamp or pay much attention to its existence, other than the fact that it served as a magnet for their enslaved people. "In relation to human purposes," a journalist wrote in 1805, "this singular swamp justly deserves the expressive name commonly given to it, that of wilderness or *dismal*, no condition of the earth's surface being more wild and irreclaimable than this."[5] The swamp has always been a tangled and snarled labyrinth of mystification to any stranger who enters: deep stagnant pools of dark water; higher ridges and mesic islands; slow flowing waterways; towering white pine, cypress, juniper and gum trees; cane briars; bushes; vines; and reeds so thick "you cannot thrust your arm through them." "They spring up as thick together as the fingers upon your hand," one nineteenth-century visitor complained, "and the briers entangle your feet and wind around your legs so that you cannot extricate yourself, and can only struggle furiously and tie yourself tighter, until you give up the undertaking in despair."[6] Fallen trees and other dead plants decay very slowly in the water of the Dismal Swamp, and thus the natural obstacles to movement multiply with time. Danger is ever-present: dry patches of land suddenly end at quagmires held up only by the matted roots of plants that look no different from the solid land they adjoin. Thick mud abounds from which it is quite difficult to extricate oneself. This is not to mention the wildlife: clouds of bloodthirsty insects, black bears, alligators, several varieties of poisonous snakes, feral cattle and hogs, and the occasional wolf roamed both bogs and dry patches throughout.

Overcoming and escaping the swamp is almost as much of a challenge today as it was in the years of the early republic. George Washington and a company of fellow speculators sank fortunes into trying (unsuccessfully) to tame the Great Dismal Swamp in the eighteenth century. Modern Navy Seals and Blackwater mercenaries approach the Great Dismal with more realism; often dropped in by parachute as part of their training, they must demonstrate superior survivalist skills to find their way out. But historically an even harder test has been finding one's way *in*.

Yet during the era of slavery, for those who slaved on labor camps, refuge beckoned within the swamp's depths. The dangers of the Dismal may hardly seem like an appealing setting to build a life, but the worst day of Dismal freedom was better than the best day in chains. The maroons of the Great Dismal Swamp—Osman in Strother's essay; the families of men, women, and children described in Jackson's narrative; and other self-emancipators whose unfettered lives unnerved and confounded whites in the surrounding region—were people who had escaped their wretched enslavement and settled into new lives of freedom in a wilderness landscape deemed worthless and inaccessible by whites.

Marronage occurred to some degree whenever and wherever slavery existed in the Western hemisphere. Originally, the term referred to escaped cattle on colonial Hispaniola—these *cimarrones* bolted into the wilderness and went feral. By the 1540s, the term was also being applied to self-emancipating human chattel, who escaped their enslavement and "reverted" to a wild state. The English became aware of the usage in the 1570s through Sir Francis Drake's Panama raids when he aligned with *Symerons* against the Spanish. "Maroon" first entered English print in early seventeenth-century accounts of Drake's campaigns.[7] Even while the nomenclature was developing, maroon communities were forming in sixteenth-century Spanish colonies in the Caribbean and Central America, and spreading through eastern South America, the rest of the Caribbean, and the southern parts of North America. Enslaved men, women, and children were emancipating themselves and establishing resistant communities where they achieved freedom beyond the reach of their former enslavers. Historian Marcus Nevius is right to call marronage "the most pervasive form of fugitive slave community formation, negotiation, and enslaver accommodation in the history of the Atlantic world."[8] It was also one of the most dynamic and impactful ways enslaved people resisted their bondage.

Though ever-present in the Americas, marronage varied significantly over time and space. Different scholars define marronage in different ways. Some follow the nomenclature of contemporary laws and categorized maroons based on the length of time a person stayed away from the slave labor camp — short-term (*petit*) and long-term (*grand*) marronage.[9] Anthropologist Richard Price describes petit marronage as more of a constant nuisance than a direct threat to the slave system: he cites French enslavers who called marronage the "gangrene" of colonial society.[10] Esteban Deive argues that only grand marronage is worthy of serious study, as it is the only manifestation of a true class struggle.[11] Some scholars only consider an enslaved person a maroon if she or he intended to remain away permanently.[12] Others, including historian James Spady, argue that marronage could even be part of a *mindset* of those who did not or had not yet actually self-emancipated. "Psychic marronage" created spaces for resistant talk and support for those who had escaped — it encompassed "a decision to withdraw cooperation with the slavers' demand that they accept domination meekly and obediently."[13] Alvin Thompson considers "individual marronage" and "collective marronage" to be broad categories of analysis.[14] Political scientist Neil Roberts proposes two novel categories of marronage: "sovereign marronage," when self-emancipating people comprise a revolutionary force that overthrows the existing political order and establishes state sovereignty, and "sociogenic marronage," marronage that transforms the very basis of the social order.[15]

American University archaeologist Daniel Sayers employs a nuanced "structural architecture" of maroon communities. In his work, maroons are categorized as "intralimital" (marronage within the geographical and structural limits of the capitalistic enslavement mode of production, or CEMP) and "extralimital" (marronage to areas beyond the limits of the CEMP). In addition, Sayers recognizes at least three diasporic "modes of communitization" in his scholarship on North American maroons: perimetrical semi-independent (marronage at the edges of a wilderness area), interior scission (exilic people who permanently removed themselves from the outside world), and labor exploitation (marronage connected in some way with slave-industrial operations).[16]

Historian Sylviane Diouf privileges geography in her analysis of marronage. She argues that, in considering the North American variety, the distinction between petit and grand marronage is less useful than thinking of maroons in terms of their proximity to slave labor camps. Thus her analysis differentiates between what she terms "borderland maroons" (those who settled on the periphery of slave labor camps) and "hinterland maroons" (those who settled in more inaccessible, isolated areas away from whites). Diouf asks readers to consider the concept of a "maroon landscape," "a space of movement, independence, and reinvention where new types of lives were created and evolved."[17]

Because their experiences were so diverse, the maroons of the Dismal Swamp defy easy classification. Though they were often intralimital, some transitioned to extralimital if they left the swamp and continued on their freedom journey to a free state or Canada. They could be described both as "hinterland" and "borderland," include instances of both petit and grand marronage, and frustrate efforts to pinpoint their community size, length of residence away from the slave labor camp, motivation, geography, or desired ends.

To accommodate the diversity of those who sought freedom in the Dismal Swamp, we must instead see their marronage as encompassing the *entire* process of self-emancipation. It extends through the whole of their "fugitive" experiences, from the first acts of escape from bondage throughout their self-earned, extralegal freedom, whether that entails a permanent settlement as part of a community or more transient life. A maroon, then, is someone who has self-extricated from enslavement, or is born to maroon parents, and lives in defiance of the laws of the enslavers that would limit their freedom. Once we begin to see the act of *marooning* as a verb, then the expansiveness of maroon life comes into focus. A person could maroon for a day or a lifetime, alone or in a village, achieve permanent freedom or be re-enslaved, settle into a quiet life in the wilderness or take up arms against their oppressor, setting their sights on the nearby plantation country for revenge, plunder, or liberation.

A great amount of social history of the past half century has demonstrated the extent to which enslaved people created emotionally, physically, and spiritually fulfilling worlds for themselves in spaces they carved out from slave systems that, it is now understood, were far from "total institutions." Enslaved people could thrive despite their enslavement. "Fugitive slaves" in the North constantly remained subject to recapture and repatriation under the terms of the Fugitive Slave Law through the Civil War and were exposed to arguably more virulent racism than they would have experienced in the South. A vast historiography is dedicated to demonstrating the resilience of self-emancipators in the largely hostile North. It was possible for these groups to prosper and to make the best of their situations on terms they set themselves; few would argue otherwise.

In many ways, maroons of the Great Dismal Swamp were better off even than self-emancipating men and women who reached the North. Indeed, most maroons consciously chose a life in the swamp over attempting to continue north. Freedom was never limited to the so-called free states or Canada, and Dismal freedom was not necessarily a second-best option in escape but a goal in and of itself that in many ways offered greater independence than if one reached a northern "terminus" of the mythologized Underground Railroad.

Outsiders described the swamp as impenetrable and unlivable, but maroons knew otherwise. In the swamp they took control of their own lives and destinies. They married, had children in the swamp, and formed families away from the control (and ownership) of white enslavers, maintained a regular cultural life beyond the supervision of whites, cultivated garden plots and raised livestock, built and lived in permanent and substantial houses and structures, and freely traded goods and services over a territory of thousands of square miles. Some people were born, lived, and died in the swamp without ever knowing another home, and others stayed for years before leaving the swamp following the Civil War. That they did so in less than ideal circumstances and with less flexibility to do exactly as they pleased only places them somewhere on a continuum of freedom and unfreedom in the antebellum South, at any point on which people could thrive relative to their circumstances.

However, only those who knew the routes or were guided could enter and live. It was and is truly a North American jungle, and there is little evidence that people sought to permanently live in the Great Dismal Swamp except those who sought a refuge of some sort, those who found themselves on the wrong side, legally speaking, of the dominant outside society. Almost immediately after the settlement of Virginia in the early seventeenth century, the Great Dismal Swamp attracted large numbers of marginalized, resistant, and often outlawed people. From the seventeenth century into the first months of the Civil War, thousands of maroons escaped to the swamp, where they established permanent communities. There they lived, worked, and died in the midst of the Tidewater Virginia/North Carolina slave society, the largest in North America. These communities facilitated resistance to the outside world run by enslavers and allowed maroons to exercise greater control over their over their own lives, labors, and destinies. The ways these communities functioned varied depending upon when and where a given community formed and what motivations individuals and groups had for marooning. Together, these communities established an extraordinary and historically significant world within the Dismal. Despite the remarkable lives thousands of maroons led in the swamp, their experiences went underrecorded in the documentary record.

This was, of course, by design. Dismal Swamp maroons were highly successful in concealing themselves, but their flight into the swamp, well beyond the gaze or reach of outsiders, has continued to be more successful in hiding them than they ever would have imagined. With no enslavers to catalog their activities beyond the point of their escape, no abolitionists around to describe firsthand the perils of swamp life, and no known internal record keeping or written tradition, the legacy of the maroons has depended on a handful of brief travel accounts, a contemporary observation here and there, a few newspaper stories, the very rare personal testimony of a former resident of the swamp, and a great deal of white paranoia, conjecture, and romanticism. These scant sources have seldom attracted the sustained attention of historians — they only hint at a story intimidating in its silence, mostly undocumented and potentially irretrievable. Herbert Aptheker noted in 1939 that maroons were only recorded in historical documents "when they were accidentally uncovered or when their activities became so obnoxious and dangerous to the slaveocracy that their destruction was felt to be necessary." Moreover, documents seldom even referred to maroons as such, denying them the association with the formidable Caribbean and South American maroons (North American maroons are most often denigrated as "outliers," "runaways," outlaws," "bandits, "fugitives," etc.). The fifty examples of North American marronage that Aptheker was able to compile were captured entirely, then, by luck. One might reasonably assume that those documented instances of marronage were but the tip of the iceberg. To skeptics, however, the documentary silences suggest a very short story without much to tell.[18]

In contrast, a rich literature is devoted to the maroon communities of South America and the Caribbean.[19] The maroons of Jamaica fought wars with colonial authorities and won a treaty of independence. The maroon *quilombo* of Palmares in Brazil numbered in the tens of thousands, persisted for nearly a century, and defeated colonial armies sent to destroy them. These communities, like other similar ones in South and Central America and the Caribbean, thus left significant records (both maroon and colonial), a boon for historians who focus on these groups.

These scholars have benefited most from a growing "fascination" with maroon history.[20] The story of the struggle of men and women of African descent to achieve freedom and maintain human dignity at the risk of great peril is an appealing one. Moreover, the study of hemispheric marronage has established the phenomenon as the very opposite of what whites asserted to be the bedrock of proslavery ideology: the idea that people of African descent were incapable of surviving without the benevolent oversight of whites, that they did not truly desire to be free, that they were, in every way, inferior to whites. Maroons were a weakness in the slave system that could not be hidden, one that directly challenged white authority and white supremacy. Accordingly, South and Central American and Caribbean grand marronage presented military, economic, and ideological threats that often compelled Europeans to action, and in the process, created a rich paper trail.

However, most North American maroon communities were much smaller and did not often interact with the white governing authorities (compared to those to their south), resulting in a dearth of source material. Thus only a few historians have taken up the challenge of uncovering the histories of marronage in the British North American colonies or the United States. Aptheker first acknowledged this history in his 1939 essay "Maroons within the Present Limits of the United States" and an eight-page addendum eight years later, "Additional Data on American Maroons."[21] However, like the brief glimpses of maroon activity he offered in his classic *American Negro Slave Revolts* (1943), these early works simply document some limited activities of maroons and lack any real analysis of their lives. They speak, in limited ways, about the phenomenon of marronage while remaining detached from the maroons themselves.[22]

Most scholars did not follow up on Aptheker's tantalizing leads. Indeed, when the topic of marronage in a North American context is not completely ignored, prominent historians of recent generations often write it off as inconsequential.[23] Eugene Genovese's take on North American marronage is perhaps the most dismissive. In his *From Rebellion to Revolution: Afro-American Slave Revolts in the Making of the Modern World* (1979), Genovese describes maroons (in particular, those of the Great Dismal Swamp) as nothing more than a "nuisance"—timid fugitives "huddled in small units," who should be called maroons "only as a courtesy." In his estimation, North American maroons were nothing more than loose bands of disorganized "desperadoes."[24]

The only thorough general overview of marronage in North America is Diouf's recent *Slavery's Exiles: The Story of the American Maroons* (2014).[25] This book is a welcome addition to a near-nonexistent historiography and examines the lives of maroons across the South from the colonial period through the Civil War. Diouf structures her history upon what she terms "the maroon landscape" that takes specificity of place fully into account in examining marronage. This is also a largely synthetic work, though it does include some fascinating original research. It does not devote more than a single chapter to any one maroon group. Timothy Lockley's documentary reader, *Maroon Communities in South Carolina* (2009),[26] though not a monograph, offers an outstanding and valuable, if brief, historiographic overview of maroon scholarship in the New World, and a fascinating glimpse into the lives of South Carolina maroons. Other historians have produced fine studies of marronage in Spanish North American colonies.[27] Yet although the Great Dismal Swamp and its human population have long held a fascinating place in American mythology, historians have only recently started acknowledging the existence, extent (population), and importance of the Great Dismal Swamp Maroons.[28]

DISMAL FREEDOM IS THE FIRST comprehensive history of the maroons of the Great Dismal Swamp. In my research over the past two decades, I have uncovered more primary documentary sources that capture the testimony of maroons themselves than were previously known to exist. Research in several regional archives and extensive work with contemporary newspapers has further fleshed out this history beyond what any historian has accomplished to date. In this book, the maroons themselves are largely responsible for helping me to speak to maroon psychology, religious life, architecture, agriculture, community relations, social structure within the swamp, health, the internal economy of the maroon communities, skillsets of maroon craftsmen, and insight into leisure activities of the swamp dwellers. All this is supplemented by research into relevant swamp industrial records, census data, registrations and sale records of enslaved people, local and national periodicals, judicial proceedings, and thoroughly situated in the secondary literature concerning Virginia and North Carolina slave society, antebellum politics and intellectual history, and African American social and cultural history.

Moreover, what also sets this work apart from prior attempts to tell the story of the Dismal Swamp maroons is my interdisciplinary work as historian for the Great Dismal Swamp Landscape Study (GDSLS). The GDSLS is an archaeology-focused research group that was initiated by Daniel Sayers in 2002. The central goal of the GDSLS has been to recover interpretable archaeological information about pre–Civil War swamp communities that existed within the current bounds of the Great Dismal Swamp National Wildlife Refuge. The GDSLS undertook archaeological fieldwork in 2003–6 and more recently 2009–13. This represents the first extensive archaeological research to ever take place in the refuge or in the historical boundaries of the Great Dismal Swamp.

I came onto the project as historian in 2009 and joined in excavations during the second phase of fieldwork. After 2010, the group's work benefited from a three-year National Endowment for the Humanities collaborative research grant. To date, the GDSLS has generated one of the largest archaeological and historical datasets on marginalized communities in North America, including the most detailed and expansive body of materials related to maroon communities currently available in North America. The archaeological fieldwork, my continued archival and documentary research, and the utilization of new technology and geophysics (ground-penetrating radar and electroresistivity) have conclusively demonstrated the existence of maroon communities or settlements throughout the swamp.[29] The work of the GDSLS has verified hunches that I had long held regarding maroon life—conjecture that I was not willing to make based solely on my earlier documentary research. No other historian has incorporated (or had access to) the archaeological record of the Great Dismal Swamp Maroons. These invaluable primary source artifacts, in addition to the documentary sources I have uncovered, finally allow this fascinating story to be told.

A note on methodology is in order. Despite my significant new findings, the directly relevant primary sources at my disposal are far from as extensive as I would like. The documentary record, especially from the perspective of a historian trained in empiricism, appears messy and problematic. There are but a handful of real primary sources—antebellum or late nineteenth-century interviews with former maroons or African Americans who had lived in the swamp and interacted with maroons, and none of these in isolation offers a complete picture of what maroon life was like in the swamp. For the most part, there is no definite way to connect the handful of primary accounts to each other or to specific locations within the swamp, population numbers are always imprecise, and the recollections of old former maroons seldom go into as much detail as a historian might wish. The archaeology provides a tremendous help in filling gaps in the documentary record, a remarkable level of detail not possible through the documents alone, and allows me to fill in gaps and thus produce a much more layered narrative, but again, maroons were and are just too good at concealing themselves.

The dearth of sources presents a clear dilemma—I can be entirely objective, limit my narrative to what the meager primary sources will support on their face, or I can attempt to tell the full story through less traditional means. So, around my known quantities I cluster evidence of secondary and contemporary non-firsthand accounts, archaeological discoveries, folklore, environmental science, and a variety of other sources to flesh out the story (think more or less overlapping concentric circles of research). In the absence of full narratives of swamp life, society, and so on, this is the best one can do to tell the tale of a people whose goal was to leave no trace, and of observers who knew next to nothing about the inner workings of the swamp. I must work with scraps of evidence, frequently written or compiled by, at worst, white enslavers, and most often from nonmaroon sources. With these, I must read these "against the grain," even listening closely for silences and/or suppression as a means to recover voices from the past.

Another way historians facing similar challenges have described this process is as "controlled speculation." Where the hard evidence is inadequate, researchers employ comparative material from other cultural or historical situations to infer crucial information that may be missing or obscured in the historical record. This is a common practice among ethnohistorians. Luckily, we have a much better understanding of other hemispheric maroons and their societies and cultures, as well as a rich social, cultural, and intellectual historiography of North American (especially Virginia and North Carolina) enslaved people and slavery.[30] My relatively limited documentary record quite often demonstrates remarkable similarities and parallels, enough so that where there are gaps, reasonable assumptions might be drawn. Hard archaeological evidence further supplements what might have formerly seemed unknowable, to fill voids around my largely faceless subjects.

The maroons were highly successful at maintaining their seclusion, which means that we cannot possibly know their entire history with absolute confidence. This book reckons with that reality by assembling generations of piecemeal scholarship and commentary on the Dismal Swamp maroons, augmenting it with new research, and going forward to tell a fascinating and important story, as fully and richly as I believe can be done. As a last resort, when absolutely necessary, this task requires me to lean on conjecture to add texture and detail that makes the most plausible sense based on the sources available. At base, all historians do this. The act of writing history itself superimposes meaning on bare evidence, some practitioners just have more "facts" to work with than others. Whenever there are gaps in this swamp history, I do my best through other related sources from the period and place to discern the contours of world the maroons would have known and the reactions they might have had. There will be more instances of "perhaps," "might have," or "possibly" than might seem normal, but these qualifiers are necessary to establish and maintain the trust of my readers, and accompanied by explanatory notes and citations. I also suspect most readers, especially regarding the stories of the Dismal Swamp maroons, would agree with past president of the American Historical Association Natalie Zemon Davis, who, in describing a project of her own that faced similar challenges, concluded, "Being speculative is better than to not do it at all."[31] In very rare cases, when I have absolutely no sources to work with, I am content to rely on what Davis calls "conjectural knowledge of possible truth" though always "held tightly in check by the voices of the past." The voices of the Great Dismal Swamp Maroons will be heard more forcefully in this work than they have in a century and a half or more.

Scholars have seldom listened for their voices, but maroon voices were at times deafening in the American South, especially in and around the Great Dismal Swamp. They collectively registered one of the most thunderous indictments of slavery, and the echoes chafed at the ideological bases on which enslavers relied to justify owning other humans. Marronage and the possibility of marronage—and all enslaved people were potential maroons—exploded the hegemony of slaver power and replaced it with an unspoken and smoldering charge of impotence to control people who, according to white supremacist orthodoxy, should have been incapable of independent thought and undesiring of independence.

Maroon voices demand a reassessment of the meaning of "freedom." Marronage in the Dismal represented an alternative to a life of enslavement. It also represented a choice, in most cases, to live free lives in the swamp, *in the South*, rather than seeking it in a free state or Canada. Maroon voices also remind us that freedom was not just an accomplishment after passage along the "Underground Railroad" but a marronage process sustained by their own heroic efforts.

Dismal Swamp maroons also relentlessly resisted enslavement and the brutalities of slavery through a method—their marronage—that at once shook fissures into the bedrock of the institution while not usually having as their goal its overthrow. As their lives and voices make clear, freedom was their primary objective, and all that was a part of their marronage, including their initial escape, helping themselves to the resources of slave labor camps, seeking to disappear in the Dismal, working alongside enslaved canal workers, and yes, even sometimes rebellion. All of these responses to enslavement landed somewhere on a continuum of resistance. Some scholars have dismissed the impact of North American marronage because these maroons did not generally wage constant and outright warfare against their enslavers (as some maroons in other locales did). However, resistance did not need to have revolution or even a direct critique of the slave system as its goal. In the Dismal Swamp, even when maroons did not direct violent attacks against their enslavers or rise up in rebellion, their very existence "in total defiance" of their enslavers maintained the *constant potential* for such action.[32] The impact of Dismal Swamp maroons' resistance was cumulatively overwhelming if not ever directly catastrophic.

Hostile voices most commonly classified maroons as "lurkers," "villains," "rogues," "runaways," "fugitives," "wild men," and "bandits." They did not recognize maroons' desire for and achievement of freedom as legitimate, and thus denigrated it and defined self-emancipators in the insulting terms of enslavers' laws and customs. Maroon voices, however, asserted their humanity and equality, and did not recognize enslavers' authority and laws. They were no longer slaves. They were not afraid. Rather, they were confident in their autonomy and security. Maroons named themselves, as did the remarkable Jack Dismal, and fully came of age as men and women through their marronage, as did the brave John Nichols. The first self-governing African American communities, North or South, whether whites recognized them or not, included the maroon communities of the Great Dismal Swamp.

DISMAL FREEDOM BEGINS BY sketching the natural history of the Great Dismal Swamp and sets the scene for the dynamic human history to follow. Chapter 1 illuminates the little-known history of the earliest European settlement in the area that would become North Carolina at the southern edge of the swamp. A handful of traders, "fugitives" from indentured servitude, enslavement, poverty, debt, or the law, and religious dissenters made their way south from Virginia as early as the 1640s. The area became a sanctuary for the renegades of Chesapeake society, with the nearly impenetrable Great Dismal Swamp between them and Virginia, the treacherous Outer Banks isolating them from the bustling Atlantic world, and the Albemarle Sound to the south. These settlers established a society outside the control of colonial authorities that fostered independence and nonconformity, valued widespread political participation, held decidedly progressive racial views, and opposed all hints of hierarchy.

The early Albemarle settlers were ultimately unable to preserve their independence beyond the Cary Rebellion of 1708–11, and they fell under the control of the elite Anglican establishment. However, sources suggest that others (likely those of mixed heritage or African descent) entered into a new life in the

Great Dismal Swamp. They were soon augmented by Native American refugees of the Tuscarora War. The first reports of established maroon communities in the Great Dismal Swamp surfaced soon after—of "ungovernable" Black, "tawny," and Native Americans raiding parties originating from its depths.

Chapter 2 follows the development of Dismal Swamp marronage through the colonial era. Although their numbers were still few and organization limited, these earliest generations of Dismal Swamp maroons began to strategically direct their aggression from their swamp base against the outside society that had oppressed them. That there was an African presence early on is made clear by an insurrection in 1709 involving Native Americans, enslaved people, and maroons. Virginia's governor, Alexander Spotswood, was also keenly aware of the diverse threat gathering in and around the swamp. He warned the colonial trade council a few years later that "Loose and disorderly people daily flock thither" to this "No-Man's-Land."[33]

After at least a generation of steady population growth in the swamp, self-emancipating men and women from the Tidewater region and beyond would have been well informed about the existence of a "city of refuge" in the Dismal, and could expect to be assisted through the quagmire by others. These maroon pioneers had already achieved their freedom in its depths, and suffered the elements and harsh wilderness environment as they carved out the first spaces for villages. These swamp elders would offer mentorship in the skills of swamp survival as well as communities to which newcomers could attach themselves. Maroon activity increased significantly in the years leading up to 1720, as refugees from the Tuscarora War entered the swamp from the South, and Africans, who were steadily increasing in number in Virginia tobacco country, fled there from the north.

This chapter also looks in detail at the surveying expedition of William Byrd II in 1728. Byrd had been hired to determine the dividing line between North Carolina and Virginia, and his journals offer fascinating insights into the swamp, swamp life for those living within its recesses, and the meaning of marronage (both in and out of the swamp) in the early eighteenth century. As Byrd surveyed, he encountered people he characterized as maroons— he called them "marooners." In his report he reemphasized the warning that his friend Spotswood had made fourteen years before, and compared the unruly population of the Dismal Swamp area to Romulus and Remus. These legendary founders of Rome had issued a call to the escaped slaves of Italy to join them in the building of a city of refuge in the wilderness. From such a beginning had grown the power of an empire, and Byrd warned that the growing maroon population of northeastern North Carolina might achieve a similar destiny if it were not checked in its early stages.

The late eighteenth and early nineteenth century comprised a new era of armed campaigns originating in and around the Dismal Swamp and striking out at the surrounding slave society. While there were no "maroon wars" in North America on par with those of the Caribbean, chapter 3 argues that the aggregate of guerrilla raids from within the swamp, maroons' involvement in the American Revolution, and connections to and participation in later slave rebellions represent the closest comparable phenomenon in North America.

Admittedly, these were often small groups, but the raids were chronic, not simply episodic, and the evidence suggests that some of these raids were part of something much larger, of plans and collaborations over a large area and among different groups of maroons and enslaved and marginalized people. Although the potentially cataclysmic nature of the maroon threat may have been more imagined than real, maroon guerrilla activity surely resulted in greater property loss than Nat Turner's rebellion or the thwarted Gabriel Rebellion. Maroons were not simply provisioning themselves through raids, either. Most maroons had once been valuable enslaved property, and their process of marooning had been, at least from a white perspective, the act of "stealing themselves" from their owner. An estimate from the 1850s that the maroons of the Dismal Swamp represented $1.5 million worth of slave property may have been a bit high for any given time, but it was actually quite low if considered from the perspective of the 200 years the Dismal Swamp served as a beacon for maroons.

The maroons themselves had as their primary goal to remain undetected. In this, they were incredibly successful. However, chapter 4 offers a closer look at the lives maroons lived, reconstructing a partial portrait of their lives from the evidence provided by contemporary documents, oral history, and recent archaeological discoveries.

To be sure, thousands of maroons did not just live in one Great Dismal Swamp "community"—that was neither possible nor practical. Simple concerns for safety discouraged large grouping, and the very topography of the swamp would have precluded the development of large villages in most cases anyway. Rather, maroons established distinct settlements across the vast Dismal Swamp that reflected the residents' diverse motivations for marooning. Recent archaeological digs in the swamp have uncovered evidence of maroon structures, as well as demonstrations of cultural features across several dry "islands." Satellite images indicate that large islands (greater than twenty acres)

and large clusters of smaller islands (fifty or more acres in aggregate) exist in
the swamp that would have been conducive to larger-scale settlement. Islands
surveyed by the GDSLS (less than 1 percent of GDSWR acreage) range from
one to thirty-nine acres, are often found in clusters with as little as fifty feet of
swamp separating them, and are as high as ten feet above swamp level in the
most isolated, deep swamp islands.

The final three decades of Dismal Swamp marronage through the end of the
Civil War represented escalation of previous eras of confrontation. As chapter 5 recounts, the proximity of the Nat Turner rebellion to the Great Dismal
Swamp and resulting white vigilance in the region significantly affected the
numbers of fugitives entering the swamp and the conduct of guerrilla warfare
from within. Nonetheless, the fact that communities continued to exist is attested to by archaeological evidence, maroon testimony, and renewed activity
of maroons after 1851 and especially after 1861. This growth, the experience of a
new generation of maroons in guerrilla warfare, and their increasing notoriety
in American popular culture had already begun to strike at the very founda-
tions of Tidewater slave society by the time many maroons left the swamp to
join Union forces in dealing a final death-blow to North American slavery.

It was also during this last antebellum decade that the accumulated intellectual burden of more than two centuries of Dismal Swamp marronage
became unbearable for white supporters of slavery in the Tidewater and beyond. Despite the apparent decrease of maroon activities from the swamp
after 1831, the symbolic shadow the Great Dismal Swamp cast over the South
lengthened. As enemies of slavery ramped up their attacks from without, the
festering sore from within that the maroons represented, and the South's inability to eradicate the actual and ideological threat therein, contributed to the
hysteria that ultimately led to disunion and civil war. A widely read description of Dismal Swamp marronage in *Harper's Monthly* and the publication
of Harriet Beecher Stowe's *Dred: A Tale of the Great Dismal Swamp*, both in
1856, centered the "great slave insurrection panic" of that year on the Dismal.
Kansas Free-Staters cited the Dismal Swamp maroons as their inspiration,
antislavery politicians weighted their rhetoric with references to the Dismal
Swamp maroons, and John Brown intended to make the swamp one of his
strongholds in his antislavery war on the South. The Great Dismal Swamp
Maroons, by virtue of their very existence and resilience, drove a nail into the
coffin of North American slavery.

The Civil War, particularly the arrival of Union gunboats in Norfolk in
1862, marked the beginning of the end of the Great Dismal Swamp Maroon
communities and the slave society from which they had removed themselves.

As the war raged around them, the already-organized maroons joined white Unionists and contrabands in a guerrilla war to disrupt Confederate power in areas surrounding the swamp, most often on the North Carolina side, where Unionist allies were more numerous. Many other maroons who left the swamp to fight did not become regulars in the Union army but rather maintained their status as guerrillas in the region. Dismal Swamp guerrillas helped provision Union forces from their raids on enslavers. Perhaps as important, dozens of maroons emerged from the swamp and served as scouts necessary for passage through the swamp. Moreover, maroon fighters already busy "spread[ing] terror over the land," in the words of a North Carolina woman, loosely joined forces with Confederate deserters as the derisively named "Buffaloes." From their base on the North Carolina edge of the Great Dismal, "Buffalo" bands set off on regular campaigns into northeastern North Carolina, both to plunder and make good on their explicit pledge to "clear the county of every slave."[34]

When the war ended, Great Dismal Swamp Maroons quietly emerged from the swamp and then disappeared again, this time into the bustle of a world where slavery no longer existed. But now they traded one set of dangers and uncertainties for another. Bears and rattlesnakes were no longer a constant threat to their safety, but many now-former maroons were a bit skittish on the outside after so many years in exile. They would have to wrestle with the ambiguous meaning of freedom, their place in Reconstruction governments, and later, a Jim Crow world that led some former maroons back to the only secure and safe place they had known, the Great Dismal Swamp.

CHAPTER ONE

The Origins of
Dismal Swamp Marronage

Freedom Wears a Cap which Can Without a Tongue,
Call Together all Those who Long to Shake of The fetters of Slavery.
—Governor Alexander Spotswood to
Virginia House of Burgesses, 1710

THE GREAT DISMAL SWAMP is one of the most massive landforms along the east coast of North America, and as such, every population encountering it has had to address its presence in one way or another—whether as foragers, settlers, or fugitives. Sprawling over 2,000 square miles, the Dismal was a hunting ground and sacred space for Indigenous people since time immemorial and hundreds of years before Europeans arrived in the region. As colonizers attempted to "subdue" the North American frontier and settle the broad Tidewater, the swamp presented one of the most significant obstacles to their advancement—it was nearly impassable, and terrifying to them in its dark mystery. However, what was an impediment for colonial society became a great defender of those who sought to escape it. Indigenous refugees, white servants attempting to escape the stifling Virginia plantation complex and often their indentures, religious nonconformists, and self-emancipating Africans put the swamp between themselves and the Old Dominion, and developed a dissident society beyond any colonial authority.

Though an open and relatively egalitarian community developed in the swamp, Virginia officials deemed the area a "rogues' harbor." When the expansion of a landed elite class with the support of colonial officials finally overwhelmed, most of this community's members despairingly resigned themselves to the dominion of the gentry—but not all. Some moved from the edges of the Great Dismal Swamp and into its interior to join a small but growing multiracial population of refugees. The swamp may not have offered a life of leisure and comfort, but it allowed its residents a free existence beyond the scrutiny and practical reach of authorities on the outside. From these origins and over 200 years, a maroon population grew that at once fascinated, terrified, and repelled white outsiders. For disaffected exiles of the Tidewater, however, the swamp drew them in like a magnet, enabling them to begin to chip away at the foundation of the planter society that had enslaved and marginalized them. There would be no "masters" in the Dismal Swamp, only free people.

The Prehistoric Swamp

The Great Dismal Swamp lays in what is called the embayed section of the Atlantic Coastal Plain, which consists of three wide and gently sloping terraces separated by longitudinal, eastward-facing escarpments, or sudden elevation changes. It is bounded to the north by the Churchland Flat (just south of the James River), to the east by the Deep Creek Swale, to the south by a transition zone surrounding the mouth of the Pasquotank River basin, and to the west by the Suffolk Escarpment—otherwise called the Suffolk Scarp—the first main character in the Dismal Swamp drama.

The Suffolk Scarp sits fifty miles inland from the present Atlantic shore, itself formerly the ocean's shore during the Pleistocene around 2 million years ago. It rises twenty to thirty feet higher than the lower coastal plain and falls eastward to the ocean. With a handful of lesser scarps and ridges south of the James River, the Suffolk Scarp laid a scene for a dramatic human drama to come. The Scarp interrupted the general west to east flow of the landscape, and of waterways and rivers, from the mountains to the sea. North of it, the James River, the Elizabeth, the Nansemond, and other lesser waterways flowed as "a superhighway" east into the Chesapeake Bay, wide open to the Atlantic and the rest of the world. South and west of the Scarp, waterways including the Chowan and Roanoke flowed more slowly and southerly into the Albemarle Sound. Though a rich and beautiful estuary, it was bottled up by accumulating sediments carried by southern-flowing longshore currents (the Outer Banks), making it, in Jack Temple Kirby's comparison, a Carolina cul-de-sac rather than a Chesapeake highway, with no safe outlet to the sea. The scarp thus created a Tidewater hinterland and determined the travel and settlement patterns of the haves and have-nots long before humans arrived on the scene.[1]

By the end of the Pleistocene and last glacial period around 12,000 years ago, a warming climate raised sea levels as well as inland freshwater tables, and in the increasingly boggy area east of the Suffolk Scarp fast and densely growing vegetation clogged stream valleys with organic matter. As the detritus accumulated faster than it could decay, it built up a layer of peat twenty

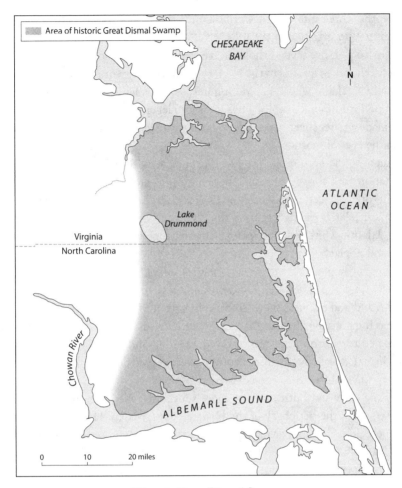

Area of historic Great Dismal Swamp

CHESAPEAKE
BAY

N

ATLANTIC
OCEAN

Lake
Drummond

Virginia
North Carolina

Chowan River

ALBEMARLE SOUND

0   10   20 miles

Historic Great Dismal Swamp

feet thick in places, at a rate of accumulation of a foot or more per century.[2]
By 4,000 BCE perhaps 1,000 square miles of the infant swamp was swaddled
with a blanket of peat. Two millennia later, a mature Great Dismal Swamp
covered 2,000 square miles and reached from what would become Suffolk,
Portsmouth, and Norfolk to the north and the Albemarle Sound to the south.[3]

Near the western center of the swamp was Lake Drummond, a roughly
three-by-five-mile (3,100 acre) oval named after the first colonial governor of
North Carolina. Today, the lake sits eighteen feet above sea level (one of the
highest points in the swamp) and is six to seven feet deep at normal levels. Five
rivers draw their waters from Drummond and the Dismal and flow out from

its depths, three into North Carolina and two into Virginia. Drummond's origins are uncertain, and theories include a meteorite impact, tectonic shift, or massive peat fire several thousand years ago. A local Indigenous legend attributes the lake's genesis to the reign of terror of the great Firebird, who lived in the Dismal and whose smoldering nest seared a hole into the center of the swamp.[4] Drummond's sublime beauty is also legendary—"One thinks if God ever made a fairer sheet of water," a hunter wrote in 1908, "it is yet hidden away from the eyes of mortals."[5]

Much of the swamp, as might be expected, is covered in water and the vegetation that thrives therein. There are miles and miles of reeds and cattails in open spaces, duckweed and cypress knees under dense swamp forest canopies. Islands of high ground dot the landscape, ridges heavily wooded with Atlantic white cedar, maple, blackgum, tupelo, bald cypress, sweetgum, oak, and poplar.[6]

Since the region's human prehistory, the Great Dismal Swamp was the central feature of the Tidewater. For thousands of years before Europeans entered their world and called it "new," Indigenous people had lived along this coast, even as the great swamp was maturing. Early Paleo-Indians (Early Woodland Adena culture, 1000 BCE–200 CE) were farming and hunting in and around the Dismal at least by the third century BCE.[7] Very little else is known of their history, beyond that they once existed.[8]

By the early sixteenth century, more substantial Native American groups had settled at the periphery of the Dismal. The Croatan, Hatteras, Chowan, Weapomeiok, Coranine, Machapunga, Bay River, Pamplico, Roanoke, Woccon, Nansemond, and Cape Fear people spoke Algonquian-related languages and had developed a culturally sophisticated, if politically unstable society. They most often lived in small coastal villages, with as many as thirty dwellings enclosed by fortified palisades. Their standard of living was not as abundant as their more numerous and powerful neighbors to the west, the Iroquoian-speaking Tuscarora, Catawba, and Cherokee, and to the north, the Powhatan.[9] But they were not alone in the world.

Europeans Settling Northern Carolina

By the early sixteenth century, European explorers had reconnoitered the area that would one day be called Carolina and Virginia. The first European ships to sail along the Dismal Coast were captained by the Florentine explorer Giovanni da Verrazzano in the service of France in 1524. Verrazzano's account of a New World Eden inspired great interest in the region. The first Spanish attempt at settlement was attacked by Indigenous people and ultimately fell to the first North American slave rebellion in 1526. When the Spanish survivors fled in the fall of that year, they left behind dozens of enslaved Africans. Four decades before the establishment of Saint Augustine and eight decades before Jamestown, dozens of Africans, nameless to history, continued their lives as free people beyond the control of Europeans. Perhaps the grandchildren of these first permanent Old World settlers made the acquaintance of those Englishmen left behind at the failed and mysterious "Lost Colony" Roanoke settlement in the late 1580s.[10]

European explorers had already made contact with Indigenous people deeper in the interior. Some they befriended, others they enslaved or killed. Many they sickened with diseases that moved faster than they did, and so Indigenous people of the Tidewater and vicinity sometimes began falling ill and dying before they ever saw a white face. Europeans were seldom far behind the epidemics they unleashed. During his celebrated journey through the Carolina colony in 1700, John Lawson made remarkable observations about the cultures, interactions, and communications among the interior tribes, and in several instances mentioned the disease and enslavement that had often befallen them. He was completely silent regarding the coastal people. Most of these, it seems, had disappeared, relocated, or merged into loosely assembled composite tribes.[11] These people retreated to the most marginal lands not yet coveted by white settlers or larger Indigenous nations, including the edges of the Great Dismal Swamp.[12]

Although the first "official" permanently settled colony was finally established at Jamestown, Virginia, in 1607, small numbers of Old World settlers had long inhabited the region to the south, though they left behind next to nothing for the historian to tell their stories. As historian Wesley Frank Craven admits, "It is impossible to speak definitely of the first permanent settlement of Carolina."[13] Their numbers grew as bound laborers, mostly white servants, escaped their indentures in Virginia and sought freedom and independence on the southern frontier.

White servants had attempted to escape from Jamestown within months of its settlement and especially during the "starving time" of 1609–10 when, rather than survive on dogs, boot leather, and the occasional desperate act of cannibalism, they sought succor from the neighboring Powhatans. "To eate," one beleaguered settler wrote, "many our men this starveinge Tyme did Runn away unto the Salvages whom we never heard of after." The exodus could not be stopped, even under threat of execution. The occasional servant prone to attempted escape might even be "bownd fast unto Trees" to keep them in place.[14] They understood that surviving starvation might only mean overwork in a tobacco field and abuse at the hand of one's master. In practice, indentured servitude differed very little from outright slavery.[15]

Servant flight remained an urgent concern of planters for decades. In March 1642, the Virginia Assembly levied fines for anyone caught aiding or abetting "runaway servants and freemen," and prescribed branding for the offending servants.[16] Some might be sheltered by sympathetic Virginians, but increasingly fugitives turned their gaze on the frontier, beyond the horizon where Virginia authorities had any real political control. The likely destination for those escaping was "the swamps and forests to the southward."[17]

Virginians had explored northeastern North Carolina in 1608, 1622, and 1643 and found little that interested them.[18] Soil conditions and topography south of Virginia were seldom attractive to planters hoping to extend their agricultural reach. As one historian puts it, Virginians exploring southward may have found plenty of "rich bottom land," just at the bottom of swamps, and not the kind on which to expand Virginia's agricultural successes. The lack of accessibility and treacherous landscape of the region further dissuaded settlers. Most problematic was its coastline, where England's first attempt at permanent settlement of Roanoke had failed spectacularly. The treacherous northern Carolina coast earned the nickname "graveyard of the Atlantic."[19] The shifting shoals of the Outer Banks discouraged the approach of large vessels, and most small farmers were forced to haul their goods overland to and from Virginia. Even the overland approach was frustrated by swamps and eastern marshlands. The Great Dismal Swamp, straddling the Carolina/Virginia boundary, was in and of itself an impassable obstacle to trade. The King's Highway, no more than a "rough road" that eventually connected Edenton, North Carolina, to the south and Norfolk, Virginia, to the north, snaked through and around the swamps, required several fords, and skirted far west to stay clear of the Great Dismal.[20]

The Albemarle Sound, an estuary situated at the confluence of the Chowan and Roanoke Rivers, was the only access most northern Carolinians had to the Atlantic. Only the Cape Fear River emptied directly into the ocean, and its mouth was 200 miles from the Virginia border and remained undeveloped until the 1720s. For over half a century of proprietary rule, most northern Carolinians lived in or around Albemarle County with no immediate access to a seaport. Other rivers used for trade emptied into either the Albemarle and Pamlico Sounds, and only small vessels could navigate the shallows from sound to ocean.[21] Even the most modest profit-seeking northern Carolinians believed their home region to be a "place uncapable of a Trade to great Brittain."[22]

Official attempts by the English to colonize the region between the James River and Spanish Florida were disorganized and ineffective. In 1620, King Charles I of England granted a charter to his attorney general, Sir Robert Heath, to establish a new colony between 31 and 30 degrees north latitude, of men "large and plentiful, professing the true religion, sedulously and industriously applying themselves to the culture of the said lands and to merchandizing; to be performed and at his own charges, and others by his example." However, Heath set no example. "Carolana" was never fully brought into existence because of the political turmoil that erupted with the English Civil War. Heath fled to France in 1645, forfeiting his charter, and the territory remained free of organized European settlement.

South of Virginia and north of Florida, there was no law and no government. For those who had been criminalized through breaking their Virginia indentures, these lands presented a spacious and convenient sanctuary. Men and women on the run could generally rest assured that no pursuit would follow them south, and in any case, there was no legal authority that could have sustained their capture and extradition. No government existed in the no-man's-land to force its residents to muster into a militia or even to tax them.[23]

The same civil war that had frustrated the establishment of English law in the Carolana grant of 1629 had also influenced the servants arriving in Virginia. Undoubtedly many of them arriving in the 1640s would have retained some of the antiauthoritarian and anticonformist spirit that had been fermenting in the mother country and had precipitated a war. Many were descendants of the victims of England's enclosure movement, which had forced thousands off common lands and consolidated great estates into the hands of the aristocracy. Others were simply England's dispossessed poor or petty criminals, sent off to Virginia to work the fields. Although only a small percentage of Virginians were of African descent (22 of 1,300 settlers were African in 1624), an increasing number of them also attempted to escape their servitude. By 1640, a distinct body of case law had been developed specifically regarding the punishment of non-white escapees.[24] By 1643, runaways represented a significant enough drain of Virginia resources that the House of Burgesses passed a law providing severe penalties for escapees and rewards for their capture. Not long after, that same body lamented that fugitive laws "have hitherto in greate parte proved ineffectuall."[25]

These initial settlers did not come on behalf, with the permission, or under the protection of any European authority or colonial government. Rather they voted with their feet in a system that otherwise marginalized and disfranchised them, and they made no secrets of their motivations for settling south

of Virginia. They were escaping the tobacco juggernaut—the labor, the exploitation, and the cutthroat culture. These were not land-hungry Virginians of
means. Rather, they were the victims of that class of people, and they quickly
established their goodwill toward and willingness to abide the authority of
their new Indigenous sovereigns, the Tuscarora.[26] As one early historian put
it, "They regarded the Indian natives as the true lords of the soil. . . . They
came among the Indians as supplicants who asked favors, not as masters who
claimed rights."[27] Although the Native population south of Virginia had already begun to feel the pressures of European encroachments, enemies of their
enemies who behaved and helped themselves to only what they needed were
welcome. According to a visitor in 1709, it was "the most free from the In-
sults and Barbarities of the *Indians*, of any Colony that was ever yet seated
in *America*."[28] A cosmopolitan assemblage of former servants that likely included speakers of at least English, Spanish, French, and Dutch, for their part,
brought a knowledge of European ways that was valuable to their hosts as they
considered how to deal with advancement of the "wrong type" of whites.[29]

The European settlement pattern comes more clearly into focus in 1648,
when white settlers who had been previously living in the area, including
Thomas Tuke originally of Isle of Wight County "and severall others," entered
into the first known land purchase agreement with Native Americans south
of Virginia.[30] A 1650 account by a Virginian explorer reported several English
people living among the Tuscarora, including one "Englishman a Cockarous."
This descriptor roughly translated from the Native *cawcawaassough* as someone
akin to a minister of state or advisor to a Tuscarora king.[31] In 1654, a Spaniard,
his "family" of thirty, and seven Africans were reported to be living among the
Tuscarora.[32] Others of various ethnicities lived scattered about the countryside
or in loose settlements, the most populous being those who established a community around the home of Nathaniel Batts. The first known permanent white
settler of North Carolina, Batts had put down roots just south of the Dismal
Swamp on the northwest edge of the Albemarle Sound.[33] He purchased lands
between the Pasquotank River and Great Dismal Swamp in September 1660
from "Kiscutanewh, King of the Yeopims."[34] The Yeopim were an eastern
client nation of the Tuscarora. Another grant from the leader of the Yeopim
to a George Durant followed six months later for lands nearby along the Perquimans River.[35]

Quaker missionary George Fox called "The Old Governor" Batts "a rude,
desperate man" after meeting him in 1672.[36] Indeed, Batts was known to carry
considerable debts in Virginia, where he had married, and his character was
not without blemish. Although he had not necessarily fled south to avoid his

familial obligations, Batts's wife, angry at his attempts to claim property right-fully bequeathed to his stepchildren, may have played a role in his permanent solo removal to Carolina (Mrs. Batts apparently never ventured down to Caro-lina to visit her husband).[37] But though Fox disparaged Batts for his roughness and called him "rude," his steadily growing group of Carolina neighbors called him "Governor." The Yeopim, Chowanoke, or perhaps both had also ceremo-nially adopted him, given him the honorary name "Secotan," and sought his counsel as a trusted advisor.[38] Batts was a primary peace negotiator between the Tuscarora client nations and new European outsiders when they sought an audience with the Chief.[39] The mutual affection between Batts and Kicko-wanna, daughter of Chief Kilcokanen, was also legendary.[40]

Thus by the middle of the seventeenth century, and before any attempt by the English to extend their dominion over the region, generations of Old World settlers and refugees from bound labor inhabited the Albemarle along-side Native American neighbors. They had acknowledged and respected the authority of the Tuscarora, elected their own independent governor, formed themselves into a body of electors and lawgivers, and functioned as a com-munity on the frontier. They may have been "rude," but the common usage of the term simply meant not of high class. One's standing back in Virginia meant very little in their new settlement. As powerful Virginia leaders grew increasingly wealthy and refined, their North Carolina counterparts remained a motley crew of misfits, proud of their "rude" repute, and well beyond the jurisdiction of Virginia or England. By the middle of the seventeenth century, there were likely at least 500 settlers squatting south of the Old Dominion.[41]

The Beginnings of Proprietary Government

With the end of the English Civil War in 1660 and restoration of the monar-chy, Charles II turned his gaze back to the land named for his father with a new approach to empire. The king's political supporters who had enabled his return to the throne required generous thanks in the form of special privileges, lands, trade, and wealth. To his supporters went shares and leadership in the Royal African Company and the Barbados Company, as did great open spaces on maps of North America. The vast and never formally settled Carolana terri-tory would also be included in the bounty of those favored by the king. Known together as the Lords Proprietors, they were Anthony Ashley Cooper, after-ward Earl of Shaftesbury; Edward Hyde, Earl of Clarendon; George Monck, Duke of Albemarle; William Craven, Earl of Craven; Sir George Carteret of the Isle of Jersey; John Lord Berkeley; Sir John Colleton of Barbados; and Sir William Berkeley, an adventurer and governor of Virginia between 1641 and

1677. These men had their loyalty rewarded with a near-kingly dominion over the land from Florida to the southern edge of the Albemarle Sound (now so named after one of the Proprietors), which would, they along with the king hoped, become a reliable revenue stream back to England.

In 1665, the king issued a new charter that amended the 1663 document. The southern border shifted closer to Saint Augustine and the upper boundary moved a half degree northward. As had been the case with the Maryland charter of 1632, the Lords Proprietors were given wide latitude to establish their authority over their new colony. The charters allowed them to establish a political and legal system (so long as its laws did not conflict with those of England), legislate, create a judicial system, build forts and organize a militia, and even wage war. They were also allowed the flexibility to establish a significant degree of representative government in the new colony, to be exercised "with the advice, assent, and approbation of the Freemen" in elected assembly.[42]

A key difference between the charters of 1663 and 1665 was the inclusion of Albemarle, the only portion of the colony already populated. But the Proprietors seemed to have been unaware of the preexistence of generations of Carolina "Freemen." Long before the Carolina charter, Berkeley had already been selling speculative land grants there, and he likely assumed that any settlers must be legitimate patent-holders. The oversight, however, did not go unnoticed in the colony as it seems to have in England. An early historian recorded that after the charter, Albemarle became an even more attractive destination for misfit Virginians. "Into this middle ground, this 'no-man's land,'" he wrote, "we are expressly told emigrants came from Virginia, because it was under *no government*; some of them may have been rogues, probably they were. The facts, however, furnish two very obvious reflections, and with them we dismiss the subject: first, these rogues came not *into Carolina*; for their hiding-place, Albemarle, was not then within her limits and jurisdiction: and secondly, had it been, they brought their roguery with them ready made *from Virginia*."[43]

Thomas Woodward, the first surveyor sent into Carolina from Virginia in early 1665, confirmed that the settlers he encountered could claim no "legal" title to their lands and were, instead, rather poor squatters who had occupied the Albemarle region for decades. Moreover, before he even arrived, their previously existing "General Assembly" had drawn up a list of petitions for their new (on paper) Lords and had begun their attempt to dictate their terms of government and how they believed the affairs of the colony should be run.[44]

The "rude" Nathaniel Battses of northeastern Carolina would hardly serve as the basis for the highly structured feudal society the Proprietors hoped to establish upon their grant. Yet the squatters were at that point the only settle-

ment in the colony, already had a self-chosen government, and could only be ignored at the Proprietors' peril. "Rich men," the surveyor reported back, "which
Albemarle stands much in need of," must be recruited to settle there in order
that the undesirable authority might be displaced.[45] If not, widespread "leveling
parity" might overrun the colony. Although he humbly noted, "I know it befits
me not to dispute your command," Woodward worried that "for the present, to
think that any men will move from Virginia upon conditions harder than they
can live there, will prove, I fear, a vain imagination." Perhaps accommodation
of the Albemarle authority was in order until "men of greater possessions" and
in greater numbers could be convinced to settle, take their rightful place atop
Carolina society, and "conduce more to the well being and good government."[46]

Berkeley, already on the ground as governor in Virginia, was tasked by his
colleagues with establishing some form of workable government in northern
Carolina. Interestingly, they authorized him to form two distinct governments for this territory—not one each for the southern and northern halves
of the colony but one for the Albemarle region itself. Their reasoning relied
on Woodward's advice. A settlement already existed "on the north-east part
of the River Chowan," a community diplomatically described by Proprietor
George Monck as being "for liberty of Contience." Until others might be
persuaded "to plant there" (that is, planters) elsewhere in the region south
and west of them, it might be wise to accommodate "all sorts of persons."[47]
Woodward the surveyor had admonished the Proprietors to not underestimate
the settlers. He had urged them "to entertain this truth as a maxim, Those that
live upon a place are best able to judge of the place."[48] And so the Proprietors
proposed to recognize the prior existence of a self-chosen Albemarle government, at least for the time being.

Whether it was from dissatisfaction with Nathaniel Batts's leadership, or,
as at least one historian argues, Batts's decision to retire from his post, the
Albemarle settlers apparently did not elect to remain entirely self-governing.
Perhaps they had sufficient confidence in the man chosen as the first colonial
governor of Albemarle, William Drummond, who was a Scot and former indentured servant himself. Like many in the community, he had also attempted
to escape the Virginia tobacco fields. He had been discovered in his attempt
and was viciously whipped for his offense. He truly detested the haughty
Berkeley and sympathized with the folks of Albemarle. An "abundance" of his
new constituency, he noted with approval, had moved into northern Carolina
after having also become "weary of Sir Williams government" to the north.[49]

The growing Albemarle population remained isolated, poor, and disconnected, and its political culture was profoundly antiauthoritarian. Proprietary

government was little more felt than the absence of government before, and the area continued as a beacon to those who sought less government rather than more, and independence rather than riches. Indeed, Albemarle became known as "Poor Carolina," wedged midway between "proud Virginians" and "upstart South Carolinians."[50]

Most of the original settlers did not seem to care that the Proprietors sought to implement new rules and laws. After all, they had migrated to northern Carolina specifically to avoid the impositions of the Virginia gentry, and would not freely accede to a remote authority, whether removed by hundreds of miles or thousands. Case in point: when Thomas Miller assumed the post of collector of customs in Albemarle County and attempted to belatedly execute the Navigation Acts there in 1677, community patriarch George Durant raised an army of 30–40 Pasquotank settlers (including "sundry fugitives"), arrested Miller and several other proprietary officials, impaneled a grand jury in his own home, and called for the resurrection of the dormant Albemarle local assembly (though never explicitly rejecting the authority of the Lords Proprietors).[51] Durant's associate John Culpeper (whose actions may not truly have earned the eventual naming of the uprising as Culpeper's Rebellion) was ultimately seized and tried before the King's Bench for treason.[52]

Yet as interesting as the rebellion might be as evidence of the independence of Albemarle, the resolution of Culpeper's case is equally remarkable. Fearing a possible revocation of their charter (and aware that they did not possess the resources to unseat the extralegal Albemarle authorities), the Lords Proprietors chose to defend Culpeper and were able to influence his acquittal. Even more noteworthy was their defense strategy. Lord Anthony Ashley Cooper, in his testimony, rejected the charge that the rebels were guilty by admitting that there could be no treason because "there hath been no legall Governmt ever settled in Albemarle," that is, the northeast corner of the colony had never truly been brought under the political jurisdiction of the proprietary government, remained under local control, and therefore was not subject to the same laws as the rest of the colony. They may have been nothing more than "ye Rabble," but the roots of the settlers' authority ran deep, and they represented a potentially valuable proprietary ally against royal interposition. They were thus sustained in their authority.[53]

Virginians were aghast at the Proprietors' seemingly backing "rabble" against the "better sort" in Carolina. They had long hemorrhaged fugitive servants into North Carolina, and had just barely survived Bacon's Rebellion, a class war that pitted frustrated white servants and African Americans against the gentry. Especially since men who had followed Nathaniel Bacon in Virginia had apparently taken up the cause of the Albemarle settlers, they increasingly criticized northern Carolina as a den of iniquity and "rougues harbor" and the colony's policies as direct threats to their own well-being.[54]

Thomas Miller had warned in his 1679 London deposition that "affaires have been carried on to ye great damage of his Majty . . . by reason sundry fugitives have been entertained among the Albemarle Instructors &c."[55] Two years later the governor of Virginia, in his official report to the Lords of Trade and Plantations, declared frankly "As regards our neighbors, North Carolina is and always was the sink of America, the refuge of our renegades; and till in better order it is a danger to us."[56] Edward Randolph, commissioner of customs to the colonies, indicted North Carolina in 1696 as the common resort of "Pyrats & runaway Servants" from Virginia, and noted its lack of "regular government." He echoed the charge four years later.[57]

The more, it seemed, might make the merrier in North Carolina and the misery of Virginia. One of the earliest known laws passed by the Albemarle Assembly was an act that extended sanctuary for debtors fleeing into the colony for a period of five years.[58] It having been common practice for some time to welcome fugitives into North Carolina, they were likely to be offered shelter "among persons of the like circumstances & principles" who had availed themselves of Albemarle's hospitality in earlier years.[59] Though vigorously denied by contemporary Carolina officials, historians have generally confirmed Albemarle's notorious reputation.[60] Unwelcome (or unfree) in Virginia, society's outcasts were gathering together just south of that colony's reach.

A "Rogues' Harbor"

A small but significant African population made their homes in Albemarle as well. Some 40 percent of Albemarle's white settlers in the mid-seventeenth century brought enslaved Africans with them (and claimed headrights for them), but a large portion of the area's African population could be counted among the "runaways" of which Virginians complained so loudly.[61] It seems that Carolina harbored not only the debtors of Virginia's elite but also their "renegade" human property. With the African rebels of 1526 and their descendants somewhere on the southeast frontier and Africans living among various Indigenous groups (and these two populations were not necessarily distinct), a multiracial renegade society was developing in the Dismal Swamp region.[62]

Whether enslaved or "fugitives" from enslavement, Albemarle's population of African descent enjoyed a degree of autonomy rare in the North American colonies. A combination of a "leveling spirit" common among early settlers, weak institutional structures and commercial markets, and the challenging

frontier environment confronting all alike reduced differences based on class
and race.[63] The enslaved and the enslavers, Black and white, worked side by side
carving an existence out of the frontier. Like men working face to face on opposite ends of a whipsaw, a sense of "sawbuck equality" obtained where "direct,
equalitarian confrontations" tempered the degree of white domination preva-
lent in Virginia and "curbed" many of the harshest features of enslavement.[64]

The lack of a large and well-defined upper class in Albemarle also resulted in
local government reflecting the region's full class spectrum, a more equal distribution of land and property, and weak church establishment—the most visible
symbol of the state. This often irked more well-to-do settlers, although they
remained a minority voice.[65] Francis Veale, one of Albemarle's early settlers
of a haughty nature, observed of his neighbors: "I will Now Just Mention
Something of their Manners & Religion theres not a clergy man in the whole
Government but they that are Religiously Inclin'd getts a Tayler or Some old
Pirate or Some Idle Fellow to Read the Services of the Church of England &
then He Hacks out a Sermon . . . but they all Live very Loving together &
comes to Meetings att one anothers' Houses, but never talks of Religion."[66]

John Urmstone, a veteran minister of the Society for the Propagation of the
Gospel in Foreign Parts, did missionary work on the outskirts of the Great
Dismal Swamp in the early eighteenth century. Though Quaker George Fox
was warmly welcomed into North Carolina homes, Urmstone more often received a cold reception. In letters back to his superiors in London, the minister
lamented his inability to make any headway with the settlers, whom he described as "a very factious mutinous and rebellious people most of them allied
to the Quakers and at all times at their Beck ready to oppose either Church or
state." There was not, he noted, any controversial view that lacked defenders
in this community that he claimed was full of "Libertines Men & Women of
loose dissolute and scandalous lives and practices."[67]

It is unlikely that Roanoke was as awash with prostitutes and moral prof-
ligates as Urmstone suggested. Their rejection of his Anglicanism was most
likely a dismissal of any representative of the establishment, not upright living
or religion itself. The embrace of Quakerism and deference to Quaker "dissenting" political leadership by many residents of Albemarle, especially those
with deep roots in the Dismal Swamp precincts, made more sense in a community built upon and dedicated to a more leveled society that what obtained
in Virginia and was developing in South Carolina.

North Carolina in the late seventeenth and early eighteenth century was
a hotbed of subversion. In 1701, it was foremost among proprietary colonies
that the Board of Trade of England had in mind when that body urged the

revocation of their charters. It had not sufficiently regulated trade and commerce, its laws were often at cross purposes with those of Parliament, and "by the harbouring of Servants and Fugitives; these Governments tend greatly to the undermining the Trade and Welfare of the other Plantations, and seduce and draw the People thereof; by which Diminution of Hands, the rest of the Colonies, more beneficial to *England*, do very much suffer."[68] Its charter was not revoked upon that initial 1701 recommendation, but again that summer, the board repeated its complaint that "they prejudice other Colonies in drawing . . . away their servants and people and harbor fugitives." Proprietary colonies like Carolina, the board concluded, "are in a state of Anarchy and Confusion."[69]

By the end of the century, however, as Albemarle's population continued to grow, its expansion included not just fugitives or misfits from Virginia but also ambitious and upwardly mobile colonists who were being increasingly squeezed out of other Caribbean and North American coastal hot spots. Opportunities elsewhere to get rich quick and/or obtain political status were becoming less common, and Albemarle was now attracting its share of opportunists.[70] The absence of a rigid political hierarchy appeared to outsiders as a power vacuum waiting to be exploited, and a new generation of settlers, many of them from prominent Virginia or English families, hoped to translate their connections and financial resources into financial success and political power in North Carolina.[71]

Such opportunists were successful in directing the colony down this path in the last decade of the century, laying the foundation in Albemarle for a new society that resembled the hierarchical rule of the British empire. This trend tended toward authoritarian politics and away from toleration of dissent and religious freedom. The old settler party in Albemarle could look north to Virginia and see discomforting similarities in the direction of their colonies: land speculators and cronies of proprietary governors began to grab up huge swaths of land, a practice very much at odds with the values of Old Albemarle. If left unchecked, Albemarle risked falling under the thumb of a landed elite, supported by an Anglican establishment to which the secular settlers did not conform.[72]

Three interrelated bulwarks remained against the imposition of a rigid hierarchy and development of a full-blown slave society in the region. The House of Burgesses, where Old Albemarle settlers and their political allies still held a majority, continued to reject any measures that might concentrate power in the hands of a small landholding elite. Also, the leveling spirit of Albemarle Quakers, a prominent portion of the Burgess delegates themselves, stood as a challenge to the elite Anglican establishment. Finally, the traditional sovereigns of the Dismal Swamp region, its Indigenous people, remained a check upon the geographic expansion of land-hungry men of the Albemarle' Chowan precinct.

These planter-elites hoped to overcome all three in one fell swoop and claim what their peers in Virginia and South Carolina enjoyed—more land, armies of enslaved people to work it, control of the government, and deference from the "lower sort." To snatch up Indigenous land, they needed the political power to be able to break decades-old agreements with Native Americans over boundary lines, especially a treaty prohibiting white expansion west of the Chowan River. Political power could only be accomplished by wresting control of the assembly from its old settler–aligned Quaker majority.

The landed gentry knew that if they could officially establish the Anglican Church in their corner of the colony, then the Quakers, the strongest ally of the old settlers and advocates of peace with neighboring Native Americans, could be weakened and possibly disqualified from office. In late 1700, the council prorogued and dissolved the assembly, maneuvering behind the scenes for favorable assembly election results the following fall. Then, two months later, it passed the Vestry Act, which imposed a new tax to construct churches and pay a minister's salary, and the Act against Sabbath Breaking. However, these acts were not ratified by the Proprietors, and the Vestry Act remained the hot button political issue in the next assembly elections in 1703.[73] The council was not able to exert the same influence then as it had two years earlier. In that election, supporters of the establishment complained that "all sorts of people, even servants, Negroes, Aliens, Jews, and Common sailors were admitted to vote."[74] Council president Henderson Walker informed the body that Quakers controlled a majority of the House of Burgesses and had "declared their designs of making void the act for establishing the Church."[75]

As the establishment of the Anglican Church remained in limbo, northern Carolina's Anglican deputy governor Robert Daniel seized upon a 1702 Privy Council order that demanded all colonial assemblymen take an oath of loyalty to Queen Anne as a qualification for taking their elected seats. Previously, Quakers had been allowed to subscribe their name in a book rather than swearing an oath, a practice they refused. Now, though, Quakers might be denied their seats, and this fate did in fact befall most of the assembly's Quaker delegates (who had held nine of ten seats in Dismal Swamp precincts). Their dismissal left many administrative and governmental positions open, and when Thomas Cary assumed the governorship in the spring of 1705, he filled them with loyal Chowan men. When the assembly met in December, the governor and his council called for new elections (with oaths required of delegates chosen) and redrew precinct boundaries. The Dismal Swamp precincts that had previously claimed five seats each on the assembly legitimately worried that their representation might be diminished. In fact, their power was diluted through the creation of several new precincts (without any input from the assembly) in Bath County.[76] The political representation of Old Albemarle seemed to have been hamstrung, and the "Plebian Route," as Virginia governor Alexander Spotswood later derisively called it, seemed blocked.[77]

The Quaker/dissenter faction dispatched representatives to London to plead their case before the Proprietors. Fearing revocation of their charter, the lords repealed the Vestry Acts, removed Cary from office, and issued new blank delegations for a fresh governor's council. William Glover, Cary's replacement, was even more ardently aligned with the establishment. Incongruously, Cary returned in 1708 and threw his support to the Quaker/dissenter group, the very constituency he had opposed in his term as governor. He was clearly not a principled politician but rather another opportunist, yet was able to win the support of the dissenters by opposing religious establishment. He still nonetheless privileged the landed elite.

Now with the support of the old settlers (called "a gang of tramps and rioters" by his political opponent) Cary managed to oust Glover from office and organize an assembly with an old settler majority, including Quakers, that required no oaths. Glover, however, refused to acknowledge his removal and organized his own rival government of backers of the establishment willing to take an oath of office. Outnumbered, however, he fled to Virginia, and Cary and his Quaker/old settler coalition was left to govern mostly undisturbed for two years. Importantly, with land-hungry newcomers out of power for the time being, pressure upon neighboring Native American groups subsided.

The open minded old settler Quaker philosophy of peace and fair-mindedness took Indigenous-settler relations back a generation to a time of more peaceable coexistence.[78] Allies of the establishment thought Cary's coalition a bunch of "roguish Quakers" without law or order. Albemarle, an Anglican minister lamented, resembled "Olivers days come again."[79] Those empowered under Cary, of course, would have taken the commonwealth reference as a compliment. They would have their own civil war soon enough.

The Development of a Landed Elite
and the End of Old Settler Power

Arrivals from across the Atlantic in late 1710 threatened the Cary government's peace and authority. Baron Christoph De Graffenried, a British peer from Switzerland, had been granted 10,000 acres by the Proprietors along the Neuse and Cape Fear Rivers to establish to establish a town of immigrants from Germany and Switzerland. Despite being ravaged by disease and plundered by French pirates during their voyage, several hundred immigrants established the town of New Bern at the junction of the Trent and Neuse Rivers. They struggled with a poor harvest and did not establish good relations with local Native American groups.[80]

Meanwhile Edward Hyde (not the former Proprietor) had arrived in Virginia in August with documents from the Proprietors naming him the new deputy governor of North Carolina. Cary did not challenge the validity of Hyde's appointment and stepped aside as the new governor called for elections. However, when Hyde aligned himself exclusively with the Chowan clique, resurrected an oath requirement for elected officials, and pushed through a new act establishing the Church of England, Cary joined an energized opposition faction that questioned the validity of Hyde's commission and demanded the dissolution of the newly elected assembly. Hyde attempted to have Cary and other dissenting leaders arrested on trumped-up charges and went after him with eighty armed men. Cary and forty followers met Hyde at a fortified position on the Pamlico, and the latter retreated before a fight could break out.[81]

Following news that Cary had been armed and provisioned by a Quaker merchant, including "a Brigantine of six Guns . . . with some other Vessells equipped in a Warlike manner," and was amassing manpower such that the governor's forces could not hope to overcome him, Hyde appealed to Virginia authorities for assistance in putting down the rebellion.[82] He could not have found a more willing partner than Virginia governor Alexander Spotswood. Spotswood was a vocal critic of the North Carolina "rabble," especially when they claimed political power. Now, as the number of people enslaved in Virginia was approaching half the colony's population, Albemarle's traditional open-arms policy regarding "fugitives" had become more of a real threat than a stubborn annoyance. In 1709 and again early the next year, the Dismal Swamp counties of southern Virginia had been shaken by rebellion plots of maroons and enslaved people, the end goal of both being a permanent escape into the Great Dismal Swamp.[83] Spotswood warned his Burgesses that "the Desire of freedom" among Virginia's enslaved population was perhaps "The Most Dangerous" threat facing the colony. The late insurrection plots along the northern edge of the Dismal Swamp proved to him "that we are not to Depend on Either their Stupidity, or that Babel of Languages among 'em." "Freedom," he continued, "Wears a Cap which Can Without a Tongue, Call Together all Those who Long to Shake of The fetters of Slavery."[84]

Freedom's call was quite loud from the North Carolina Dismal Swamp region. Virginia's council determined to help settle the "great commotions" in

North Carolina before its "bad influence" extended back across the Dismal, "encouraging the servants and negroes and other persons of desperate fortunes to run from hence in hopes of protection from the party in arms there."[85] When Cary rejected Spotswood's mediator, Virginia mustered a detachment of its militia into Hyde's service and sent several Royal Marines who had been stationed north of the Dismal.[86]

Before the troops from Virginia arrived, Cary's men went on the offensive. They attacked Hyde's fortified position in Chowan, but through a series of strategic blunders, the rebels managed to lose possession of one of their ships (and along with it all big guns and ammunition), and many troops by capture. After this loss, Cary's popular support quickly began to erode, especially when it became known that Royal Marines were set to engage the rebels. The presence of the queen's soldiers was evidence of the real power the establishment faction truly held over the old settler population—an attack upon them by the rebels would have been an act of treason. With no path forward, rebel leaders "disbursed themselves": they either fled the colony (Cary and some of his closest associates were arrested attempting to sail for England) or retreated into the anonymity of the Carolina interior frontier or the Great Dismal Swamp.[87]

The "Quaker-Leveller republic" had fallen, and it would not be long before yet another bloody conflict would strike northern Carolina.[88] Less than two months after Royal Marines marched over what was left of Old Albemarle, and while Hyde's forces and the marines were still hunting down enemies in and around the Dismal Swamp, the Tuscarora War erupted.[89] Tensions had been building for some time between Native Americans and North Carolina settlers south and west of the Dismal. As long as the Albemarle settlers were faithful to the commonsense of their first generation, their relations with their Indigenous neighbors had remained peaceable. However, as the European population grew and settlement expanded south of the Albemarle Sound in the 1690s, friction sometimes flared up into conflict. The settlements of Bath and then New Bern were built upon Tuscarora land, raising tensions further. The Tuscarora had been accused by settlers of sheltering runaway slaves.[90]

In August, the Tuscarora seized De Graffenried and North Carolina surveyor general John Lawson while they were on a scouting trip up the Neuse. De Graffenried was mistaken for Governor Hyde himself. Lawson was already notorious as the surveyor who laid out towns on land that was not his to claim. King Hancock of the Tuscarora invited forty other regional chiefs to an "Assembly of the Great" where they considered the fate of their valuable prisoners and pledged themselves to a pantribal alliance to oppose further European expansion.[91]

After torturing and executing Lawson (De Graffenried had managed to

prove that he was not Hyde and struck a favorable deal in exchange for spar-
ing his life), hundreds of Indigenous warriors swept through the river valleys
south of the Albemarle Sound, attacking the settlements in their path. In the
first day's offensive, they killed over 130 whites (mostly men) and took dozens more women and children prisoner. The Tuscarora alliance continued to
spread out across the region south and west of Albemarle and wreaked havoc
and destruction over the next several weeks.[92]

At least one historian has called the Tuscarora War an unbroken continuation of the Cary Rebellion.[93] It might seem that way, for many reasons.
Although all extant contemporary sources of the conflict come from Hyde-
aligned establishment figures and do not confirm a connection between Cary
supporters and the Indigenous alliance, the behavior of rebels in the Dismal
Swamp counties, in the words of another historian, "overwhelmingly" suggests
that they at least agreed to remain neutral while the attacks pushed back the
previous decade's incursions south of the Albemarle Sound.[94] Hyde accused
rebel John Porter of encouraging Indigenous attacks "on the Western Shore of
Chowan, that has been the only subjects to her Majesty that on all occasions
has expressed their loyalty."[95] Spotswood believed that the rebels maintained
"a traitorous correspondence with the Tuscarora Indians wereby they have en-
deavoured to incite and stir up the said Indians (by promises of reward) to cut
off Her Magesties good subjects of the said province of North Carolina."[96] De
Graffenried had accused rebels of having "defamed Govr. Hyde, in the opinion
of the Indians, to such a degree that they held him for their declared enemy."[97]

Moreover, Hyde was unable to muster militia from among Dismal Swamp
rebels to fight the Tuscarora. Quakers, Spotswood pointed out, had will-
ingly taken up arms "to pull down the Government" but "now fly again to the
pretence of Conscience to be excused from assisting against the Indians."[98]
Settlers of Old Albemarle who had never attended a Quaker meeting also
refused to take up arms for the establishment against their Indigenous good
neighbors. After all, they were not endangered by the attack—there would
be no attacks on the Dismal Swamp counties, only upon their political opponents.[99] Even faced with a five-pound fine for not responding to the call
to arms, "few or none would go out." Rebels, Thomas Pollack protested, attempted to "hinder and dissuade" their neighbors "and will not so much as
send their armes to those who are willing to go." Further, they concealed
those who feared being impressed or who were still wanted fugitives from the
previous uprising.[100] Only through the ruthless intervention of South Carolina
settlers and 300 allied Native Americans was the North Carolina colony, south
of the Dismal Swamp, saved from destruction in the Tuscarora War.

Most of the defeated Tuscarora were unwilling to submit to the authority of Tom Blount, who had been installed as a puppet "king" of the Tuscarora by colonial officials. They attempted to go north through western Virginia to join the Iroquois Confederacy in June 1713. Though many succeeded, some whose path of retreat led north through the protection of the Dismal Swamp found themselves cut off by Virginia troops who had been stationed by Spotswood at its northern edge to keep them from passing through the eastern part of his colony. These were hemmed into the swamp without an outlet to escape.[101] Even those who coalesced under Blount were limited to their old Skanwaknee hunting grounds north of the Roanoke River in present-day Bertie County, at the edge of the Dismal. The swamp, then, became an extension of their settlement. Moreover, still falling occasionally under attack from their settler-allied Indigenous enemies, they found that the swamp provided a close, and for some, permanent refuge. There, too, they would encounter other Indigenous people who had already taken up residence in the swamp. The entire remnant of the Matchapunga had been forced "into the recesses of the Great Dismal Swamp" by James Moore's South Carolina forces in early (probably February) 1713.[102] With light canoes, they had taken refuge in the "most distant extremities" of the Dismal, "in which it was impossible for the whites to follow them."[103]

The final barrier to North Carolina's transition to a plantation society, controlled by a cadre of establishment landed elites, had been removed. Powerful interests to the north and south agreed that Albemarle's sanctuary society had represented a threat to the health and expansion of their own slave societies, and so they decisively intervened to squash it. Old Albemarle and its allies had held their own for seven decades in their leveled society.[104] However, following the Tuscarora War, the consolidation of powerful forces seemed to squeeze them further and further into the margins. Free of any Native American threat, white planters swarmed across the colony and established slave labor camps. From fewer than 1,000 before the Tuscarora War, the number of enslaved people mushroomed to 6,000 by 1730. "The introduction of slaves," one early historian wrote of this period, "may be considered as unimpeded."[105] It certainly was for Maurice Moore, a South Carolinian who had led forces to the rescue of North Carolina against the Tuscarora, and who remained in Albemarle after his victory. In 1725, he moved with his family and brothers into the Cape Fear region of the northern colony. The Moore family, described by a contemporary as "of the set known there as the Goose Creek faction" imported hundreds of enslaved people from their South Carolina plantation empire into their new land of opportunity.[106]

In 1714, twice as many ships arrived in North Carolina as had in any previous year to transport out a dramatic increase in exports.[107] In 1715, the government passed its first slave code, enacted laws to encourage internal improvements and thus the production of cash crops for an external market, provided for the establishment of sawmills and gristmills, made provisions to combat runaways from enslavement, and declared "no Negro Mulatto or Indians shall be capable of voting for Members of Assembly."[108] North Carolina was being belatedly shaped in the plantation society image of its neighbors.[109]

For those of the old settler faction who remained, the successes of the new elite usually translated into marginalization and financial struggle. Those who were enslaved could watch as the frontier was replaced by endless rows of tobacco, and outlets for their escape were nearly closed off. Once-powerful Indigenous groups knew this progression well; they had tracked its advance for a century. The forces of change were bearing down on Old Albemarle, and all those who had opposed it—Black, white, and Indigenous—could either face it with their backs to the Dismal or seek relief from the constricting grip of the slave society. Some chose swamp life, and joined the small but growing community who had called the Dismal home already for a generation, forging the swamp into a conspicuous landscape of refuge and resistance.

The world was closing in, but the swamp could not be squeezed. It was right there, in the center of a bourgeoning plantation society, resolute, unconquered, unmapped even, overlapping and oozing into two colonies, and, misfit landscape that it was, sheltering society's misfits. The Dismal Swamp had truly become, as John Culpeper warned in 1681, "the sink of America, the refuge of . . . renegades."[110] There, swampers thumbed their noses at Virginia and English authority, ignored Carolina laws, and continued to welcome fugitives, now fugitives themselves.

Colonial officials noted with alarm the increased rate and numbers of people fleeing their jurisdiction into the Dismal. Spotswood reported to the Lords Proprietors that "great numbers of loose and disorderly people daily flock thither."[111] Plantation society's outcasts were assembling in the swamp, staying in the swamp, learning the swamp, applying a ready-made political and social structure to a new landscape, and welcoming and guiding others into the swamp. Experienced swampers shared their accumulated knowledge of survival. Certainly the first generation had experienced great adversity in carving out their swamp homes from the wilderness, but together they were learning how to adapt to and coexist with their natural protector. Shared circumstances encouraged the development of a unique community, deep in the swamp and far from the gaze of the outside world.

CHAPTER TWO

Dismal Swamp Maroons
in the Colonial Era

Landscapes are culture before they are nature; constructs of the imagination
projected onto wood and water and rock . . . once a certain idea of landscape,
a myth, a vision, establishes itself in an actual place, it has a peculiar way
of muddling categories, of making metaphors more real than their
referents; of becoming, in fact, part of the scenery.
—Simon Schama, *Landscape and Memory*, 1995

AT THE TURN OF THE eighteenth century, the southern edge of
"civilized" Virginia society butted up against an amorphous and
subversive southern hinterland with the Dismal Swamp at its head
and Old Albemarle below. In the first two decades of the century,
North Carolina elites fostered the development of a new plantation society
patterned on the examples of its neighbors: Virginia, the "Old Dominion,"
whose leaders helped the North Carolina establishment faction defeat its
political opponents, and South Carolina, whose military strength cleared away
the Native Americans who had been seen as a hindrance to expansion.

But the Dismal was a natural obstacle even more difficult to dispatch than
Indigenous warriors. White Virginians and North Carolinians alike looked
with frustrated disgust at the massive and threatening wasteland along their
shared eastern border. Worse, maroons seemed able to navigate the Dismal
with ease, claiming an agency they supposedly should not possess, slipping
into its depths effortlessly, and sometimes even striking back from its refuge.
Yet there was little the Tidewater whites could do to bring the swamp and its
people under their control.

Dangers of the Dismal

The Great Dismal Swamp was a black hole of unproductivity in the eyes of
Tidewater leaders. As enslavers churned out great profits from the lands surrounding it, the enormous swamp remained conspicuous for its refusal to yield

an easy passage from the Chesapeake Bay to the Albemarle Sound, dry land to the plow, or profits to anyone. As much as the fertile fields of the Tidewater were blessed with bountiful yields year after year, the Dismal seemed cursed. The edge of the Dismal was the edge of the "civilized" English world. On the other side was darkness into which no law extended, where monsters and beasts prowled, and where outcasts gathered into maroon communities. It was a landscape befitting the name *Dismal*.

A swamp, of course, is not only a natural landscape, and the Great Dismal Swamp of North Carolina and Virginia is something especially different. As archaeologist Daniel Sayers argues of the Dismal, it is no more a fully natural space than a city block, a residential yard, a shantytown, or a holy site. The historic Dismal Swamp emerged because of an alienating process of the "nonflow of capital" during the colonial period. This was a landscape in the way of "progress," threatening development that was forced to avoid and work around it.[1] It, along with the shifting Outer Banks of the Albemarle Sound, had been serious impediments to the early commercial development of Carolina. Virginia lawmakers looking down their noses south declared the Dismal "altogether useless."[2]

"Outlaw" Virginians of the mid-seventeenth century viewed the treacherous region more positively, and used the swamp's protection to their advantage as they sought refuge from Virginia authorities and Chesapeake overcrowding. Even they, however, mostly moved around it and not through it. They did not move *into* the Dismal in sizeable numbers until they had to as a last resort as the squeeze of development and political oppression pressed in against the swamp in the early 1700s.

Few questioned this wisdom. The Dismal Swamp was considered one of the most inhospitable tracts of land on the eastern seaboard. Dense vegetation reportedly choked out even the sun, and deadly wildlife lurked in the shadows. Besides the imposing swamp terrain, congested with dense vegetation, wildfires—"most dreadful conflagrations"—regularly swept through the swamp in warmer months when water levels dropped and dry peat became as flammable as tinder.[3] Depending on whose stories one might hear, the swamp was also plagued by ghosts, bewitched, cursed, the realm of a dragon, and the haunt of Satan himself.

Until the nineteenth century, swamps in general and the Dismal in particular were understood to cause sickness. The Dismal's peat bogs, standing amber waters covered in a layer of green duckweed, were considered together a "mire of nastiness," and a "filthy quagmire" from which dank vapors emerged to carry dread diseases.[4] The "miasma theory" of disease held that "miasma"

"The Beasts of Carolina."
From Lawson, *A New Voyage to Carolina.*

(or "pollution" in the ancient Greek), a noxious, contaminated form of dirty air or mist, contained particles of decomposed matter (miasmata). These particles, when inhaled, infected those who breathed them with malaria (Latin, literally "bad air"). Hippocrates taught his students in the fifth century BC that malaria disrupted the four humors of the body. Marshy lowland areas were to thus be avoided at all costs.[5]

The Dismal was believed to exhale nothing but miasma and poison vapor. William Byrd, the surveyor, noted a buzzard flying far above his head over the Dismal; he believed that it "flew prodigiously high to get above the noisome exhalations that ascend from that filthy place."[6] No doubt he was worried for his own health, since the "exhalations that continually rise from this vast body of mire and nastiness infect the air for many miles round, and render it very unwholesome for the bordering inhabitants. It makes them liable to agues, pleurisies, and many other distempers, that kill abundance of people, and make the rest look no better than ghosts."[7] He had already complained of the uncertain footing of the swamp, the occasional "island" of higher elevation that was home to venomous serpents and deadly beasts, and foul water. Added to this was the very atmosphere of the swamp that threatened one at every breath. If the beasts of the swamp did not kill you, the swamp itself might.[8]

Whites living on the margins of the swamp appreciated its dangers and respected its sovereignty. They warned outsiders who dared consider entering the swamp of the perils to their health and lives. Penetrating the swamp, they cautioned, was suicidal; at best, outsiders could only claim a perilous détente with the massive Great Dismal by clinging to its edges. William Drummond, the first official governor of northern Carolina, had once become so thoroughly lost in the Dismal that he nearly died of exposure.[9] Many a huntsman who followed game into the Dismal did not return. In the swamp, the hunter might easily become the hunted.[10]

Thus as colonization and settlement intensified in the region surrounding the swamp, the Dismal itself was conspicuous in its refusal to be developed or inhabited by people of means. In the "chaotically transformative" Tidewater and Mid-Atlantic region, the Dismal Swamp could not have seemed any more remote or static.[11] This physical inaccessibility frustrated outsiders to no end, but it also tormented their psyches, increasingly tied up with concepts of mastery—mastery of the natural world, mastery of a man's household, and mastery of one's subordinates in society.

English colonists in North America embraced the elements of the eighteenth-century Georgian order. European mindsets expected landscapes, spaces, and places to be "controlled, divided, and denaturalized."[12] From the Enlightenment focus on progress and the ability to control nature through the rationalization of space grew cultural patterns that emphasized control. Surveys grew increasingly rectangular. Builders designed houses to be more functionally structured and compartmentalized inside and symmetric outside, often extending to a symmetric formal garden. Landowners composed landscapes to express power and control, to make clear planters' dominance over nature and society. This order was considered necessary to bring harmony to an era of apparent disorder, and to symbolically discourage any breakdown of or attack on the established order.[13] In Jamestown, it worked. Ironically, this "order" was so thoroughly expressed through the material culture of the eighteenth century that it was eventually mistaken as itself being natural.[14]

The Great Dismal Swamp, then, was both natural and unnatural. It was set apart from the "true" and appropriate nature of things that could be and were subdued by men, but its thorough indomitable naturalness was also what gave the lie to that conception. Outsiders hated the Dismal for its refusal to conform, to submit. It was reviled as a deformity on the Tidewater landscape that by midcentury had otherwise been conquered, subjugated, and laid out to reflect colonial spatiality. Large numbers of square acres were consolidated in rectilinear landholdings, random natural patterns were overlain with symmetry, and order was imposed on the landscape through usage patterns, that is, areas denoted specifically as places for fields, homes, streets, business districts, and commons.[15] The Dismal Swamp could not even be categorized as land or water, liquid or solid. It did not have clear borders or boundaries. It was ambiguous, dangerous, and abject, made so, as philosopher Julia Kristeva writes, by "disturb[ing] identity, systems, order . . . the in-between, the ambiguous, the composite."[16] The Dismal was a place that blurred meaning and authority.

The wild Dismal Swamp was, put simply and literally, out of control. It was a physical reminder that for all the symmetry and precise angles of the world exterior to the swamp, the ideal ordered world of the Tidewater could never be fully achieved.[17] Moreover, as the swamp increasingly developed into an affront to the Georgian "order" of the natural world, it was also becoming dangerous for the sanctuary it offered the equally untamed "dregs" of society who were, it seemed, settling together in the Dismal. White, Red, Black, and "tawny," the swamp beckoned to them as an outlaw's haven. It was, in the words of J. F. D. Smyth, himself most likely a "fugitive" servant from Virginia in the 1760s, a "general asylum for everything that flies from mankind and society."[18]

What made the marronage of these outcasts even more vexing to white elites was the notion that they had actively rejected "civilization," embraced the wildness of the swamp, and regressed into barbarism, an animal state of nature (or *back* into it, as they believed the case to be with Africans). As historian Alvin Thompson argues, whites viewed marronage in the wilderness "as the call of the wild, the evidence of man at his uncivilized worst."[19] The swamp sat dark and disturbing on the periphery, a fecund, creeping, supernatural thing that would engulf cleared land if neglected. Its maroons, sheltered in its depths, often issued from it to strike at and overrun the plantation world. Neither submitted to "civilization." Neither seemed particularly inclined to respect the boundaries and limits of the outside world.

Compounding the doubly uncivilized "menace" of the swamp and its inhabitants to whites was the fact that despite the Dismal's common description as impenetrable, it very obviously was not. Rather, it seemed only to be navigable by society's rejects. For a white "gentleman" to enter the swamp, it was feared that he would lose all ability to control his fate (few dared without placing their lives in the hands of an enslaved guide). In contrast, maroon outcasts, for possibly the first time in their lives, seized control of their own destiny as they intrepidly entered into the swamp. The Dismal and its unique inhabitants became, as Anthony Wilson suggests, "a persistent reminder of the limits of civilization's conquest of nature and of the divine right of social class."[20] The disorder of an intractable natural space that defended and embraced "civilization's exiles," who flouted the law as well as the social and racial hierarchy, was unbearable.[21] And yet nothing could be done about either.

Resistant People in a Resistant Landscape

In 1672, a group of enslaved Africans escaped their Virginia labor camp. This in and of itself was not particularly remarkable, yet once they reached a wilderness area, settled there, and withstood all attempts to retake them, the fact of their marooning became a serious concern to colonial authorities, especially since the maroons appear to have encouraged other oppressed people to become a part of their community there.[22] A wild and untamed landscape, adjacent to settlements of "civilized" slave labor camps, that provided sanctuary to a potentially multiracial rabble, was a serious matter. As the maroons continued to haunt the developed periphery, the planters' greatest anxiety was that "other negroes, Indians, or servants . . . [might] fly forth and joyne with them." In response, Virginia lawmakers passed "An Act for the Apprehension and Suppression of Runawayes, Negroes, and Slaves," which allowed maroons to be killed with impunity for the good of the state.[23]

Four years later part of that nightmare came true, as poor whites and African Americans joined forces in Bacon's Rebellion. Although that conflict began as a movement against Native Americans, Virginia officials were horrified when ethnic cleansing shifted into multiracial class warfare. Bacon's death decapitated the rebellion, but elites could not escape the realization that if all of Virginia's disaffected laborers came together to oppose the planters' society, the results could be disastrous.[24] The Great Dismal Swamp, everyone knew, could become their fortress.

That possibility explains the obvious panic that a group of southern Virginia planters evinced in a letter to a Virginia magistrate in March 1709 recounting details of the first recorded maroon raids originating from within the Great

Dismal Swamp. They described the maroon campaign as "most remarkable" because it was a multiracial affair, planned and undertaken by African and Native American allies in a region already known for white servant fugitivity. There had been, the planters reported, "a Late Dangerous Conspiracy, formed and Carried on by greate numbers of ye said negroes and Indian slaves for making their Escape by force from ye Service of their masters, and for ye Destroying and cutting off Such of her Majesty's Subjects as Should oppose their Design." The conspiracy had stretched across the Dismal Swamp counties of Surry, James City, and Isle of Wight, all part dry, part bog, part plantation, and part swamp. The fugitives had made good use of the protection the swamp had offered them, allowing enough security to plan a potentially massive rebellion.[25]

The plot was ultimately betrayed, and white authorities rounded up and examined large numbers of conspirators. The transcript of those examinations (which the petitioners had attached to the magistrate's letter) has been lost, or otherwise the rebels' names, numbers, and details of what may have been the largest slave rebellion plot to date would be known. Most of the "greate numbers" were interrogated in an extralegal proceeding, summarily "punished," then delivered back into the hands of their masters, presumably for further abuse.

The "Principle Contrivers," however, remained imprisoned "in ye Goal [jail] of the County" awaiting further orders from magistrates as to how they might be made an example of. Salvadore was described as the charismatic "great promoter and Incourager" of the rebels, while Tom Shaw had "allways been . . . very rude and Insolent." Scipio had been the highest ranking lieutenant of Angola Peter, "the Cheif promoter . . . of that wicked and pernicious designe." Salvadore and Scipio were hanged, drawn, and quartered, with parts of their bodies displayed in towns across the region in "the most publick places" as an example to others. Peter eluded capture, was "outlawed" for his plot "to levy war," and almost certainly returned back into the Dismal Swamp to avoid the price placed on his head dead or alive.[26] In fact, just as the reward was announced, Peter, from his Dismal Swamp base, may have been at the head of another massive Surry County and Isle of Wight County insurrection plot of "great numbers" "for levying war in this colony" on Easter Sunday 1710. This design was frustrated by the betrayal of Will, who was given his freedom as a reward but had to go into hiding since it was believed the maroons he had given up "Laid Wait for his Life."[27] Peter was never captured.

In a landscape enduringly resistant to development, marronage was becoming just as enduring a form of resistance against slavery in the Tidewater.

Maroons hit at their enslavers' interests initially and directly by "stealing themselves," a "theft" that not only removed a valuable chattel from the ownership of the enslaver but also compounded the loss by prohibiting an enslaver from the benefit of that chattel's labor. Maroons also adroitly claimed unruly space that confounded whites. They created an alternative landscape where they were, to a great degree, independent of the outside, dominant society.

It is noteworthy that the first recorded maroon raids from the Dismal Swamp were directed against Virginia and not North Carolina. While the Dismal Swamp counties in North Carolina remained true to the spirit of Old Albemarle, few people there felt the need to exile in the swamp, and the few who did had no desire to direct attacks against their allies, families, and friends to the south. Rather, it was Virginia, the colony that oppressed and enslaved the maroons, that faced guerrilla campaigns like those of 1709 and 1710 and felt the effects of "troublesome Indian renegades," "lawless Englishmen," and African "Rogues" striking north.[28] Besides outright armed engagement, maroons commonly picked off the cattle and hogs of Virginia planters who allowed their animals to graze and forage on the rich western edge of the swamp, and supplied themselves from the storehouses of southern Virginia slave labor camps.[29]

With the Virginia Dismal's multiethnic maroon population significantly augmented by representatives of the same ethnic groups from North Carolina, the swamp was now possibly the most cosmopolitan place in British North America. Native Americans had utilized the swamp for hundreds of years for hunting and ceremonial purposes, and their collective memory informed the ability of Europeans and Africans to use the swamp as a refuge from colonial oppression. They relied on Indigenous guides to find their way into the swamp and to survive once concealed. By the early years of the eighteenth century, a triracial outlaw culture and society was developing within and around the Dismal Swamp, starting and raising families, trading, making a living, and for the most part remaining out of the eye of the powers outside the swamp.

And outlaws they were. In Virginia, or perhaps even (beyond Albemarle County) North Carolina, many of these residents were "fugitives" from servitude, slavery, debt, or any number of statutory provisions. Some might have even been generational outlaws back to their ancestors of the previous century. In and around the swamp they were literally outlaws—outside the reach of any "law." They resided in what was still for all practical purposes a no-man's-land. Settlers in and around the Great Dismal Swamp thumbed their noses at any and all authority, ignored the laws of Virginia and North Carolina, and continued to welcome fugitives. They may have technically been located *within* the boundaries of a jurisdiction, but it was never clear whose.

Since authorities of both colonies were interested in determining just whose scofflaws these were, officials on both sides of the swamp sponsored numerous attempts to establish an official line through it. The border between North Carolina and Virginia had never been clear. It had never been accurately mapped, lying as the diving line did through some of the most rugged terrain in American through which no colonial had ever ventured, much less a capable surveyor. A joint 1710 survey fell apart heated as accusations flew between Virginians and Carolinians over each other's qualifications and the shoddiness of inaccurate surveying equipment. Through almost the entirety of proprietary rule in North Carolina, no one knew where one colony ended and the other began. Of course, maroons did not care whose laws were in force—the only law in the Dismal Swamp was their own.

Surveying the Virginia / North Carolina Boundary

To counter the swamp's geographical uncertainty came the 1728 surveying expedition of William Byrd II. Colonel Byrd was a wealthy planter in Westover, Virginia, and shared with the elite of that colony a general disgust at their "rude" southern neighbors. Byrd wrote two accounts of his experience, one titled "The History of the Dividing Line betwixt Virginia and North Carolina" and another bawdy and sarcastic version he intended to keep hidden from public view.[30] Both versions betray his contempt for North Carolinians. Byrd's Virginia patrons craved a precise survey of their southern border. Mapmaking demanded it, and tax rolls could not be filled without it. Virginians like Byrd also craved an official line to separate fair and civilized Virginia from the barbaric riffraff of North Carolina.

Byrd was accompanied by two other Virginia boundary commissioners, as well as a chaplain who might minister to any unbaptized heathen North Carolinians they might encounter along the way.[31] Four North Carolina commissioners (unprepared and unprofessional, in Byrd's opinion) accompanied them as well. Byrd nicknamed his North Carolina counterparts Judge Jumble, Shoebrush, Plausible, and Puzzlecause in his "secret" account.[32] With several gear-porters and surveyors, the men drove a stout cedar post into the sand on the north shore of Currituck Inlet where they determined the border latitude of 36 degrees 31 minutes north, and set out due west from it.[33]

Byrd initiated the survey by insulting the first North Carolinians he encountered, "a marooner, that modestly called himself a hermit," and his companion, "a wanton female." They lived in a bark hut on the south shore of the inlet, and Byrd assumed they subsisted largely upon what shellfish they could lazily gather and what milk they could "moisten their mouths with" from their neighbors' cows. They were shabbily clothed, scandalously shared labor between the man and woman, and Byrd seemed to have been confirmed in his prejudices: "Thus did these wretches live in a dirty state of nature, and were mere Adamites, innocence only excepted." The first person the survey team spied the next day tried to avoid them by hurriedly paddling in the opposite direction, because, Byrd figured, he must have believed the men were "officers of justice."[34] Byrd's failure to note the race of these Dismal Swampers (when his normal habit was to capture the experience in great detail) suggests his uncertainty regarding those categorizations.

Three days later, Byrd's team knocked off early for the day and decided to explore out about a half mile from the line. This was near the Northwest River, approximately 6.5 miles into the swamp from the cedar log on Currituck Sound. Not entirely unexpectedly, Byrd encountered a maroon family. He described them and their situation as "a family of mulattoes that called themselves free, though by the shyness of the master of the house, who took care to keep least in sight, their freedom seemed a little doubtful." He did not record anything else about these people, although he did use the encounter as an occasion to include some commentary on marronage and fugitives in the Great Dismal: "It is certain many slaves shelter themselves in this obscure part of the world, nor will any of their righteous neighbours discover them. On the contrary, they find their account in settling such fugitives on some out-of-the-way corner of their land, to raise stocks for a mean and inconsiderable share, well knowing their condition makes it necessary for them to submit to any terms. Nor were these worthy borderers content to shelter runaway slaves, but debtors and criminals have often met with the like indulgence."[35] Byrd had clearly already been made familiar with the existence of marronage in the Dismal and subscribed to his Virginia peers' opinion of the swamp as the "sink of America."[36] He did not miss the chance to mark maroons' exotic presence along with the swamp's flora and fauna, they being but slightly removed from the latter in his mind.

In his manuscript, Byrd also issued a stark warning to the government of North Carolina. He pointed out that early Rome had also welcomed society's outcasts to grow its population. The city's legendary founders, Romulus and Remus, like the maroons of the Dismal Swamp, had issued a call to the exiles, dispossessed, and self-emancipating people of Italy to join them in the building of a city of refuge in the wilderness. From such similar beginnings had grown one of the most powerful empires in history, and Byrd warned that if the growing maroon population of the Dismal Swamp were not soon checked, a dangerous power base hostile to the surrounding country might emerge.[37]

After a week of difficult work, the group reached the point at which the Dismal became too thick for the gentler folk of the expedition to traverse. Cocksure of their ability to continue on, the actual surveyors arrogantly celebrated their pioneer abilities on the eve of their entry into the depths of the Dismal. Shrewd edge-dwellers, however, attempted to dampen the surveyors' enthusiasm before going in. "Ye have little reason to be merry, my masters," said one solemn-faced man. Then he warned, "I fancy the pocoson you must struggle with to-morrow will make you change your note, and try what metal you are made of. Ye are, to be sure, the first of human race that ever had the boldness to attempt it, and I dare say will be the last. If, therefore, you have any worldly goods to dispose of, my advice is that you make your wills this very night, for fear you die intestate to-morrow."[38] Byrd reported that "these frightful tales were so far from disheartening the men, that they served only to whet their resolution." The next morning, though, the team found the formidable swamp not "one Jot better than it had been painted to them."

Byrd went on to write the first detailed account of the deep interior of the Great Dismal Swamp (derived secondhand, of course, from his crewmembers who actually attempted the journey). The swamp was, overall, "a filthy bog" full of thickly growing and intertwined "gall bushes" and "bamboo-briers." The ground, where it was above water, was "moist and trembling under our feet like a quagmire, insomuch that it was an easy matter to run a ten foot pole up to the head in it, without exerting any uncommon strength to do it." They found the ground so spongy and saturated that the dark amber colored water oozed up to meet them—"every step made a deep impression, which was instantly filled with water."[39]

However, they apparently did not see the "Lyons, Panthers, and Alligators" locals had warned them about. In fact, Byrd wrote that they

laid eyes on no living creature: neither bird nor beast, insect nor reptile came in view. Doubtless, the eternal shade that broods over this mighty bog, and hinders the sunbeams from blessing the ground, makes it an uncomfortable habitation for any thing that has life. Not so much as a Zealand frog could endure so aguish a situation. It had one beauty, however, that delighted the eye, though at the expense of all the other senses: the moisture of the soil preserves a continual verdure, and makes every plant an evergreen but at the same time the foul damps ascend without ceasing, corrupt the air, and render it unfit for respiration. Not even a turkey buzzard will venture to fly over it, no more than the Italian vultures will over the filthy lake Avernus, or the birds in the Holy Land, over the Salt sea, where Sodom and Gomorrah formerly stood.[40]

Byrd's surveying team was meant to hack their way west, while the colonel and other gentry went north and around the swamp. They made plans to meet on the eastern side of the Dismal in eight days' time. After offering a benediction to "the Almighty to prosper your Undertaking, & grant we may meet on the other Side in perfect Health & Safety," Byrd and his surveyors parted ways.[41]

The men could make no more than a mile and a half headway per day. In fact, they could not clear a way quickly enough to avoid getting sucked down into the bog. The reeds were ten feet high and thick, briars pierced their skin at every turn, and the unseasonable March heat was stifling, especially since no breeze penetrated the jungle to cool them. The more perceptive of them would have also had the uncanny feeling of being watched from a distance— maroon sentinels patrolled the swamp and carefully observed the activities of any outsiders.[42]

When the surveyors did not emerge from the swamp on the appointed day, Byrd became concerned. Had they succumbed to the elements, been sucked down by boggy peat or quicksand, been attacked by bears or panthers, or, most terrifying, been waylaid by maroon "bandits" who had intimate knowledge of the swamp and a powerful motivation to defend their refuge? Byrd ordered guns fired and drums beaten, hoping for some response from the men, but none was heard. The reason, they later found out, was that the surveyors had only been able to penetrate one-third of the way into the swamp in eight days and had run out of supplies. They had developed an understandable "dread of laying their bones in a bog that would soon spew them up again," abandoned the survey, and hurried due west as fast as they could slog it through the swamp (about four more desperate miles that day). By the end of the next, they had reached Peter Brinkley's home near Coropeake, North Carolina, overcome with hunger and exhaustion.[43]

After a short recovery, the surveyors returned to the swamp and continued their "dirty march."[44] With nothing to do but wait on the crew's reemergence, Byrd suffered through his confinement with his North Carolina hosts. "It was really more insupportable than the greatest fatigue," he wrote, "and made us even envy the drudgery of our friends in the Dismal." For their part, the surveyors bore three more solid days pulling their survey chain through the muck, and covered the remaining five miles of swamp before finally treading again on dry ground.[45]

Maroon Legislation

Most people noted Byrd's achievement in determining where North Carolina ended and Virginia began. However, by confirming that the Tidewater's outcasts were finding refuge in the Dismal Swamp, he stoked long-standing fears of the development of the swamp as a seat of fugitive power. In 1680, in response to increasing rates of marronage and slave unrest, Virginia lawmakers had passed "An Act for Preventing Negroes Insurrections," aimed at curtailing any enslaved person who dared "lift up his hand in opposition against any christian," and especially maroons who "lye hid and lurking in obscure places, comitting injuries to the inhabitants." In the case of such resistance, "it shal be lawfull for such person or persons to kill the said negroe or slave soe lying out and resisting." This death sentence was commonly called "outlawing," the granting of full license to whites who might execute an offender, and a threat that would lurk over many Dismal Swamp maroons over the next century and a half. This 1680 law was to be printed and publicly proclaimed every six months.[46]

In 1691 the colony passed "An Act for Suppressing Outlying Slaves." Aimed again at "negroes, mulattoes, and other slaves [who] unlawfully absent themselves from their masters and mistresses service, and lie hid and lurk in obscure places killing hoggs and committing other injuries to the inhabitants of this dominion," the law provided strategies for their capture, including authorizing a sheriff "to raise such and soe many forces" as he thought necessary "for the effectual apprehending [of] such negroes, mulattoes and other slaves." If the maroons "lying out as aforesaid shall resist, runaway, or refuse to deliver and surrender him or themselves" to the authorities, "in such cases it shall and may be lawfull for such person and persons to kill and distroy such negroes, mulattoes, and other slave or slaves by gunn or any otherwaise whatsoever."[47]

Virginia expanded its seventeenth-century maroon laws into a comprehensive slave code in 1705: "An Act Concerning Servants and Slaves." Among its many provisions, this code created monetary incentives of up to 200 pounds of tobacco for white Virginians to "take up" maroons, provided for runaways to be whipped, prohibited the enslaved from possessing a "gun, sword, club, staff, or other weapon," and called for the seizure of "all horses, cattle, and hogs" owned by enslaved people. An entire section of the law pertained specifically to maroons, described again as enslaved people who "run away and lie out, hid and lurking in swamps, woods, and other obscure places, killing hogs and committing other injuries to the inhabitants of this her majesty's colony and dominion." These could be outlawed, and it would be lawful "for any person or persons whatsoever, to kill and destroy such slaves by such ways and means as he, she, or they shall think fit." If one chose not to kill a captured maroon, dismemberment or similar punishment "as they in their discretion shall think fit" was encouraged for "any such incorrigible slave, and terrifying others from the like practices." Since preventing such occurrences was in the public interest, owners would be compensated for their lost or mutilated property.[48]

North Carolina followed the lead of its northern neighbor in 1715 by passing legislation with the same exact title and nearly verbatim text. This included prohibitions on enslaved people traveling beyond their labor camp without a pass and provisions for maroons "who lie out hid and lurking in the Swamps, Woods, and other Obscure Places." People successful in marooning could be killed with impunity after a period of two months.[49] In 1741, hoping to avoid its own Stono Rebellion, North Carolina strengthened its punishments for recalcitrant enslaved people in new legislation. This code included prohibitions against enslaved people carrying weapons of any sort or "rang[ing] in the Woods, upon any pretence whatsoever," and death sentences for those maroons who "run away and lie out hid and lurking in the Swamps, Woods and other Obscure Places" or who might "consult, advise or conspire to rebel."[50] Here the law's authors acknowledged how "contagious" marronage was. The 1741 code was passed again in similar forms three more times in the colonial era.[51]

Effective laws that are consistently followed do not have to be passed and re-passed a half dozen times, or publicly published and proclaimed every few months as a reminder that they remain in force. Legislative revisitation suggests ineffectiveness, the psychological discomfort of legislators, or, as was most likely the case, both. Moreover, the verbatim-repeated language regarding maroons in the legislation over nearly a century and across colonial boundaries spoke volumes about the real terror maroons struck in the hearts of white planters in the Tidewater.

The rate of bound labor mushroomed at the beginning of the eighteenth century, especially in Virginia but also in North Carolina. Enslaved people comprised nearly 30 percent of the population of Virginia around 1700. Their numbers had grown more than 500 percent between 1680 and 1700, while the white population actually declined.[52] The year North Carolina passed its first slave code, a third of its residents were enslaved.[53] As the number of enslaved people increased, so too did evidence of resistance to their enslavement, including marronage.[54]

Maroon activity in and around the Dismal Swamp steadily increased through the first decades of the eighteenth century. The swamp's population likely grew daily as Virginia governor Alexander Spotswood feared, enough to inspire a series of legal enactments to curtail it.[55] Maroons cut out cattle and hogs from Virginia herds, sheltered other fugitives from enslavement and the law, purloined the property of whites for themselves, and claimed an agency otherwise denied by their former enslavers. The swamp region was, as Spotswood declared in 1711, "a common sanctuary to all our running servants and all others that fly from the due execution of the laws."[56]

Spotswood consistently complained about the maroon threat to law and order — maroons refused to acknowledge his authority (his own bound laborers were apparently also prone to escape) and that of the colony of Virginia.[57] But others betrayed a fear that bordered on panic in their commentary regarding the Great Dismal Swamp and its maroons. Some colonists described maroons with the same invectives then being applied to the pirates marauding up and down the coast.[58] Their number, which may have only recently surpassed 100, was exaggerated into legions, and from the swamp, like a deadly miasma, spread a hardly suppressed panic of "marauding hordes."[59]

The Specter of Insurrection

The feared cataclysm was not long in developing. In the summer of 1730, unusually large numbers of enslaved people across Virginia, but especially in and around the Dismal Swamp counties, were noted to have absented themselves from their labor camps and held "many meetings and consultations . . . in order to obtain their Freedom." Officials mobilized local militia units to break up these groups of maroons and enslaved people and get them back to their quarters. Governor William Gooch noted that these operations pushed the soldiers to exhaustion, and kept them on patrol at the height of harvest season. Some of the ringleaders were eventually captured and placed "under severe chastisement by whipping for rambling abroad."[60]

The roundup was ineffective in breaking up the insurrection conspiracy or the maroons, at least in the Dismal Swamp counties of Norfolk and Princess Anne. Six weeks later, a group of several hundred had marooned in the northern Dismal, organized themselves into fighting units, and elected "officers to command them in their intended insurrection."[61] Again, however, the plot was foiled and several maroon leaders "taken up and examined." The great majority ("above three Hundred") retreated deeper into the Dismal, from which they continued to commit "many outrages against the Christians . . . and did a great deal of Mischief." With the help of some Pasquotank Indians, authorities eventually recaptured twenty-four of the maroons and hanged them.[62] The "Chesapeake Rebellion" of 1730 was mostly bloodless (for whites), yet it was also most likely the greatest entry of maroons into the Dismal Swamp until the 1770s.[63]

Governor William Gooch had said plainly, "We are in no small danger from our slaves," especially, it seemed, from self-emancipated maroons "lurking" in the swamp shadows.[64] His friend William Byrd agreed. Byrd was one of the very few white colonists to have ever encountered a group of maroons within the swamp, so in a sense he was a North American authority on marronage. In a July 1736 letter to colonial official John Perceval, he expressed his fear that Virginia might "some time or other be confirmed by the name of New Guinea," a much more nuanced fear than Gooch's. Byrd was aware of what historians would later confirm—that "outlandish" Africans (that is, those born in and kidnapped directly from Africa) marooned at a disproportional rate compared to "seasoned" African Americans. In the mid-eighteenth century, even as the overall ratio of Africans declined in Virginia and North Carolina, they still remained a large percent of the runaways, as much as three times more likely to escape and maroon than seasoned enslaved people, and they were the most likely to maroon in groups.[65]

Byrd thought it best if "insolent" Africans no longer be imported into Virginia. They might have a strong influence on poor whites and other bound laborers, potential fugitives themselves, and "dispose . . . them . . . to pilfer."[66] Yet the occasional group of maroons who raided a granary or smokehouse on the periphery of the swamp seemed far less a threat than the large numbers who might congregate in its depths and rise up to overthrow their captors and colonial authority. Byrd was well aware of the First Maroon War that was then raging in Jamaica and feared the same fate for Virginia, especially following the Chesapeake rebellion of 1730. Like Jamaica, Virginia had inaccessible places maroons could lay out unmolested and "do as much mischief" as they were then making in the Caribbean. "We have already at least 10,000 men of these descendants of Ham fit to bear arms, and their numbers increase every day." Who knew if a North American Cudjo already lurked in the Dismal Swamp, a maroon leader "of desperate courage . . . exasperated by a desperate fortune [who] might with more advantage than Catiline kindle a servile war"? Indeed, had not Angola Peter already launched such a campaign in 1709, and hundreds of maroons just recently joined swamp forces under military leaders of their own election? "Such a man," Byrd warned, "might be dreadfully mischievous before any opposition could be formed against him, and tinge our rivers as wide as they are with blood."[67]

Byrd dealt with recalcitrance on his own slave labor camp by brutalizing his human property into submission. If his enslaved people "fell short" of expectations, that behavior was identified and demarcated, the people forced to submit to his exceptionally brutal mastery. If all went according to the master's plan, the aberration was destroyed.[68] The torture and sexual assault Byrd inflicted upon his human property were entirely within his legal rights. Master and slave were as distinct as night and day. Yet the Dismal had been beyond his capacity to master or subdue. He had been able to confirm the placement of an imaginary surveyor's line through the swamp but could not muster the fortitude to traverse it himself as a member of the survey crew. The ambiguities with which he wrestled were quite intellectually unsettling, and unusual in his experience. There was no order in the swamp—no law, no clear jurisdiction, no productivity, no society (as he would recognize it). Vines and leaves choked out the sun, animals stalked men, gasses from the muck arose to sicken people, and with every step, water and dry ground refused to remain distinct from one another. White and Black blood mingled in the veins of the swamp's inhabitants, and no one could tell slave from free.

The specter of servile insurrection had long haunted him. A younger Byrd had been stricken with nightmares following Angola Peter's maroon campaign of 1709–10. In his dreams, Virginia was threatened with apocalypse. In one particularly disturbing nightmare, a fireball in the night sky burned as a sign of judgment that awaited Virginia slave society. As it struck him with terrors as he slept, Byrd the dreamer could not warn his fellow planters of the looming catastrophe. Historian Anthony S. Parent interprets Byrd's dream as a manifestation of his extreme anxiety when he contemplated the fallout from the rebellion. Byrd's powerlessness to protect against a potential disaster and inability to fully understand it figured into his proposals to deal with the recalcitrant swamp years later.[69] Even if he lacked the physical strength to combat the Dismal, he believed he possessed the political and social authority to eliminate his dark nightmare.

Byrd's Proposal to Drain the Swamp

Byrd dealt with the ambiguities of the swamp by encouraging its complete destruction, though it would be through the efforts of others. Byrd would never set foot in the Dismal again after the survey, and it would remain, in his estimation, nothing more than a "vast body of dirt and nastiness."[70] "It would require a great sum of money to drain it," he admitted, "but the public treasure could not be better bestowed than to preserve the lives of his majesty's liege people, and at the same time render so great a tract of swamp very profitable."[71]

Later that year, Byrd petitioned the king with a plan to bring the swamp into productivity. The Dismal Swamp, he wrote, was a "vast extent of bogg, which is now of no value to the crown, nor ever can be, in the condition it lyes at present." Draining it would make the surrounding country "much more wholesome . . . by correcting and purifying the air, which is now infected by the malignant vapours rising continually from that large tract of mire and filthiness." Moreover, the dry swamp could be profitably utilized for lumbering, shingle production, the production of tar, and growing of hemp, rice, and corn. Canals too could be cut through the swamp to connect the Chesapeake Bay and the Albemarle Sound. Labor was to be extracted from enslaved workers, families specifically, whose natural reproduction would allow the swamp activities to continue indefinitely "that their breed may supply the loss," which would be considerable. Not only would women and children defray "the mortality that must happen," but their presence would also prevent the men's marooning to the remaining recesses of the swamp and fraternizing with established refugee communities. Marronage of the men would cause "many great inconveniences." After *only* ten years (of backbreaking enslaved labor), Byrd predicted, "Dismal will be made as good land as any in the country, with at least 300 negros working upon it."[72] Redeeming the Dismal for agriculture and rendering it useless as a sanctuary for outlaws, Byrd's scheme would substitute the "right" type of Africans (enslaved people) for the wrong ones currently inhabiting the swamp (maroons).

Byrd, of course, would not be the man to tame the Dismal Swamp—deep down, it terrified him too much. For more than a generation, whites outside the swamp continued to be intimidated by it and largely ignored it (or rather closed their eyes and pretended the danger was not there at all). No one but the "wrong sort" made any inroads into the massive blank space on the Tidewater map. To Byrd's credit, plenty of "negros" were indeed at work in the Dismal, but rather for themselves, free of the bonds of enslavement, working to provide for families and building independent communities. He had documented at least one maroon family, and described the skills of other swampers of questionable legal status in evading the outsider's gaze. We hear nothing from his team that actually dragged the surveyor's line through the swamp, the only whites known to have traversed the morass by that point. However, archaeologists have recently excavated village clusters of maroon-built structures deep in the swamp whose construction likely predated Byrd's expedition by a century, as well as others that may have been under construction by maroon carpenters that spring of 1728.[73]

Plenty of evidence in later years documents maroons' continuing active presence in the swamp in the generation after the survey. J. F. D. Smyth documented a significant population of maroons who had been living in the swamp for more than three decades, raising their own livestock and crops near swamp-built cabins possibly in the 1730s and earlier.[74] Another maroon craftsman was living in the swamp by at least 1748 producing goods (musical instruments and furniture) from materials available in the swamp, most likely for internal trade with other maroons.[75] These are isolated glimpses of marronage in the Dismal, but each suggests maroons existing within networks and communities of other maroons — other swampers who were fed from maroon gardens, who raised families over decades, or who sat on the porch of a swamp cabin listening to an elder pluck a handmade banjo.

Despite all the fuss North Carolina and Virginia officials made over the rising incidence of marronage, Dismal Swamp maroons, with a few noteworthy exceptions, spent more time tending garden plots than plotting rebellion in the early eighteenth century. Over more than a century of marronage in the swamp, maroon activity seldom registered as more than a nuisance to the outside slave society. The *potential* for more destructive activities emanating from the swamp was real, especially as the maroon population grew over the first half of the eighteenth century (and indeed would be realized later), but the actual impact was initially of little real consequence. In some ways, marronage was a safety valve for the slave society that surrounded the swamp. Although marronage did keep alive a constant ethos of resistance among those who self-emancipated, it offered them an attractive alternative to rebellion.

The biggest threat posed by marronage, like the Dismal Swamp itself, was an intellectual one. Despite all the legislation on both sides of the border, the maroon population of the Dismal had continued to grow. The Dismal resisted development, and the notion of capturing maroons from the swamp was even greater folly. The powerlessness enslavers felt at their inability to stop the growth of untouchable resistant communities in their own backyard was matched only by the impotence they felt at the intractable nature of the swamp itself.

The Dismal Swamp Company

By the 1750s ambitious white entrepreneurs were looking to the swamp as a challenge that might actually be met. The combined populations of North Carolina and Virginia had reached nearly half a million people, and the Dismal beckoned as 2,000 square miles of potentially redeemable wilderness surrounded by bur-geoning development.[76] For too long, they believed, it had hindered economic development, and to enterprising outsiders the potential of the vast territory was being wasted on the refugee maroons who had settled it as a squatters' oasis.

In 1753, the Virginia Council granted the entire portion of the Dismal Swamp within its borders to four businessmen, agreeing with them that the swamp was "at present altogether useless" and ought be redeemed.[77] This par-ticular association undertook no work to drain their portion of the Dismal, and so their grant eventually expired. In the spring of 1762, one of those busi-nessmen, former Norfolk mayor Robert Tucker, claimed 1,000 acres of eastern Dismal Swamp land and sent in an enslaved crew to hack a drainage causeway through his patent. As work commenced, Tucker and a group of eleven new business associates (including a thirty-one-year-old Virginian named George Washington) began discussing a new potential business venture that they hoped might conquer the swamp once and for all.

In May 1763, Washington, his brother-in-law Fielding Lewis, and two others reconnoitered a portion of the Virginia side of the Dismal. Washing-ton's meticulous habits as a surveyor informed his close observation of the swamp. The edges were a bit too sandy to be of much use, he believed, but further into the swamp, dense evergreens and thick brush appeared to be rooted in a heavily organic soil that Washington believed might be the equal of any other Virginia farmland already under plow. He and his group slowly trekked to the swamp's central Lake Drummond (which Washington called "the Pond") and there camped on its shore. Continuing through the swamp, Washington remained excited by the potential of the dark topsoil, and the apparent fecundity of the entire swamp. Virginians and North Carolinians nearby expressed their certainty that the businessmen were putting too much stock in this "low sunken Morass, not fit for any of the purposes of Agricul-ture," but Washington would have none of it. It would eventually prove, he steadfastly believed, "excessive Rich."[78]

That most of the land was underwater was not exactly an afterthought, but it was not enough of an obstacle to discourage Washington and his colleagues from incorporating the Adventurers to Drain the Dismal Swamp (later the Dismal Swamp Company, hereafter DSC) to begin the process of not only "draining Improving and Saving the land" but also enriching themselves with the products of its bounty.[79] The incorporation of the DSC involved merely drafting documents and affixing signatures on the appropriate pages. The ac-tual work of subduing the Dismal would be done by enslaved laborers. Paths

"Washington at Lake Drummond, Dismal Swamp" (1880).
The Miriam and Ira D. Wallach Division of Art, Prints and Photographs,
Print Collection, The New York Public Library Digital Collections.

and ditches had to be cut, trees cleared for camps and fields, and other arduous labor undertaken by a bound workforce.

The Virginia Council granted the investors "a considerable Quantity of Land lying in the Counties of Norfolk and Nansemond and bounded by the North Carolina Line, known by the name of the Great Dismal [which] has lain entirely waste and unpatented hitherto—approximately 40,000 acres of the swamp's northwest quadrant (additional grants would bring the total nearer to 200,000 acres). Two days later shareholders met together in Williamsburg and pledged financial contributions to support the corporation's startup. Byrd had suggested that drainage could begin with the labor of ten enslaved workers, but the shareholders assessed themselves five "able male labouring Slaves" each. They also accepted Washington's offer to survey the company's tract.[80]

Dismal Swamp Company officials established a base of operations on another adjoining 402-acre property six miles from Suffolk leased from Virginia planter Miles Riddick. They called it alternately Dismal Town or Dismal

Plantation. There, the enslaved workers built houses and other outbuildings, grew corn, rice, and other crops, and raised livestock, all for their own support while they were to hack a way through the wilderness and bring the swamp into submission for their enslavers.

In July 1764, Washington took up a brief residence on the slave labor camp to "to receive & set ye People to Work."[81] When the enslaved workforce arrived, another observer dejectedly described them as "the worst collection that ever was made—they seemed to be the refuse of every one of the Estates from whence they were sent." This was at least partially true—Washington assessed his partner John Robinson, then Speaker of the Virginia House of Burgess, an extra twelve pounds for sending him enslaved workers fully incapable of confronting the harsh tasks at hand.[82] Washington himself only sent two enslaved people from Mount Vernon to labor in the swamp: Jack and Caesar. Four others, named Harry, Topsom, Nan, and a child named Toney, he bought on the cheap to round out his personal company assessment. Toney's value was appraised the lowest of all company workers sent to slave in the swamp in 1764.[83]

Washington's younger brother John soon assumed management of the labor camp. As the resident overseer, the younger Washington compelled the forty-three enslaved men, nine women, and two children to clear sections of old growth cypress and cedar trees and newer red and white oaks, maples, and elm, and from these trees to carve 10,000 eighteen-inch shingles for sale out of Norfolk.[84] He also drove them to dig by hand a ditch three feet deep and ten feet wide from Dismal Town five miles to Lake Drummond.[85] This was perhaps the most brutal task an enslaved person could be given in the swamp. One man forced to do such work called it "very severe." The ground was always saturated with swamp water, and the enslaved crew were constantly at least partially submerged in the muck, "cutting away roots and baling out mud." "If they can keep their heads above water," he remembered, "they work on."[86]

The following December, as their enslaved work crew attacked the company's swamp tract with axes and mattocks, the shareholders purchased another thousand acres in Nansemond County alongside the road connecting Suffolk to Norfolk. They hoped to connect it to the Nansemond River with a canal dug, of course, by enslaved laborers and assessed themselves five more enslaved people each.[87] They had also received the remarkable permission from the General Assembly to send them to dig canals or causeways on *any* land adjacent to the Dismal Swamp, even if it was owned by private landholders, in the interest of "publick utility."[88]

Of the sixty new enslaved people brought in to work the swamp, 20 percent would be women. Although it is unlikely that any of the shareholders had read William Byrd's unpublished thirty-year-old plan to drain the swamp, they had learned a lesson he had also discussed in his proposal—that a severely imbalanced gender ratio would cause the men to "run about" and maroon into the swamp away from Dismal Plantation.[89] The presence of women may have retained some of the men, but the excruciating labor, sweltering heat in summer and biting cold in winter, poisonous snakes, bloodthirsty insects, and near-constant immersion in water and swamp muck were obvious factors that nonetheless encouraged marronage in the Dismal.

Jack and Venus were just two of the enslaved people who embraced a life of marronage over the grueling labor demanded by the Dismal Swamp Company. Robert Burwell had sent them to the swamp in 1764 as his contribution to the labor force (his partial share of the company only required a pair of workers). The married couple had been together on Burwell's Smithfield, Virginia, slave labor camp, then slaved under John Washington's direction until 1765. They were returned to Isle of Wight County, and from there they made their escape together in 1771. Thirty-five-year-old Jack was described as "slim, clean-made, talkative, artful, and very saucy." Venus was thirty-two and described as "stout made" and "very smooth tongued."[90] Jack, at least, was recaptured, but he made his escape yet again less than two years later. In a 1773 notice, Burwell advertised for his return with a similar description as in the first ad, except that now the maroon was styled "a Negro man named JACK DISMAL."[91]

Tom was another who took his chances in the swamp. He broke away from his company work gang in April 1767 (exactly when, his captors could not state). His marronage may have gone unnoticed for some time due to the decentralized nature of most swamp labor (other than canal-digging), or possibly his escape was kept a secret by his fellow enslaved workers, but eventually his absence was recorded. After Tom was in the swamp, away from his captors, for more than a year, John Washington placed an ad for him in the *Williamsburg Gazette*: "Nansemond, June 20, 1768. RUN away from the subscriber some time in April 1767, a new Negro man named TOM, belonging to the proprietors of the Dismal Swamp. He is about 5 feet 6 inches high, has his country marks (that is, four on each of his cheeks.) Any person that apprehends the said fellow, so that I may get him, shall have three pounds reward, paid by JOHN WASHINGTON."[92] Another ad appeared in the *Gazette* sixteen months later and seems to be describing the same Tom, this time placed by his owner, John Mayo. Tom, it seems, had not been retaken. The new ad reminded readers to be on the lookout for him. To the earlier description was added Tom's "roguish look" and the fact that he had "lost part of one of his ears," possibly as punishment for an earlier escape attempt. He was supposed to be at work in the northwestern company tract but was likely marooned in the swamp somewhere further east. The reward for his capture had been raised to five pounds.[93] After nearly another year, Tom remained at large and was assumed to still be secreted in the Dismal, possibly "low-down" now in the North Carolina section. The reward for his capture had been doubled to ten pounds.[94]

Runaway ads paint a painfully incomplete picture of the people they describe, one that was always written from the perspective of the enslavers. They might offer a first name (even an earned "Dismal" surname, as with Jack), physical description, marital status, or last known whereabouts. However, the more tantalizing details of their personalities and experience of marronage are just beyond the reach of readers more than 200 years later. It is almost a certainty that people enslaved by the Dismal Swamp Company were aided by, collaborated with, and eventually settled among groups of maroons already living in the swamp. These "artful," "saucy," and "roguish" men and women powerfully and constantly resisted their enslavement. What traditions of Africa did Tom retain in his maroon life? Did Jack intend his 1773 escape down the Rappahannock River to end back in the Dismal, reunited with Venus, who remained in the swamp?[95] Unfortunately, these ads can only confirm so much, and leave too much forever unknown. However, unlike most historical figures, maroons' disappearance from and invisibility in the historical record is powerful evidence of their ultimate success. Venus Dismal may have finally found her permanent freedom.

The Dismal Swamp Company, in contrast, seemed to be struggling in its contest with the swamp. Reclaiming the Dismal was much slower work than any of the company investors anticipated. Chronic marronage often left the enterprise shorthanded. Torrential rains in June and July 1766 made any farming of reclaimed lands nearly impossible. Once the rain stopped, a severe drought parched the region, accompanied by heat so intense that enslaved people died toiling in the company rice fields.[96]

By 1769, the company's only revenue was from the sale of shingles. There was a seemingly inexhaustible supply of cedar and cypress in the swamp, but this was hardly the fortune investors anticipated. The ranks of the enslaved at Dismal Plantation had been "considerably lessened" by death and marronage. The company had not even been able to complete the surveys necessary to retain its grant and had to beg the Virginia Assembly for a seven-year extension.[97] This the company was allowed, but six years later in 1775, it had still accomplished little, much less subdued and drained the mighty swamp. The

DSC (or more accurately, its enslaved laborers) had built up Dismal Plantation and cut a five-mile drainage ditch to Lake Drummond. The company grazed around thirty head of cattle on drier swamplands, had a meager stock of sheep and hogs "not worth mentioning," and could not even find a local buyer for a crop of rice grown by enslaved company workers. John Washington left his post as overseer of Dismal Plantation in 1775 to join the Virginia militia and left company affairs "in a good deal of confusion." There had been fifty-four enslaved workers at the beginning of the company's operations, and despite regular levies upon shareholders to send more laborers, in 1775 there were but fifty, death and marronage having taken a constant and significant toll. The company adjourned its last shareholders meeting before the American Revolution with no concrete plans for new swamp business.[98]

On the eve of the war, the swamp remained a liminal space between two things at once. The whites whose interests lay in conquering it were disappointed and defeated. They were repelled by its dangers, its mysteries, and its refusal to conform to the demand to be productive. George Washington would find greater success against the British Army than against the Great Dismal Swamp. Indeed, the swamp was not done with Washington and his fellow enslavers, and fast-growing communities of maroons in its depths would claim their revenge in their own contributions to the war. Washington and the Dismal Swamp Company had failed in their endeavor to drain the swamp and could only make any real profit from the wood products that were but by-products of the original stalled enterprise. Enslaved laborers and maroons took some satisfaction in the disappointments of their oppressors, but their true hopes and dreams had never really been to see their tormenters fail. To them, the swamp was their powerful guardian, protection against the outside world that would enslave them, and a dark paradise that offered them a most unlikely gift—freedom in the midst of Tidewater slave society. Those who did not foolheartedly attempt to destroy the swamp might be embraced and nourished by it. The maroons of the Great Dismal Swamp would play their own part in the drama of the next American generation's battle for independence.

CHAPTER THREE

North American Maroon Wars,
1775–1831

To the whole south, it seemed that in those horrid recesses
of nature the avenging genius of slavery crouched but for
a moment before covering the land with desolation.
— *Petersburg Index*, 1869

THE MAROONS OF the Great Dismal Swamp waged battles every day, whether against the elements and the swamp, whites' notions of the physical and intellectual capacities of the people they held (or tried to hold) as property, or in actual combat with enslavers themselves. There were no maroon wars in North America comparable to those fought in Jamaica, Surinam, Haiti, and other Caribbean and South and Central American locales, but in the aggregate, the chronic maroon skirmishes emanating from the Dismal, often coordinated with wider rebellion plots of enslaved people or military contests in the region, resulted in greater property loss and human casualties than all other North American rebellions of enslaved people in the half century following the American Revolution.

Guerrilla warriors from the Dismal kept the swamp region on edge through constant martial pressure on white communities nearby. They were agile, adaptable, and mobile fighters who chose when and where to engage their enemies. They took advantage of their environment to strike fast and disappear just as quickly. Moreover, with 2,000 square miles of swamp as their headquarters, maroons could coordinate with each other and their still-enslaved brothers and sisters in the region to plan larger rebellions and insurgences. The militant maroon threat was constant, if not immediately calamitous. Their belligerence was real, whether inspired by hunger or revenge. The North American maroon war they waged from the fastness of the Dismal Swamp left deep scars—physical, economic, and psychological—on enslavers in the Tidewater and beyond.

IN EARLY NOVEMBER OF 1775, George Washington was at the Cambridge, Massachusetts, headquarters of the Continental Army, of which he had taken command in July. He was far from his Mount Vernon home, and his Dismal Swamp Company business was even further from his mind. By the end of the month, however, his attention was wrested back to the Dismal Swamp region and what he called the "diabolical Schemes" of the colonial governor of Virginia, John Murray, Lord Dunmore, which not only threatened Washington's own business interests but also heightened the menace of mass marronage, slave rebellion, and the "total destruction" of all of the Old Dominion. "Nothing less than depriving him of life or liberty," Washington wrote of Lord Dunmore, "will secure peace to Virginia."[1]

Following his victory over Patriot forces at Kemp's Landing (just east of Norfolk and on the northern edge of the Dismal), Dunmore had moved to reassert royal authority in rebellious Virginia. On November 15 he declared martial law. Though admittedly "most disagreeable," Dunmore believed the move was necessary to combat the open war being waged upon the king's ships and the formation and approach of a rebel army from Williamsburg. Such treason could not be contained through the "ordinary Course of the civil Law." Patriots like Washington read the proclamation as clear evidence of heavy-handed imperial tyranny. The most shocking provision, however, was found in the proclamation's closing section, which declared "all indented Servants, Negroes, or others, (appertaining to Rebels) free, that are able and willing to bear Arms, they joining his Majesty's Troops, as soon as may be, for the more speedily reducing this Colony to a proper Sense of their Duty, to his Majesty's Crown and Dignity."[2]

Dunmore had accused the patriots of treason, but rebel colonists judged his response as potentially murderous. Yet Dunmore suggested that he had only ratified a phenomenon that was already occurring. Enslaved people had been fleeing to his banners for months seeking refuge, and rumors of slave rebellion already abounded in the Tidewater region. Dunmore had warned of a large-scale insurrection in Surrey County in April of that year, and the following month he issued a public proclamation reminding Virginians of their vulnerability to their peculiar "internal weakness."[3]

He admitted to William Legge, Lord Dartmouth, that the chaos that followed his decree was not only of his creation, and such thinking rather changed "the effect into the Cause."[4] Still, he intended the proclamation to intimidate Tidewater whites by striking at the core of their economy, social structure, and sense of mastery. The Virginia convention's response said the same: Dunmore had assumed "powers which the king himself cannot exercise, to intimidate the good people of this colony into a compliance with his arbitrary will . . . and hath offered freedom to the servants and slaves of those he is pleased to term *rebels*, arming them against their masters, and destroying the peace and happiness of his majesty's good and faithful subjects, whose property is rendered insecure, and whose lives are exposed to the dangers of a general insurrection."[5] To be sure, Dunmore was not concerned with the peace and happiness of rebellious colonists, only restoring order. If it had to be accomplished with "a Force from among Indians, Negroes, and other persons," then so be it.[6]

Within a week, hundreds of African Americans had joined Dunmore's forces, and before he left Virginia in 1776, perhaps 1,500 had rallied to his standard—men, women, and children in families and as individuals. The men able to fight were enrolled in an outfit called Dunmore's Ethiopian Regiment, and wore sashes across their breasts that read "Liberty to Slaves!" Dunmore heartily believed in the ability of people of African descent to fight valiantly, and he employed the Ethiopian Regiment the next month at the Dismal Swamp Battle of Great Bridge. Following this defeat, the British evacuated mainland Norfolk and moved the Ethiopian Regiment north to protect a strategic freshwater supply at Tucker's Point on the Elizabeth River.[7]

Through July 1776, Dunmore maintained a "floating town" of ships offshore of Norfolk. Along with an array of Loyalists, Dunmore's flotilla sheltered hundreds of Africans and African Americans, many of whom came to the British standard after having previously worked and/or lived in the Great Dismal Swamp. One young man, for example, had been kidnapped from the Gambia at the age of twenty-three, bought and renamed Harry by George Washington, and put to work slaving in the Dismal Swamp for three years for the DSC. There he had lived with Nan, another person Washington enslaved. After being separated from his companion and returned to Mount Vernon, Harry escaped from Washington in 1771, was recaptured, and escaped again in 1775 to Dunmore's call. When Dunmore sailed north for New York in August, Harry remained with him, joined the newly formed "Black Pioneers," and now *Corporal* Harry Washington earned, in one historian's estimation, a reputation among Black British soldiers comparable to that of his former owner among the Patriots.[8]

George Washington, whose own formerly enslaved men now fought on behalf of his enemy Dunmore, appreciated the threat the Ethiopian Regiment represented. "If that man is not crushed before spring," he wrote to Richard Henry Lee, "he will become the most formidable enemy America has; his strength will increase as a snow ball by rolling: and faster, if some expedient cannot be hit upon, to convince the slaves and servants of the impotency of his designs."[9]

There are indications that maroons made up a not-insignificant portion of Dunmore's troops, and that they may have been in on his plans months before the November 1775 proclamation. In May, Dunmore had revealed his plan to recruit Black soldiers "on the back Parts of the Province of Virginia," not limited to but certainly including the legendary Dismal Swamp maroon communities. Secret negotiations would have been much easier with maroons than enslaved people on a farm or labor camp. Moreover, in the fighting by the Ethiopian Regiment within the Dismal, Dunmore's Black soldiers demonstrated skills that would have been common to Dismal Swamp maroons. Maroons knew intimately the swamps and waterways flowing east from the Suffolk Scarp and the Dismal. They included Joseph Harris, who was said to be well acquainted with the swamp creeks and tributaries of the Nansemond River, and Caesar, who despite his reputation as "a very great Scoundrel" knew the marshes and waterways of southeastern Virginia like the back of his hand.[10]

Back at Dismal Plantation, the compound fell into disrepair as company officials busied themselves with war matters unrelated to their swamp venture. The company's enslaved people were largely left to their own devices in the swamp under minimal oversight. Many escaped and marooned deeper in the swamp, while others sought Dunmore's lines. A British raiding party descended upon Dismal Plantation in 1781 and destroyed buildings, commandeered food and supplies, and liberated many of the enslaved people. Over the course of the war, at least thirty people enslaved by the company disappeared into the swamp or British lines, and by the end of the war, only a few young Black girls worked the plows on what was left of Dismal Plantation's dilapidated fields.[11]

Even after Dunmore's retreat to New York, however, maroon raids from the Dismal Swamp kept the region destabilized. Josiah Phillips, born at the edge of the Dismal in Princess Anne County, was a landless white laborer who had been given a commission by Dunmore in 1775 and had begun plundering the area in the summer of 1776. His band numbered around fifty, including a large number of African Americans. They were offered shelter and support by the Dismal Swamp maroons, and many of Phillips's "swamp banditti" had been recruited from their numbers.[12] Together, the "party of desperadoes" raided Norfolk and Princess Anne Counties, burned slave labor camps, freed enslaved people, and carried off livestock and other provisions.[13]

Virginia governor Patrick Henry offered a $500 reward for Phillips's capture, dead or alive.[14] However, men organized (in some cases impressed) to hunt down Phillips's band refused to pursue him, and a quarter of those who began on the mission deserted, such was the terror that the maroons produced. The commander of the Norfolk and Princess Anne militia, citing his men's "cowardly disposition," wrote the governor that "scarce a man, without being forced, can be raised to go after the outlaws" in the Dismal.[15] Only after the Virginia legislature passed a remarkable law that authorized the capture or killing of Phillips and any of his men was he captured and hanged on December 4, 1778 (along with two captured maroons). The remnants of his gang continued to raid and retreat to the swamp through the rest of the war.[16]

By the end of the war, the Dismal Swamp counties had "neither civil nor military law," Gen. William Caswell complained, and desperadoes wrought havoc in the region, raiding livestock and plantations among other "daring outrages," and then settled unmolested deep "into their strong Swamps."[17] Even when some outlaws allied with the British sought terms of surrender to Patriot Virginians, "the great offenders" who had ravaged the region for the previous five years and who were still at large in the swamps were explicitly excluded from any possibility of immunity.[18]

Thousands of African Americans evacuated with the British in 1783. Among this group was Col. Harry Washington, formerly of the Dismal Swamp Company and enslaved and by the Founding Father himself, later leader of Black troops against him. Jack Dismal, the former maroon also once enslaved by the company, made his final escape onboard a British ship. "Stout wench" Sukey Dismal, who escaped her slave labor camp on the north edge of the swamp in 1778, sailed out on the *Nisbet* bound for Nova Scotia. With her were her children Nancy and George, both born free in British lines.[19] How many others with Dismal Swamp connections evacuated with the British will never be known.[20]

The Dismal Swamp Maroons' Revolution Continues

Their Virginia and North Carolina captors had succeeded in their rebellion. They were now free to live their lives, to enjoy liberty, and to pursue happiness to their hearts' content. They also remained free to enslave others. The Dismal Swamp maroons' war was more complicated. Some had fought on the losing side but by doing so confirmed their freedom. Some who had not been maroons before their escape to Dunmore had gained valuable intelligence on the Dismal during their service, and sought the protection of the deep swamp afterward.[21] Although significant numbers of maroons emerged from the swamp toward the British standard or Josiah Phillips's leadership, probably other enslaved people took advantage of the wartime instability to seek freedom within the swamp and avoided the war whenever they could. The maroon population of the Dismal is believed to have "mushroomed" toward the end of the military conflict.[22]

Of course many had never left the swamp, and resistant community life went on, inward-facing, as it had for generations. Maroon resistance did not require encouragement from Redcoats. The Dismal was described the year after the war ended as remaining a "perfectly safe" permanent retreat for "run-away Negroes," who "with the greatest facility elude the most diligent search of their pursuers."[23] Long-term Dismal Swamp marronage was noted in published travel narratives of 1784 and 1799 and an anthropological study in 1784.[24] Readers of *New York Magazine* would have learned of "run-away negroes" living deep in the Dismal, "many of whom live here to be old, without the least danger of being discovered."[25] How writers had gained this information was unclear, but a certain consistency among the different accounts (and corroboration by closer authorities later) suggests postwar readers were hearing some truth about deep swamp marronage that had survived the Revolution intact.

Other maroons settled around the swamp's edges in Virginia and North Carolina, continuing a constant campaign of pressure on the outside world of their enslavers. African Americans, bears, and wildcats from the swamp killed all of the Dismal Swamp Company's hogs in 1784.[26] Maroons like "the General, who was with the British Army in the American war," had done what they could to frustrate the Patriot "freedom" struggle. In the next generation, he would again be involved in a rebellion plot that spanned the entire Dismal.[27] The rate of self-emancipation soared in eastern Virginia and North Carolina, which led the General Assembly in the latter to pass legislation specifically empowering sheriffs to pursue "lurkers" in the Dismal.[28]

The settling of maroons deep in the swamp or even occasional raids from the swamp periphery did not represent an immediate direct threat to the Tidewater system of enslavement. Occasionally, maroons and enslaved people did use the swamp as a staging ground for larger-scale rebellion. However, the *potential* for them to do so—motives of revenge and freedom shared by an accumulating army of disaffected maroons—was perhaps just as frightening to whites as actual instances of insurrection.

Their own colonial war had sparked an age of revolution, and whites kept abreast of continuing freedom struggles in the hemisphere. Developments on this front were of great interest to African Americans in and out of the swamp. In the summer of 1791, maroons and enslaved people had risen up in rebellion in Saint-Domingue and began waging war against French colonials. Marronage was, in the estimation of historian Jean Fouchard, "the dominant feature of all Haitian history," and the Haitian Revolution was won through the unceasing heroics of "maroons who were seasoned by two centuries of guerilla warfare."[29]

African Americans in the Dismal Swamp region could follow developments in the Caribbean. Those who could read and had access to newspapers learned of the heroics of maroon guerrillas like Sylla, Sans-Souci, and Boukman, and of course read tales of Toussaint Louverture. They passed along news of his victories over French enslavers to those who were not literate. What was more, some newspaper editors unwittingly helped readers in the US South make the direct connection between North American maroon wars and those in the Caribbean. For instance, adjacent to its reporting on an extensive insurrection plot in Norfolk, the *Balance and Columbian Repository* ran a story headlined "LIBERTY. EQUALITY. ARMY OF ST. DOMINGO."[30] Although not naming his source, one early historian quoted the enslaved as emphatically asserting in the 1790s that "what one Negro had done, others might do."[31]

Some of Haiti's maroon counterparts in the Dismal did in fact attempt to follow their example, and the swamp was central to rebellion plots that unfolded in the Tidewater region over the next decade. In 1792, there seems to have been a coordinated insurrection of African Americans stretching from Richmond to the Dismal Swamp and through into northeastern North Carolina. On May 5, the Northampton County militia lieutenant Smith Snead received an urgent warning from six local residents that "a variety of circumstances" had convinced them that a rebellion was being planned and urging Snead to prepare for an assault. The next day, he wrote the governor requesting "a hundred weight of powder, and four hundred of lead" to protect against the impending attack.[32] The "circumstances" of that plan were detailed in a May 17 letter from Petersburg. Close to 900 African American "banditti" were reported to have gathered together in Northampton County, Virginia, and had organized themselves into fighting units under the command of a man named Celeb. They had been raiding the region over the span of nearly two weeks, and had been in "general communication" with at least 300 African Americans on the Dismal side of the Chesapeake Bay in "the lower parts" of Norfolk County (that is, the swamp). Together, they made plans "to commit some violent outrages" along the northern fringes of the Dismal and "to blow up the magazine in Norfolk, and massacre the inhabitants."[33] Norfolk resident Thomas Newton wrote the governor that he was certain "a number of strangers," meaning enslaved Haitians brought to the city by recent West Indian refugees, were prepared to join any insurrection when it broke out.[34]

Before the rebels could combine, the Eastern Shore contingent was apparently "taken up" and overcome. They had in their possession "a barrel of musket balls, about 300 spears, some guns, powder, provisions, etc."[35] Still, there was suspicion among officials from July to November, as far south as Charleston and as far north as Richmond, that remnants of the same conspiracy stretched there from the Dismal. After maroon activity on the Virginia side of the swamp picked up in the fall, there was a period of relative silence until the following summer of 1793, when in Richmond John Randolph overheard three Black men discussing their plot "to kill the white people soon in this place." The one "who seemed to be chief speaker" pointed out the success of the Haitian Revolution: "You see how the blacks has killed the whites in the French island and took it a little while ago."[36]

Randolph's July 1793 deposition made the discovery of a letter in Yorktown the next month even more ominous. The letter addressed "Secret Keeper Richmond to secret keeper Norfolk" referred to a "great secret that has been so long in being with our own color," although the author was concerned that "some on our Town has told of it," presumably the conversation overheard and reported by Randolph. The scope of the plot was great:

> We have got about five hundred Guns aplenty of lead but not much powder. . . . I hope you have made a good collection of powder and ball and will hold yourself in readiness to strike whenever called for and never be out of the way. . . . It will not be long before it will take place, and I am fully satisfied we shall be in full possession of the [w]hole country in a few weeks. . . . Since I wrote you last I got a letter from our friend in Charleston[:] he tells me has listed near six thousand men, there is a gentlemen that says he will give us as much powder as we want, and when we begin he will help us all he can, the damns brutes patroles is going all night in Richmond but will soon kill them all, there ain't many, we will appoint a night to begin with fire clubs and shot, we will kill all before us, it will begin in every town in one nite. . . . Keep ready to receive orders, when I hear from Charleston again I shall [k]no[w] and will [w]rite to you, be that give you this is a good friend and don't let any body see it, [w]rite me by the same hand he will give it to me out his hand and he will be up next week. . . . Don't be feared have a good heart, fight brave and we will get free. . . . I had like to get each [illegible] but God was for me, and I got away, no more now but remain your friend.[37]

Nothing more became of this plot, however. The identities of both "Secret Keepers" remained a mystery, as did the extent of the involvement of maroons from the Dismal Swamp. What *was* clear was that what Julius Scott calls "the common wind" of the age of the Haitian Revolution also blew through the Great Dismal Swamp.[38]

President George Washington had hoped to help suppress the Haitian Revolution by sending $726,000 to French planters there, as well as approving supplies of provisions, arms, and ammunition to the colonials. This, the only attempt by the United States to suppress a foreign slave revolt, proved to be a failure.[39] Clearly, several national interests contributed to the decision to commit the United States to this intervention, but Washington's own nagging problem with maroons and fugitives in his Dismal Swamp Company experience may have motivated him as well. By the time of the Haitian Revolution, the swamp, especially its maroon contingent, was getting the best of the company and driving its investors into fits. The frequency at which people enslaved by the company marooned was so great that it had great difficulty hiring enslaved laborers in the years following the American Revolution. Company agent David Jameson admitted in early 1787 that "no person inclines to hire their Negroes to work at the Swamp." Without the availability of a stable bound labor force, John Driver advised Jameson that Dismal Plantation was not worth maintaining. A "Remnant of worn out Negroes" would certainly not sustain the enterprise.[40]

Canals Cut into the Swamp

Still, the shareholders refused to give up the venture. In 1783, their thoughts had returned to the original scheme to "subdue" the swamp: to drain it by digging ditches and canals and impose *some* order upon it.[41] Washington had long envisioned digging a proper canal, and one of the company's largest undertakings after establishing Dismal Plantation had been to have enslaved workers dig a "ditch" (called Washington Ditch) from the company farm to Lake Drummond in 1768. Perhaps *real* profits might be made by opening up a way for North Carolina and Virginia—the Albemarle Sound and the Chesapeake Bay—to be linked together through the swamp. The initial idea was to link the southern branch of the Elizabeth River in Virginia with the upper reaches of the Pasquotank in North Carolina (through Lake Drummond and across Dismal Swamp Company lands). The company could then capitalize on the shipment of North Carolina corn and grains directly to a burgeoning and hungry Virginia, and also open a cross-swamp canal to public traffic and charge tolls for its use. To be sure, roads already skirted the western edge of the swamp, but they were slow, cumbersome, and dangerous. A canal directly through the Dismal would be far more efficient, even with the potential burdens of tolls.

In December 1783, the Virginia House of Delegates first considered a bill to authorize a canal through the swamp. By 1790, the legislatures of both Virginia and North Carolina had passed laws authorizing the digging of a "Dismal Swamp Canal" and chartering a company to undertake the project. Shares of the Dismal Swamp Canal Company (DSCC) went on sale in the spring of 1791, and the Dismal Swamp Company become its largest shareholder apart from the state of Virginia, despite the fact that the official proposed route would take the canal east of Lake Drummond.[42]

Construction of the canal commenced three years later in Virginia at Deep Creek, a tributary of the Elizabeth River, eleven miles by water from Norfolk. In North Carolina, excavation began at South Mills, seven miles south of the state line, where Joyce's Creek met the Pasquotank River. Between 1794 and 1805, crews of hundreds of enslaved workers cleared dense underbrush, cane, and briars, cut down immense pine, cedar, and hardwood trees and cleared their roots, and shoveled by hand thousands of tons of peat, soil, and general muck (dodging alligators and snakes all the while).

Virginia farmer Edmund Ruffin described a Dismal Swamp canal construction site on one of his visits to the swamp. "The surface of the swampy ground is," he wrote, "in many places, so nearly level with the water, and the earth is so generally a quagmire of peat, and so full of dead roots and buried logs, under the water, and of living trees and roots over and at the surface, when but very little above water, that the difficulties of removing such obstructions are very great." There was "such a mass of sound wood" that he imagined the ditching could be undertaken "not by the spade, but principally by the axe, the saw and the mattock." He thought the idea of excavating these canals by hand "insuperable," even though enslaved people had already cut miles of canals by the time of his account.[43] The work, as historian David Cecelski writes, was "the cruelest, most dangerous, unhealthy, and exhausting labor in the American South."[44]

The canal was meant to be at least eight feet deep and wide enough to accommodate vessels with a fifteen-foot beam. The full length of the canal would be twenty-two miles.[45] Approximately 14 million cubic feet of swamp would need to be excavated by hand. Work progressed very slowly, despite (or maybe because of) supplies commonly being withheld unless the work quotas of enslaved ditchers were met. A full day's labor of an army of enslaved workers would advance the project less than ten yards. Officials expected the two canals to meet by the end of 1799, but two years later there were still miles between ditching crews.[46] Had Virginia and North Carolina's waters mingled in a Dismal Swamp Canal that was completed on schedule, the bloody events of 1800–1801 in the swamp region might have turned out quite differently.

Rebellion Flares Again

In the spring and summer of 1800, Gabriel, a blacksmith enslaved near Richmond by Thomas Prosser, and several free and enslaved coconspirators planned a campaign to attack Richmond and win the freedom of enslaved participants estimated to reach into the thousands. The planned August 30 uprising was ultimately betrayed by two enslaved men who knew of the plot, but it was also made impossible by torrential rains and flooding that made the rebel army's march into Richmond impossible. By the next day, patrols were searching for the ringleaders and detaining suspects.

Gabriel's rebellion in Richmond had been meant to signal other simultaneous uprisings throughout Virginia. Testimonies of conspirators identified parallel revolts to be launched from Petersburg, Manchester, and even as far away as the northern edge of the Dismal Swamp. There, around 150 enslaved people, "mulattoes," and "some whites" from Norfolk and Suffolk had gathered at Whitlock's Mill just outside of Norfolk for the signal to strike. That signal, of course, never came, but their testimony once captured undoubtedly shook the white population of the swamp region: they had gathered at the ready "to do what those in Richmond were about to do."[47]

Gabriel fled south. Although his destination was probably not the Dismal Swamp proper, he hoped to make it to Norfolk on the northern edge of the swamp and from there onto a ship away from the Chesapeake. There he was captured, almost a month after the planned insurrection. Although he never made it to the Dismal, he and his rebellion became part of the collective memory of maroons and enslaved people in the region.[48]

Abolitionist Martin Delany provides what historian James Sidbury calls "as reliable an image as exists" of the vitality of Black folklore around the Dismal that claims Gabriel as a part of their own freedom campaign.[49] The hero of Delany's novel *Blake, or, The Huts of America* (1859) visits with Dismal Swamp maroons who claimed to have been confidants of "General Gabriel." The maroons had kept Gabriel's name alive through half a century "in sacred reverence" and remembered him as one of "the greatest men who ever lived." As Gabriel had hoped to raise an army to take Richmond, those who kept his name and mission alive, the maroons of the Dismal Swamp, believed themselves numerous enough "to take the whole United States."[50] The swamp was becoming, in Sidbury's assessment, "Virginia's primary mythic locus of Black freedom."[51]

Even as Gabriel's body swung from the gallows, the spirit of revolution continued to grow among Virginia and North Carolina African Americans in a remarkable period where organization among the enslaved merged with maroon guerrilla warfare.[52] Sancho, an enslaved ferryman who labored on the Roanoke River, had recruited sympathetic African Americans to Gabriel's cause. After Gabriel's rebellion was put down, Sancho continued to solicit a small core of conspirators to join him in a new assault on the lower Chesapeake.

Plying the waterways of southeastern Virginia, Sancho's lieutenants circulated the conspiracy plans across the region in the winter of 1801.[53] Word reached Norfolk and the northern Dismal Swamp through enslaved watermen soon after Christmas. There, Will, enslaved in Princess Anne County but hiring himself out on the Norfolk docks, sought to organize other conspirators, including whites and enslaved and free African Americans.[54] Norfolk whites were aware at least by March that there was "a regular correspondence carrying on between the negroes of the different states" orchestrated by "a *cunning black fellow* . . . strongly suspected of being the confidant of the discontented negroes" on both sides of the Dismal.[55] Thomas Mathews of Norfolk may have been referring to the same man when he reported to governor James Monroe that "an emissary" was delivering correspondence through the Dismal Swamp to Elizabeth City, North Carolina, and then further into northeastern North Carolina.[56] Despite his plans to capture the man, Mathews was unable to apprehend him before he slipped back into North Carolina.[57]

Collaborators there believed themselves to be part of something wide-ranging. Davy, a literate man enslaved south of the Dismal, knew that the "head negroes" were in Virginia, and that whoever the leader was "was at work under the ground . . . & that when the fight was begun all the negroes were to join those who commenced."[58] A core of coconspirators from Virginia to North Carolina thus planned a wide-reaching and surprisingly cohesive rebellion to be begun the weekend of Easter 1802 (some time between Good Friday and Easter Monday).

However, Sancho's plan became overextended. Rumors of the plot were freely circulating by the end of the year. In January, a patrol in Nottoway broke up a planning meeting and arrested supposed head men, Bob and Joe, as well as several others. Although the trial that followed made clear that Bob and Joe were not the plot's masterminds, only local leaders, the two were found guilty and hanged. The same happened in Brunswick in February and Norfolk in April. In North Carolina, there were executions in Camden and Currituck

Counties beginning in April.[59] Sancho himself was captured, tried, and executed on May 16 in Halifax County.[60] By late May, "the spirit of insurrection seem[ed] to be a little checked," though whites were far from at ease.[61]

As the roundup of alleged conspirators continued, the jails north of the Dismal were so full of "convicted slaves" that their maintenance had become "burthensome and their safe keeping inconvenient." It was proposed that the offenders be sold off or transported out of the country.[62] On the North Carolina side of the swamp, the Elizabeth City jail was reported to be at capacity by the end of May. After quick trials, one white observer hoped to see "some of the savages *pulling hemp*."[63] Many did find the end of a rope; there were mass arrests in Hertford and Bertie Counties, North Carolina, and hangings of rebels in Halifax, Hanover, and Princess Anne Counties as well as in Norfolk.[64] Though authorities were terribly low on arms and ammunition, they were able to capture enough from the maroons that they prayed with "trust under God, we shall be able to suppress this infernal attempt."[65]

Yet the North Carolina continuation of Sancho's rebellion took on a life of its own, one centered in a Dismal Swamp maroon camp north of Elizabeth City. There, Tom Copper, who had been outlawed, led a maroon band that numbered at least thirty-eight, and likely many more. "General" Copper and his lieutenants recruited other rebels to his heavily armed maroon camp and had them pledge their loyalty to the "plot to kill the white people" by signing their names on a muster roll. Mingo, an enslaved man later taken up and interrogated, claimed to have been to the camp and seen the paper, and testified that men including Lawrence, David, Big Charles, Old Will, George, Old London, Jack, Dick, Little Isaac, John, Aaron, Jesse, Drew, and two Jacobs had all signed.[66] Their plan was to continue Sancho's design to destroy Richmond and hit other Virginia targets, but they intended to use the southern Dismal Swamp as a refuge and base of operations for strikes against North Carolina targets as well.[67]

While Copper and his men planned, "alarmed" whites continued to crack down on enslaved people they suspected of being some of the "deluded wretches."[68] At one point, Copper himself was captured and thrown in the Elizabeth City jail.[69] He was not held long, however, because in the last week of May, "six stout negroes, mounted on horseback," orchestrated a jail break and were able to free him. Four of the "stout" associates were taken in the rescue, losing their freedom so their general could retake the field.[70] It seems that Copper remained marooned (or at least no identified record notes his recapture) and continued his campaign. The first week of June, an anonymous African American informant warned authorities that "their [*sic*] has been expresses going in Every direction for some days to see all the negroes they could . . . to make the arrangements and conclud what time it is to commence and at what plasis they are to assemble."[71]

The level of organization in these efforts was remarkable. Besides a vast communication network running through the Dismal Swamp and connecting two states and perhaps a dozen counties, Tom Copper's military organization was becoming more sophisticated. A letter found in a cotton barrel owned by one captured conspirator (corroborated by testimony from others) showed that by early June, the maroons served under "Captains" assigned to each Dismal Swamp county. Below them served an unknown number of "officers," who commanded maroons "embodied in large companies, armed, in the Great Swamp, near the Virginia line." Rendezvous points were planned out and communicated well in advance.[72]

In the early summer came reports of large numbers of armed African Americans and violent confrontations between Blacks and whites in Hertford and Bertie Counties.[73] By August, however, the threat seems to have passed. It is unclear what events transpired or what happened to General Tom Copper and his officers. Perhaps the hypervigilance (even possibly paranoia) of North Carolina and Virginia authorities ultimately broke the back of the resistance by thoroughly decimating its ranks. Conservatively, over a hundred of the alleged conspirators were captured, jailed, and tortured, and most were either executed, punished and returned to their masters, or condemned to be transported out of Virginia or North Carolina.[74] Buyers wishing to purchase condemned slaves on the cheap appeared to have trouble identifying sufficient numbers remaining in the jails by the end of the month.[75]

Although their public statements may have suggested confidence, whites across two states remained petrified by the maroons' campaign of summer 1802. One observer later wrote that they were "as horror stricken and insecure as are people in volcanic countries when the everlasting hills begin to shake and the mountains pour forth fire and ashes and melted rocks and stifling gases."[76] Citizens remained on edge because of the number of African Americans in their midst from "the French Islands" who might be easily convinced to help "reduce [Norfolk] to ashes."[77] Enslaved people also could sense whites' terror, which lasted much longer than the immediate threat of the 1802 plot.[78]

Even though the panics of 1802 were calmed, insurrection activity centered around the Great Dismal Swamp continued with some frequency. Hot spots included Isle of Wight County, Virginia, in 1805; Chowan County, North Carolina, in 1807; and Norfolk County, Virginia, and Albemarle County, North Carolina, in 1808.[79] Edenton residents were so thoroughly alarmed by the looming unrest that they proposed a series of Black Codes, a curfew for African Americans, with "a sufficient number of vigilant and trusty men" as enforcers.[80] Their plea was raised again the following year over fears that "one desperate and unprincipled villain" was poised to descend upon their town and lay it to waste. Writing as "Mentor," one resident pointed out the special dangers of their town situated on the southern edge of the Dismal Swamp, where "we, our wives and our children" were "surrounded by desperadoes, *white and black*, who perhaps would 'laugh at our calamity and mock when our fear cometh.'"[81]

The "villain" Mentor had in mind was likely a notorious maroon leader and preacher named General Peter. Peter's camp was in Isle of Wight County in the northern part of the swamp, and, like Tom Copper eight years earlier, he commanded a wide-ranging network of enslaved people, maroons, and even some whites across the vast Great Dismal Swamp. Also like Copper, Peter planned a coordinated insurrection to strike from both sides of the Dismal, in this case the night of June 9, 1810. Starting on the North Carolina side, rebels planned to fight with "clubs, spikes, and axes" then quickly move north and "help the Virginia negroes." There would be "an Earthquake" on the same night in Virginia and North Carolina.[82]

Peter also relied on a sophisticated communication network across and around the Dismal Swamp. His plan was to establish a network of agents on the plantations of eastern Virginia and North Carolina for communication purposes, planning, and eventual coordinated action. He relied especially on fellow "negro preachers" to disseminate plans for the rebellion. He aimed to build upon the relationship between maroons and their still-enslaved brethren by linking them through the efforts of underground plantation spiritual leaders who commonly preached to maroons in the swamp, to those still in bonds on slave labor camps, and sometimes to groups that included both. Under cover of religious meetings, these men preached rebellion as "the great and important object" of their messages, an insurgence so great that the destruction of white society and freedom for the enslaved was certain. Their accessibility and mobility made the preachers, in the opinion of Richard Byrd of Smithfield, Virginia, just north of the swamp, "more dangerous than any other description of blacks."[83]

Now that the Dismal Swamp Canal had been completed (the two ends had met in 1805, slightly north of the state line) and a sandy road created from what had been excavated from the canal beds that flanked the waterway, what had been a grapevine telegraph across the swamp became a potential superhighway of information. Although the canal bed was not level, and there were not yet any locks or a reliable flow of water, its shallow draft was usually plenty for the shingle flats, canoes, and small craft of the swamp's African American watermen, and, in some instances, Black preachers.[84]

Some suspected conspirators were taken up along the northern edge of the swamp in late May. After twenty lashes, "a negro boy" gave up the details he knew about the "'intended works' in Carolina." One of the men he named as a conspirator corroborated many of his statements upon his capture. However, others who were eventually interrogated were much less accommodating. The man who announced the impending "Earthquake" on the Virginia side of the swamp defiantly declared that he "was entitled to his freedom, and he would be damned if he did not have it in a fortnight." Another told his enslaver that a full accounting of the plot "would make her heart bleed."[85]

Governor John Tyler learned of the insurrection plot in a May 30 letter, although he doubted the full veracity of this report. Still, the Virginia government ordered 100 copies of the letter printed for distribution to military officials in the eastern part of the state.[86] Vigilant authorities there and in North Carolina continued to arrest many African Americans believed to be involved in the "works," and the interrogations that followed led to more arrests. By May 30, the threat seemed to have passed. Perhaps, as Richard Byrd suggested, the two-state dragnet swept up enough of the cross-swamp messengers that it became impossible for groups of rebels to communicate. "I think it probable," he wrote the governor Tyler, "that we have broken the chain by which they were to be linked."[87] After the suppression of the cross-swamp and cross-state rebellion plots of 1802 and 1810 there would be no more coordinated North Carolina/Virginia campaigns for another decade. Maroon offensives went from plans to hit big cities in coordination with large numbers of enslaved people to precision guerrilla strikes. These were arguably more effective and even more terrifying. Terrorism, the threat to strike anywhere and at any time, was a valuable tactic. Marronage continued apace, just on a more local and personal level.

Consider the North Carolina maroon campaign of Pompey Little in the early 1820s. He had been enslaved on W. P. Little's "Littleton" plantation in Hertford County, North Carolina (just south of the Albemarle Sound), before he marooned in 1815. Although in describing his former slave in an advertisement Little had assigned him the same surname, Pompey was in fact a giant of a man—well over six feet tall and "heavy-set." He joined a maroon community in the Gates County portion of the Dismal Swamp and for seven years developed a reputation as a "notorious outlaw" in the region. He was a masterful guerrilla strategist, skilled in planning attacks then disappearing back into the swamp. He fought with whatever implements were available, but his weapon of choice was a "long two-edged knife." Pompey was known to brazenly attack travelers in the middle of the day, and had no qualms about his victims knowing his identity. In fact, the man who eventually shot and killed him first threatened to publish Pompey's description in the Suffolk newspaper, to which the maroon leader declared that he was "welcomed to do so and could add his name, Pomp."[88] Pompey Little had no fear.

In the summer of 1818, a multiracial "gang of desperate wretches . . . all armed and officered"—at least twenty-eight maroons from Dismal Swamp in southeastern Princess Ann County, Virginia—"openly declared themselves at war with the inhabitants of Black Water." From their swamp base, they committed a string of "the most atrocious outrages and depredations on persons and property." For some time they had frequently raided local farms and slave labor camps in midday, taking cattle, hogs, and poultry at will. They meted out justice to those who had wronged them when they were enslaved (in one instance maroons dragged one such man into the swamp and beat him to death with clubs). As they raided, they recruited more people to join their maroon community, which eventually included men and women, young and old. In a late June raid, an *"old woman"* was one of the maroons shot and killed along with their "captain" while hog-tying livestock.[89]

Less than a month later, these maroons appear to have regrouped under the command of the so-called murderous Mingo and his right-hand man, Ned Downs, who had been with them for several months. Mingo, who proudly bore a scar from a bullet grazing his head during one raid, led the "gang of negro desperadoes and runaways" in (by his own admission later) theft, killing cattle, arson, firing upon local farmers, and "the commission of many a heinous crime and deed of blood" over the next six months from their Dismal Swamp base. Mingo's deeds, and the "ferocity" of the band of maroons he commanded, were said to "have given rise to many strange stories" among the locals, enough to "furnish out a volume of no small dimensions, and no little interest."[90]

In November 1818, the maroons participated in the murder-for-hire of Alexander Taggart, a South Carolina slave trader in Princess Anne County on business. Harper Ackiss, a man "whose negroes were known to be in league" with the maroons, agreed to pay Ned and Mingo $100 each to kill Taggart and take the "large sum of money" he had on his person. This they did, and then buried him in a shallow grave in the swamp three miles from Ackiss's house, where he was discovered three days later.[91]

Ackiss aroused suspicion when, just days after Taggart's disappearance, he paid off a significant debt and purchased two enslaved people (in the exact denominations and amounts as Taggart had noted in his cash account book).[92] Ackiss was arrested on capital charges. On December 7, two justices of the peace received "satisfactory intelligence" of the involvement of "Negroes Mingo and Ned and other runaway negro slaves" that were "lying out hid and lurking in swamps, woods and other obscure places."[93] They authorized local lawmen to raise whatever troops were necessary to hunt down the maroons. The force of 140 infantry and cavalry of Princess Anne militia could turn up no trace of them.[94]

Mingo was ultimately betrayed by one of his confidants named Cox. Under the pretense of celebrating their escape from the militia, Cox got Mingo drunk then led him into an ambush. He got Mingo so worked up in telling tales of his many escapes that he fired off his musket in a "feu-de-joie" celebration. With Mingo's barrel empty, Cox quickly disarmed him, gave the signal that brought out the concealed militiamen, and attempted to assist in his capture. Mingo, however, put up a spirited fight, drew out his knife, and severely wounded one of the men before being subdued and tied up. Even after being bound, Mingo "made a violent effort" to attack Cox, biting and scratching him until he was pried off of his betrayer. Following a quick trial in Norfolk (for arson, curiously, not murder), Mingo was sentenced to death and jailed in Kempsville.[95]

However, following a citizens' appeal, the governor commuted Mingo's sentence to "transportation" out of Virginia. Outraged, a large group of leading citizens, including a man Mingo had once attempted to murder, requested that the governor reconsider his decision based on the maroon's having waged "open war against the property and even being of our citizens." The governor was unmoved, despite the fact that the petition was signed by 663 residents of Princess Anne County, a number that represented nearly two-thirds of all white males in the county over sixteen. As Mingo was being transported from Kempsville to Norfolk, where he was to be placed onboard a steamer bound for Richmond (where he was to be sold), a mob attacked the sheriff's transport and assassinated Mingo. They shot him in the head "with his brains and blood running out, without a single struggle or groan."[96] Thus, as an early Norfolk historian put it, "the soul of the hardened criminal was accordingly hurried into eternity . . . and his body unceremoniously deposited in a hole hastily dug by the roadside, about seven miles from the city."[97]

Of all the things that terrified lower Virginia about Mingo, the most troubling may have been the close relationship that the maroon captain and his followers seemed to have had with local whites. At Mingo's trial, witnesses testified that whites had known of his activities, held extensive conversations with him, and even assisted him in some of his deeds. Eight white men admitted that Mingo had informed them of his plan to kill the Princess Anne County sheriff, and none of them had taken measures to stop him. Harper Ackiss, of course, had paid Ned and Mingo to assassinate Taggart, and two of his white friends may have been in on the plot as well.[98]

Following the loss of Mingo, leadership of the northern Dismal Swamp maroons passed to Ned, who quickly took up Mingo's "cruizing ground." By the end of 1818, this had expanded from Black Water to Northwest River Bridge. Not long thereafter, leadership of these maroons appears to have passed to the "notorious and even formidable" Bob Ferebee. It is not known what happened to Ned. Ferebee continued to lead "a formidable gang of . . . ruffians" in the Dismal Swamp, maroons "in league" with people still enslaved.[99] Over the next six years Ferebee's group was blamed for "many atrocities" in Norfolk and Princess Anne Counties.[100] Their sporadic attacks kept residents near the swamp in a panic because of "the too apparent fact that their lives are at the mercy of a band of lurking assassins, against whose fell designs neither the power of the law, or vigilance, or personal strength or intrepidity, can avail."[101]

A correspondent to the *Raleigh Weekly Register* described the maroon threat to his readers: "The desperadoes are runaway negroes (commonly called outlyers) who find a secure retreat from pursuit in the neighboring swamps, in which some of them have been all their lives employed in cutting timber or getting lumber and with the dreary haunts of which they are perfectly familiar . . . The topography of that section of the county being calculated to favor their murderous purposes and to shield them from discovery, detection in the execution of their horrid purposes is almost impossible without an accident." These maroons had regularly raided nearby farms and plantations, robbed travelers on the roads, stockpiled guns and ammunition, and killed numerous local citizens. The targets of their plunder were most often to obtain chosen goods for their own subsistence in the swamp, but some of the killings seem to have been specifically chosen "objects of vengeance," perhaps those known to mistreat their enslaved people or militia members who had been especially active in attempting to hunt them down. Although unsuccessful, the maroons attempted to assassinate a "General Foreman," a well-known veteran of the War of 1812, Norfolk magistrate, minister, and enslaver of people, as he passed through the swamp. "No individual after this," a Norfolk writer warned, "can consider his life safe from the murdering aim of these monsters in human shape."[102]

A detachment of 200 infantry and cavalry went out in late May to "scour the country in search of them," but by the next month, only three maroons had been apprehended.[103] One of them, however, appears to have been Bob

Ferebee, "chief of the party of outliers."[104] Ferebee was jailed and charged with crimes — including murders — dating back at least five years, and sentenced to be executed on July 23. The other two captives, Lewis and Jerry, preceded Bob to the gallows, and one relieved newspaper editor hoped "their fate [would] have its due influence on preventing the recurrence of those horrible atrocities for which they are doomed to suffer."[105]

The executions had no such influence. Indeed, the North Carolina maroons remained quite active as Virginia maroons regrouped.[106] Maroons in the southern section of the Dismal Swamp had become so active by 1822 that the North Carolina legislature passed "An Act to Encourage the Apprehension of Runaway Slaves in the Great Dismal Swamp." Among other provisions, the act incentivized the incredibly "dangerous and difficult work" of entering into the swamp in search of maroons who had "secreted themselves" there for a period exceeding three months by providing a captor one-fourth the appraised value of the maroon apprehended.[107] This was no small sum. At a time when the average price of an enslaved male was close to a thousand dollars, the prize for the capture and return of a Dismal Swamp maroon could be five to ten times the usual reward offered by enslavers in advertising for their "fugitive" property.[108]

Still, few hazarded slave hunts in the swamp. The rare man who actively attempted to bring maroons to justice and out of the swamp had a way of ending up dead. One Dismal Swamp farmer, as soon as he had made known his plans to rally a posse to apprehend some of Mingo's notorious swamp maroons, was shot in his fields and died at the feet of his terrified wife.[109] Three years later, Elisha Cross was killed by the very maroons he had been working to apprehend in the Gates County area of the Dismal. "No one was more active than Mr. Cross," a reporter wrote, "in endeavoring to bring these wretches to justice, which had so excited their resentment that they had threatened to take his life so soon as an opportunity should offer." Their chance was not long in coming, and they shot Cross in the back, stabbed him numerous times, nearly cut off one of his thumbs, slit his throat, and sliced his face "from each corner of his mouth to that in his throat."[110] The last week of June 1823, maroons attempted to kill Henry Culpepper at his home on the North Carolina side of the canal (near the hostelry of Maj. William Farange). Culpepper survived the first attack by playing dead after being fired upon, but two months later, his determined attackers returned and shot him with seven slugs from two guns. He died four days later.[111] Assassinations like these were not common, but they demonstrate maroons' tenacity and willingness to go to any length to maintain their freedom.

Beginning in 1822, a "considerable gang" of heavily armed maroons based in Gates County, North Carolina, renewed cross-swamp operations. Under the leadership of a self-emancipated man named Bob (alias Sam) Ricks, maroons raided plantations in the Virginia counties of Sussex, Southampton, and Nansemond, and Gates County, North Carolina, back and forth across the border for several months. In September 1823, four of them (Willis, Elisha, Jim, and Jack) were captured and jailed, but they were freed ten days later in a daring jailbreak. Another of their raids was on a slave coffle of seventeen people passing near the Dismal Swamp bound for the Deep South. Six of Ricks's men ambushed the coffle and demanded "the surrender of the negroes they had in possession." The enslavers Whitefield and Tomkins "were compelled to fly for their lives," leaving chained men, their wagon, and all their baggage in the hands of the maroons. Although some of the coffle were afraid to join the maroons, others, including the brother of the man believed to have killed Elisha Cross, enthusiastically joined up and were "furnished with arms."[112]

In early June 1824, four of Ricks's men were captured attempting to sail to New York with forged "free papers." They were transported to the jail in Gates County, North Carolina, and the $1,200 reward for their capture was paid to the ship's captain who had betrayed them.[113] Jim was condemned and executed for the murder of Elisha Cross; his last words from the gallows were his unrepentant confession.[114] Bob Ricks's name does not appear again in the record after the capture of his friends. It may be that he was ultimately successful in sailing the maritime Underground Railroad to a different type of freedom, or he may have remained marooned in the swamp.[115]

Maroons had kept the Dismal Swamp region in a state of near-constant rebellion for decades. There was no question in many enslavers' minds that their escaping property was endeavoring to reach the Great Dismal Swamp. Their fears were widely published in runaway ads. An understanding developed that some maroons sought scission from the outside world, while others were engaged in guerrilla warfare. Even those maroons who were not actively engaging with enslavers were doing comparable damage to the proslavery gospel that held African Americans incapable of survival outside of white oversight and as benefiting from and appreciative of their enslavement. That growing numbers of maroons were doing just fine on their own in the most inaccessible wilderness in America, arming themselves and even stockpiling weapons to turn against those who would enslave them, inspired terror.

There had been rumored rebellion plots involving Dismal Swamp maroons in the previous three decades that, if real, were larger and potentially more cataclysmic than those of Gabriel in 1800 or Denmark Vesey in Charleston in 1822. Moreover, African American unrest in the Dismal Swamp region far exceeded that of any other distinct region of the South. There was the real fear that disaster was imminent, and no one knew when the "earthquake" maroons had warned of in 1802 might strike. That it hadn't rocked their society in the decades since only added fear that the building pressure would be even more destructive. When it finally came, however, it was not from the Dismal Swamp but dry land in an unexpected corner of Virginia.

Dismal Swamp maroons, though, may not have been so surprised. Bob Ricks, after all, had been enslaved in Jerusalem, Southampton County, Virginia. Ricks's slave labor camp was not far from the slave labor camp of Samuel Turner. When Bob Ricks was around twenty-five in 1811, he would have heard about the escape of a man Turner enslaved named Abraham, who was believed to have marooned to the Great Dismal Swamp. This almost certainly was not the first Ricks had heard of the Dismal, but if Abraham had escaped there, Bob would have from that point associated that place with freedom, and of course he himself escaped to the Dismal eleven years later.[116] Maybe Abraham was with Ricks when his maroon band roamed far afield from their Dismal Swamp base to strike back at their home Southampton County in the 1820s. Ricks remained at large, and his name remained one of the most feared on both sides of the Dismal for a decade. It would be eclipsed in 1831 by Abraham's son, Nat Turner.

The Nat Turner "Cataclysm"

On August 21, 1831, Nat Turner led around seventy other African Americans in the largest rebellion of enslaved people in the antebellum era just twenty-five miles east of the Dismal Swamp. Perhaps this is what Abraham had meant when he said his son "was intended for some great purpose."[117] Starting with the Travis family, Nat's captors, the rebels began going from house to house, killing about sixty white men, women, and children, and recruiting new followers. By midday on August 22, the group began a march toward the county seat of Jerusalem, but on the way they encountered alarmed whites and a quickly organized militia unit. The two armed groups clashed, and Turner's followers scattered and became disorganized. After regrouping overnight, Turner's rebels attempted to attack another farm but were repulsed and several rebels captured. The white militia, by this point reinforced by state and federal forces including three companies of artillery, killed or captured many of the remaining insurgents.

Turner, however, escaped and remained at large. As news of the rebellion spread out from Southampton County over the next few days, speculation about the conspiracy and fate of its leader ran wild. While solid information remained scarce, some white officials and newspaper editors sought to reassure a panic-stricken public. In an effort "to correct exaggerations," the editor of the *Richmond Constitutional Whig* assured his readers that "serious danger, of course, there is none. The deluded wretches have rushed on assured destruction."[118] The plot, another editor wrote, "is believed to have originated only in a design to plunder, and not a view to a more important object."[119]

But there were other, more terrifying possibilities, and as the actual death toll became clearer, it was obvious that something truly terrifying had occurred. Exaggerations and conjecture quickly took over interpretations of the raid—Nat's army continued to roam the countryside undeterred; hundreds of enslaved people were rushing to his standard; thousands of whites lay dead in the streets. But the most terrifying possibility, and not at all an unreasonable one, was that the rebellion had been launched from the Great Dismal Swamp. The growing army of disaffected African Americans, armed and angry, guerrilla fighters whose martial skills and strategies had been honed for a century, had finally undertaken what whites in the region always feared: the maroon revolt to end all revolts. One editor believed "this rebellion was the work of runaway slaves, who had found an asylum in the Dismal Swamp, and had issued from it for the purpose of robbery and rapine."[120] Another source reported that "the number of insurgents had reached fourteen hundred; including six hundred and fifty who had organized themselves in the Dismal Swamp, but had not yet formed a junction with the others."[121] Another assumed that after the rebellion, the rebels had fled "probably with the view of retreating into the Dismal Swamp, whence it will be difficult to dislodge them."[122] Indeed, with the various militia groups closing in on them, a Norfolk writer assumed, the rebels would "be anxious to bury themselves in the recesses of the Dismal Swamp" from whence the majority of them had issued, triggering "well-founded uneasiness to the inhabitants of the surrounding country."[123]

Of course, no white person could sleep well with the knowledge that Nat remained at large. "It is yet unknown," one man wrote, "to what part of the country he has bent his course." Many, he noted, "strongly suspected that he had secreted himself among the thick brush of Dismal Swamp." If he was successful in his retreat, his inability to take Southampton County might turn out to be but a minor setback once he could rally the scores of maroons in the

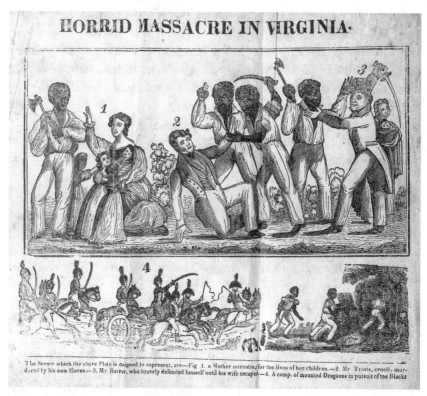

"Horrid Massacre in Virginia." From Warner, *Authentic and Impartial Narrative.*
Note the escape to the swamp illustrated at the bottom right.

Dismal. If Nat and his men made it to the swamp, he would find there "as secure a retreat as did the almost inaccessible mountains of St. Domingo to their black brethren of that island." The scenes of the Haitian Revolution were certainly a possibility here, the writer believed: "Similar scenes of bloodshed and murder might our brethren at the South expect to witness, were the disaffected Slaves of that section of the country but once to gain the ascendency: In a 'General Nat,' they might then find a wretch not less disposed to shed innocent blood, than was the perfidious Dessalines [from whom] little mercy could be expected!"[124]

Whites mobilized militias in ten counties in North Carolina and Virginia to stop the rebels' retreat to the swamp and to try to hunt down their leader. The militias of Nansemond, Norfolk, and Princess Anne Counties, reinforced by a unit of the US Army from Old Point Comfort, rather than march toward Southampton "with the rest of the Anglo-Saxon Upper South," were ordered to the northwest edge of the Dismal to await the rebels advance.[125] These local troops knew better than anyone else that there were maroons waiting to guide retreating rebels deep into the swamp to disappear. Despite the vigilance of the white militia units, there is evidence that some of Nat Turner's followers made it safely to the Dismal.[126]

Those who did not experienced great suffering. The white reprisal to Turner's rebellion was a bloodbath. Hundreds of African Americans were captured and jailed, and perhaps 200 indiscriminately "exterminated."[127] A correspondent of the *Niles Weekly Register* from Norfolk described the immediate carnage: "The roads were strewed with the carcasses of the negroes killed, and up to the 25th ult. [previous month] neither these nor the corpses of the unfortunate whites had been buried."[128]

There also followed the first large-scale assault on the maroons within the Dismal. From both North Carolina and Virginia, local militia units attempted to penetrate the swamp. However, despite reports that the whole swamp was "thoroughly scoured even to its darkest and deepest recesses," it is more likely that incursions into the swamp were limited to the fringe, canals, and adjacent dry ground.[129] Even in these superficial sweeps of the swamp, however, "a great many runaway slaves [were] found therein."[130] There is no indication that any people taken up in these raids were involved in the rebellion in any way.[131]

Nat Turner was not among them. If his plans had ever been to escape to the Dismal, the fallout from the rebellion quickly and certainly made that impossible. In the days following the failed insurgency, Nat's closest circle of collaborators scattered to the wind. He and two other lieutenants were able to conceal themselves in the woods near Jerusalem, and Nat sent them out in search of others and to gather supplies. They never returned. Nat next gathered some provisions from the house of his former captor and hid out in a hole he had dug under some fence rails in a nearby field. For six weeks, he did not leave his hole during the daylight hours, and only abandoned his makeshift cave when he believed he had been discovered. He then dug out another hole under a fallen tree nearby but was found and captured there two weeks later, still twenty-five miles from the Dismal Swamp.[132]

The swamp, it turned out, had not been the epicenter of the earthquake as so many whites had feared. Not yet, anyway. By running through so many nightmare scenarios centered in and around the Dismal, whites had actually more fully articulated just how much of a threat and danger the maroons of the swamp could potentially pose. That Nat and his rebellion had *not* figured the swamp into their plans seemed quite a surprise once dozens of writers took the opportunity to educate the general public on the Dismal. One of the earliest lengthy commentaries on the rebellion (written and published even before Nat's capture) offered a full natural and human history of the Dismal Swamp in four pages (more than 10 percent of the entire pamphlet), including accounts of maroon families who, the author wrote, would prefer to suffer and die than be retaken and placed again "under the goading yoke of bondage."[133]

Even once Turner was dead and gone, the Dismal Swamp loomed larger than ever. It remained, overwhelmingly, a black hole into which self-emancipating people disappeared, and next to nothing of substance was known about its innermost reaches. Was the maroon population of the swamp 2,000 or 3,000, as some estimated at the time of the Turner rebellion?[134] The 40,000 of another estimate some years later?[135] Impotence in the face of the unknown was truly terrifying.

Almost forty years after Nat Turner's rebellion, the editor of a Petersburg, Virginia, newspaper published without comment a memory of the near-cataclysm that had occurred so far yet so close to the Great Dismal Swamp. "The Virginia Swamp has a historical memory clinging to it," the account's author suggested, "somber as its cypress and mosses . . . For six weeks, to the whole south, it seemed that in those horrid recesses of nature the avenging genius of slavery crouched but for a moment before covering the land with desolation."[136] The Dismal Swamp maroons, though in the depths of a swamp, cast a long, dark shadow.

CHAPTER FOUR

Maroon Life in the Great Dismal Swamp

The poor slave, when his patience is clear exhausted and maddened beyond endurance at the hardships of his lot, betakes himself to these impenetrable fastnesses, to associate with wild beasts less savage than man.
—H. Cowles Atwater, *Incidents of a Southern Tour*, 1857

They used to say that if you drank the water of the Dismal Swamp, it was guaranteed to make you free.
—Lisa Mizelle, Suffolk, Virginia resident, 1994

His master told him he could not take care of himself, if given his liberty. He told him he was willing to try the experiment.
—B. S. DeForest, *Random Sketches*, 1866

THE GREAT DISMAL SWAMP was a beacon to self-emancipators and society's outcasts, and few people reached it without some fore-knowledge of where they were heading and why. Whether they had traveled a thousand miles or five, come into the swamp from routes south, east, or even *north*, these men, women, and children had already successfully eluded detection and recapture through the riskiest part of their ordeal into freedom. Once safely in the swamp, maroons most often joined one of dozens of communities made up of people with similar motivations for living there. The varying geography of the swamp determined what kinds of community formations would emerge and be sustainable, ranging from large permanent villages deep in the swamp completely cut off from the outside world to smaller groups of maroons who settled along the swamp's edge or lived among enslaved canal or shingle workers.

Life in the swamp was never easy, but maroons knew it to be better than lives enslaved. Few outsiders ever witnessed maroon life in the Dismal. The most imaginative could not have conceived just how fascinating a society was concealed in the swamp.

THE EXISTENCE OF MAROONS in the Great Dismal Swamp was widely acknowledged by the early eighteenth century. More than two centuries later,
outsiders' actual knowledge of how the Dismal was populated and what went
on in its depths remained negligible. "How these people managed to travel 30
to 40 miles without being seen," one white Dismal Swamp resident wondered
in his old age in 1902, "I could never understand." It had been a "mystery" to
him how these people seeking the swamp's protection knew just which paths
to take, where to shelter en route, and just what to do if they encountered
obstacles in their way. Only much later did this observer learn that nearly
every enslaved person for fifty miles around was "thoroughly informed" about
the Dismal through the efforts of "colored news carriers" and guides. "The
woods were full of them," one newly free person told him.[1]

Enslavers were well aware of the swamp's pull, of course. In countless runaway ads, jilted claimants of newly free people listed the Dismal as their likely
destination. It was known to be "difficult to keep slaves" in proximity to the
Dismal, and a Norfolk merchant complained of the swamp that "over one
million and a half dollars worth of slaves were in this place."[2] Beyond this,
though, enslavers seemed to have very little understanding of just what lay
within the darkness of the swamp and the lives their former enslaved people
were living there.

Their abolitionists' nemeses and other nonlocals were not much better informed. An immigrant around the time of the American Revolution had described the maroon landscape as uniform throughout the swamp—it was "the
general asylum for everything that flies from mankind and society."[3] In 1852
abolitionist Edmund Jackson generally described the maroons of the Great
Dismal Swamp as a "large colony of negroes, who originally obtained their
freedom through the grace of God, and their own determined energy." "How
long this colony has existed," he admitted, "what is its amount of population,
what portion of the colonists are now Fugitives, and what the descendants of
Fugitives, are questions not easily determined."[4] Even allies could claim only
superficial knowledge of Dismal Swamp maroons.

Fundamentally, the Great Dismal Swamp did not shelter a single large maroon colony, despite what many contemporaries on the outside assumed. Com-
mentators after the Civil War eventually understood that what whites *thought*
they knew about the Dismal and the lives maroons had *actually* been living
were two very different things.[5] In fact, self-emancipators formed dozens of
separate maroon communities across the swamp. Modern satellite imaging
indicates that large mesic islands (greater than twenty acres) and large clusters

of smaller islands (fifty or more acres in aggregate) exist in the swamp that would have been conducive to larger-scale settlement. Archaeological excavations on some of these sites have produced evidence of continuous maroon occupation throughout the seventeenth, eighteenth, and nineteenth centuries. Islands surveyed by archaeologists to date range from one to thirty-nine acres, are often found in clusters with as little as fifty feet of swamp separating them, and are as high as ten feet above swamp level in the most isolated, deep swamp islands.[6] Yet these islands spread over thousands of square miles, and though some are close enough to have been utilized by the same group of maroons, most are not. To be sure, there were large communities deep within the Great Dismal, but the basic topography of the swamp, social structure of the communities, and concerns for defense and safety preclude any possibility of their being more than loosely joined.

The overall maroon population of the Great Dismal Swamp likely fluctuated widely over two centuries, and it is impossible to give precise numbers for any given time. Frederick Douglass, whose published writings suggest a more extensive knowledge of the Great Dismal Swamp Maroons than most, spoke of "uncounted numbers of fugitives," certainly a very accurate assessment.[7] A frequent figure estimated for the Great Dismal maroon population, 2,000, derives from the militia estimate at the time of the Nat Turner revolt.[8] Maroons themselves had no idea how many others shared their swamp home, and were likely unaware of all maroon settlements across the swamp.

The Great Dismal Swamp Landscape Study has uncovered compelling evidence of "heavy" maroon use and dense populations deep in the swamp. Though considerably less than 1 percent of the Great Dismal Swamp National Wildlife Refuge acreage has even been surveyed, every area of dry ground visited by the GDSLS was determined to be an archaeological site or an isolated find.[9] The most extensive excavation to date, known simply as the "nameless" site, represents just 0.1 percent of the twenty-acre mesic island upon which it was located. At the island's highest elevation, in a twenty-by-twenty-meter area, GDSLS has excavated what are believed to be a minimum of ten significant structures and cultural landscape features (or feature complexes), including at least six sections of rectilinear structural footprints, a defensive structure (fort/ammunition depot), and several other postholes and pits of unknown purpose.[10] With the concurrence of the documentary sources indicating that the swamp population was quite large, one could say with confidence that at least dozens of maroons settled at any given time on this excavated spot, and as the GDSLS has only uncovered a tiny fraction of likely settlement locations,

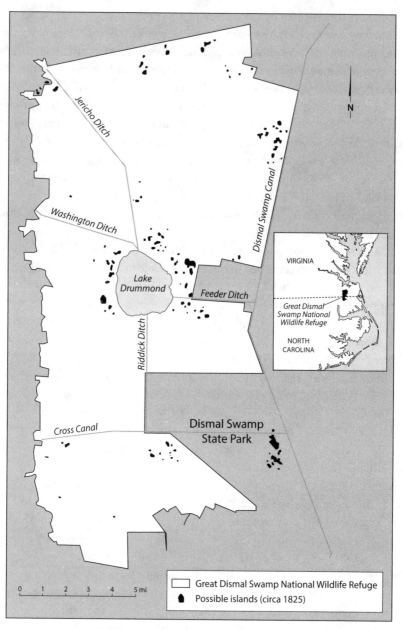

Possible islands (ca. 1825) in present-day Great Dismal Swamp National Wildlife Refuge and Dismal Swamp State Park. Adapted from "Composite Topography Map," in Peixotto, "Glass in the Landscape of the Great Dismal Swamp," 9, and "GDSNWR Water Control Structure and Ditch Network Flow Direction Map," US Fish and Wildlife Service.

the aggregate population of the Great Dismal Swamp Maroon communities at any given time after the early eighteenth century likely numbered in at least the hundreds, and likely the thousands.

Where maroons settled within the swamp depended on a number of factors. The residents of the Dismal Swamp developed distinct communities, and newcomers would have generally found (or been brought into) groups of people with similar motivations for living in the swamp. The varying landscape also determined what kinds of community formations would emerge and how they might be sustainable. For example, islands in the deepest interior of the swamp would have best supported one type of very settled marronage, while dry areas at the edge of the Dismal would have supported another much more dynamic type of community formation. The different varieties of marronage would have been significantly structured by the degree to which they depended on and remained connected to the economic and social networks of the external world.

Three different types of marronage developed in the Great Dismal Swamp. Though there were cases where a maroon transitioned from one type of marronage to another, these were almost always in the direction of more structure and independence than less (at least through the nineteenth century). *Fringe Maroons* settled at the edge of the swamp, strategically situated for easy access to both the interior of the swamp and outside world if and when they needed it. These were often the most transient maroons who were not necessarily seeking to remain in the swamp for extended periods of time. Before the significant encroachments of agriculture, lumbering, and canals in the late eighteenth century, these maroons sometimes formed small temporary communities, but as the swamp's edge receded in the nineteenth century, Fringe Maroons appeared only as very small groups or as individuals. As this transformation was occurring at the swamp's periphery, *Liminal Maroons* developed as a distinct population alongside corporate and industrial enterprises in the swamp. These maroons often lived alongside enslaved swamp laborers. They did not necessarily seek to limit contacts and connections with the outside world, and in fact were largely dependent on it for their survival. The *Deep Swamp Maroons* were those who sought to separate themselves physically, socially, and economically from the exterior world as much as possible. These were the most permanently settled maroons of the swamp, often living for years (or decades) in their isolation.

Fringe Maroons

The most ephemeral Dismal Swamp residents were the Fringe Maroons. These men and women settled at the natural perimeter of the swamp and generally fell into one of four subcategories. The first were transient refugees from en-slavement who availed themselves of the swamp's secrecy and protection for a time before moving on to another location, often a step closer to a free state or Canada. The North Star meant freedom to thousands of self-emancipating slaves over the years, and the Dismal Swamp was a bright spot lit on the path north from the Deep South.

The Dismal Swamp earned a reputation as a busy station of the "Under-ground Railroad." This was a very loose organization of abolitionists, most African American, who helped coordinate and facilitate the marronage of self-emancipating people. Traditionally, most emphasis has been placed upon the actions of those offering assistance along a particular route (south to north). In the standard narrative, thousands of enslaved people "were freed" through the Underground Railroad. The self-emancipators themselves are often lost in the process and overshadowed by, as Daniel Sayers calls it, feel-good "racially mosaic efforts, assistance, civil disobedience, and the potential of this version of history to help heal modern social ills."[11] More attention is paid to the fact of escape itself, rather than escape as a constituent part of the full lived maroon experience.

Dismal Swamp maroons are occasionally included in the telling of these stories, but seldom as the central heroic figures their experiences have mer-ited. It would be more accurate to mention the Underground Railroad as one of many processes that comprised marronage. The example of maroons in the Dismal Swamp demonstrates that, while the process of flight (and even assistance in escape) is very important, the exciting story does not end after a maroon extricated themself from enslavement, nor did it necessarily lead outside the bounds of the Slave South.[12] As one "in-the-know" abolitionist pointed out in the 1850s, "there is a Canada in the Southern States. It is the Dismal Swamp."[13]

Whether a step in a long journey or end unto itself, the Dismal was a beacon to freedom-seekers. The swamp's proximity to busy port cities like Edenton, North Carolina, and especially Norfolk, Virginia, made it a convenient refuge for planning while awaiting a northern berth on the ship of a known sympa-thetic captain or crewman, or as a stowaway. The utility of the Dismal for this purpose was well known to both the enslaved people of the region and their captors.

Harriet Jacobs's former enslaver assumed that enslaved people who fled his labor camp near the swamp would take advantage of its shelter before at-tempting to get "on board some vessel bound for the northward."[14] Another enslaver's ad seeking the return of Jerry assumed he would "endeavor to get to

Norfolk, and from thence to Baltimore."[15] Banister Midyett believed a man he had enslaved named Moses was making his was to Edenton through the Dismal Swamp, much as John was "lurking" near the swamp's edges "waiting for an opportunity to get away in some vessel."[16] Toney, who had been enslaved in Princess Anne County, Virginia, before marooning in the Dismal, had boldly declared his intention "to ship himself onboard the first vessel going out of the country."[17] Self-emancipators who marooned in the Dismal Swamp knew just how close they were to these bustling ports, and many had sought out the protections of the swamp specifically because of the proximity to northbound shipping lanes. Many runaway ads published near ports adjacent to the Dismal Swamp, such as an ad from Edenton seeking the capture of George and Harry, warned "masters of vessels . . . against carrying them off at their peril."[18]

Enslavers' worries were not unfounded. New England abolitionist captain Daniel Drayton recalled that "no sooner, indeed, does a vessel, known to be from the north, anchor in any of these waters—and the slaves are pretty adroit in ascertaining from what state a vessel comes—than she is boarded, if she remains any length of time, and especially over night, by more or less of them, in hopes of obtaining a passage in her to a land of freedom." He personally attested to instances where enslaved people hid out in the swamps for even a year or two "waiting for an opportunity to escape on board some vessel."[19] Alfred Fountain, captain of the *City of Richmond* out of Norfolk, transported dozens of formerly enslaved people into the care of northern abolitionists, and was even known to sail the Dismal Swamp Canal to rendezvous with prearranged maroon passengers.[20] Others stowed away alongside the products of the swamp in ships' holds.[21] Mills, formerly enslaved in Buckingham, Virginia, declared his intent to escape with his wife into the Dismal Swamp and stay there until they could make a bid for a free state.[22] Benjamin Randolph had waited in the Dismal for seven months before cautiously boarding a northbound ship.[23] George Langdon lived as part of a Dismal Swamp maroon community near Suffolk for eighteen months before making his escape on a schooner loaded with shingles. He arrived in New York to a new life as a tanner and mason but always carried with him birdshot lodged under his skin from being shot while marooning in the swamp.[24] Daniel Carr had marooned in the Dismal for three months, when, on a nighttime visit to see his wife in Suffolk, he fortuitously met the ship's captain who would eventually help him escape to Philadelphia.[25] Of course, not all maroon attempts were as successful. Recall that four of Bob Ricks's maroon band were jailed after their attempt to board a New York–bound ship was foiled by its captain.

Harry Grimes depicted marooning in the Dismal. "Living in a Hollow Tree."
From Still, *Still's Underground Rail Road Records*.

Of course, most ships' captains did not offer pickup in the swamp (as Alfred
Fountain sometimes did), and the process of finding and soliciting a sympathetic seaman was very risky. Slaveholders published descriptions of their
runaways in harbor towns, on trees at the ends of the Dismal Swamp Canal,
and local periodicals and warned those who might take up a Dismal Swamp
passenger of the dire criminal consequences of their actions.[26] Sometimes, an
enslaved person employed as a shingler or waterman in the Dismal Swamp
might help a maroon get access to someone in port who could arrange a berth,
but these were always dangerous missions where a single misstep or loose word
might doom a freedom seeker.[27] It could also be a supreme test of endurance,
sometimes requiring months of patient solitude. Harry Grimes marooned in
the Great Dismal Swamp for a year and a half before sailing on Fountain's
ship. "While in the woods," he remembered, "all my thoughts was how to get
away to a free country."[28]

Others made the trek through the Dismal on foot. Charlie was one man
who marooned in the western Virginia portion of the swamp. He had originally been led into the swamp by a close friend on the outside who knew
secret entrance pathways, then decided after some time living in a maroon

community that he wanted to continue his marronage journey to Canada. He left using a well-known route and an oft-utilized plan (at least among Dismal Swamp maroons). Charlie took pains to keep that route a secret—"'I suspect I better not tell the way I came; for there's lots more coming the same way I did."[29]

Sympathetic whites, free African Americans, and more settled maroons around the perimeter were known to shelter self-emancipators, offering them temporary respite from the worst dangers of escape and advice for the next leg of their journey. Local white abolitionists were scarce, yet they did what they could to support maroons and assist self-emancipators on their way. These were most often devoutly religious adherents to the Christian Golden Rule, such as a fiercely abolitionist Arminian Baptist family who lived near the Dismal Swamp Canal in Virginia, or the antislavery family who lived at the swamp's edge near Deep Creek and at night "stole into the swamp with provisions for the fugitive slaves."[30] Abolitionist Emily Pearson wrote about Elihu Woodman, a man who lived in a hidden cabin slightly off the Dismal Swamp Canal. Proclaiming that his "sympathies were alive for the slave," Woodman worked to "help slaves into the swamp settlement."[31] Virginia maroon Larinda White struck up a friendship with a white family at the edge of the swamp who had "often befriended" other maroons and made sure self-emancipators knew who could be trusted and which "meddlesome neighbors" to avoid.[32]

Poor white people living at the swamp's edge who might have balked at being called abolitionists still sometimes assisted maroons.[33] Besides frequently providing food, necessities, and shelter to Fringe Maroons, whites sometimes abetted marronage simply by withholding information from inquisitive outsiders. As early as the 1720s, poor residents of the swamp borders frustrated a party of planters reconnoitering the area. The deflective stories they told were dismissed as "hardly credible." They "pretended" to know nothing of what was hidden in the swamp's depths, and the planter investigator concluded that "there was no intelligence of this terra incognita to be got."[34] Over a hundred years later, Edmund Jackson visited the edge of the swamp from Massachusetts (he was an abolitionist, but an outsider nonetheless). "Those best enabled to gratify [his] curiosity" about the Dismal maroons refused to speak a word on the subject within his hearing.[35]

Free African Americans were also of great assistance to transient self-emancipators in the Dismal Swamp. William Johnson Hodges, a Black preacher living in the Blackwater area of the Dismal, was jailed for writing free passes for local enslaved people's use in journeys northward. Imprisoned in Portsmouth, he orchestrated his escape along with seven other free and enslaved men and hid out with them in the swamp before arranging passage to Canada. Thus William's brother Willis, who also "swore eternal war against slavery" during his brother's persecution, well knew the routes to freedom beyond the swamp when he helped enslaved people escape to Canada fifteen years later.[36] Alexander Keeling, a free Black minister to Dismal Swamp maroons, was known to deflect whites' questions about people living or passing through the swamp. More directly, when whites would post fugitive notices around the edge of the swamp, Alek was said to tear them down to protect his maroon brethren.[37]

The swamp's edges also offered a welcome refuge to those people who might have been enslaved locally and for some reason did not wish to permanently separate from the area where they had been enslaved. The cruelty of slavery had pushed them to escape it, but the bonds of family, friends, and home often kept them from fully severing their ties. Family ties and Dismal freedom were not incompatible. Jack marooned on the southern edge of the Dismal to be close to his wife.[38] Daniel was believed by his enslaver to be "endeavoring to make his way to the dismal swamp," but only after passing through Elizabeth City for his wife.[39] Diver was assumed to be "lurking about among his relations" who lived near the Dismal.[40] Jim would frequently venture out of the Dismal Swamp to the cabin of his wife and children.[41] A mother and two children marooned in the Dismal Swamp in the 1820s near her husband, who remained enslaved on a labor camp so that he could provide for them.[42]

Folks back at the slave labor camp provided more than provisions. Often as valuable to maroons was the information their friends provided. While maroons were concealed in the swamp, allies back on the slave labor camp ensured that they were kept abreast of important developments outside the Dismal. Without the help of still-enslaved informants, maroons would have been much more vulnerable to being discovered. This aid could range from news of heightened patrol activities, alerts about traps set for them back on a labor camp, or intelligence regarding a potential traitor in their midst. Knowledge could be the difference between slavery and freedom, life and death.[43]

Maroons also developed a very simple yet efficient communication system with loved ones on labor camps that helped them visit safely. A garment hung in a certain way and visible from the woods' edge might signal that the coast was clear, that there was no danger of being caught. At night, a light might be displayed in a certain window or flashed in a familiar pattern. Maroons might have a secret knock to identify themselves to those inside a cabin, or give a familiar whistle or call that confirmed the coast was clear.[44]

These networks across nearby slave labor camps, over canals and waterways, and through the woods and swamps of the whole Tidewater region, together made up the infrastructure of the "grapevine telegraph." This system of knowledge, passed from person to person, helped these men and women remain free and safe in the swamp yet in touch with loved ones still in bonds who were unable to visit them. News of escapes spread quickly through the Black population of the Dismal Swamp region, and even those not quite willing to take the risks inherent in marronage usually did what they could to help those who were.[45] They curated a secret repository of resistant knowledge and, in empowering others, they empowered themselves. They also, even if only momentarily, appropriated spaces claimed by enslavers to facilitate other resistant activity. This "psychic marronage" created spaces where marronage could be deliberated and supported even if their efforts, for whatever reason, did not extend to self-emancipation.[46]

In a description of Dismal Swamp maroons circa 1817, a visitor to the area commented on these connections: "When one has run away they all take an interest in his escape; and though there are usually 30 or 40 who know where he stays & who supply him with provisions . . . a constant intercourse is maintained between runaways [in the swamp] and those who remain."[47] Forty may have even been a conservative estimate. Quarters for the enslaved were often situated very close to one another, and in some cases two families might live under the same roof, divided (if at all) by only a thin wall. As historian Sylviane Diouf notes, at least a dozen enslaved people within a few feet of one another might easily know if a maroon visited a house at night. Within fifty feet, sixty people and several families might share that knowledge. That maroons felt safe enough to take this risk demonstrated the degree of their confidence in their brethren still in bonds.[48]

These networks could extend well beyond immediate family and friends to span several labor camps and free communities. Such widespread support could help maintain marronage for years.[49] Some, like John Salley, "ran away and didn't ever come back. Didn't go anywhere either. Stayed right around the plantation." John relied on hogs and chickens from his former home for his survival.[50] In the 1930s, Sis Shackelford remembered traveling as a child many miles from her home in Phoebus, Virginia, to the northern edges of the Dismal Swamp to carry bread and fresh meat to maroons.[51] In North Carolina (and likely elsewhere), there was "an understanding" among enslaved people spanning multiple labor camps and communities that food and weapons would be secreted at predetermined hiding places in the hinterland for the use of any future maroons among them.[52] There was support on the labor camps, from men and women who might have marooned and received vital support in the past, from some who anticipated such a need themselves in the future, or from others who simply chose to live by the Golden Rule. Within every enslaved person dwelt a potential maroon.

In these and other similar ways, enslaved people resisted by aiding and abetting maroons. They may not have joined maroon communities or led them, but they played integral roles in the process of marronage. Their fidelity was appreciated from within the swamp—those who risked their lives to protect maroons could expect the same if it became necessary to repay the favor. "There's many of them in the swamp," one writer familiar with the maroons remarked, "that would die for [their enslaved allies]."[53] Vincent Harding credits the partnership of maroons and their "silent black partners" with making "signal contributions to the heritage of black radicalism and black struggle."[54] John Blassingame describes the quiet delight still-enslaved people felt when someone close to them marooned: "each escape of a fellow sufferer produced prayers of success, fed the rumor mill, fired dreams, and raised the level of curiosity about freedom throughout the quarters."[55] In this the impact of maroons on those still enslaved is underscored. Maroons had chosen to resist their enslavement through self-emancipation, but their circumstances also influenced the resistant activities and life choices of those still enslaved. Marronage was a phenomenon that impacted the entire region.[56]

Maroons also depended on the support and protection of free African Americans in and around the swamp. Eighteen-year-old Harry, enslaved in North Carolina by Richard Blount, was believed to be marooned in the Pasquotank County section of the Dismal, "where he probably expects aid and succor from the free blacks of that county."[57] The free Skeeter family of the northern Dismal Swamp area had a long tradition, dating back to the eighteenth century, of providing food and clothing to swamp maroons while assisting them in whatever ways they could.[58] This might even include assisting maroons in nighttime incursions on nearby labor camps. It was assumed by whites that free African Americans and maroons were often in cahoots.[59]

"Uncle Alek" Keeling, a free preacher and beekeeper, was a close ally of and minister to Dismal Swamp maroons. In addition to tearing down runaway notices that enslavers posted along the canals, he earned a reputation among maroons as one of their most active protectors—he said that "they all knew that [not] the whipping post, nor jail, nor nothing could make him tell on them, and that he always gave them matches, and divided his tobacco with them."[60]

For a number of reasons, petit marronage on the edges of the Dismal sometimes also included an eventual return to enslavement after a period of "lying out." Enslaved people frequently sought temporary refuge in the Dismal

Swamp from the weight of their enslavement.[61] One man remembered that it "was an every-day occurrence" for enslaved people to maroon to the Dismal Swamp "when they were tired of work."[62] Besides frequent respites from overwork, the Dismal also protected short-term maroons from abuse. Will had been "beaten pitilessly" before seeking refuge in the Dismal Swamp.[63] Another woman, with her child, escaped to the Dismal "because I was afraid old massa would kill me." Unfortunately, the child she carried into the swamp died soon thereafter from a beating meted out by an overseer.[64]

Some slaveowners tolerated petit marronage because they viewed it as a useful safety valve.[65] Short-term maroons may have felt some sense of empowerment by registering their discontent and withdrawing their labor from their enslaver rather than leading a rebellion, lashing out on the labor camp, or fleeing permanently. Pompey's enslaver whipped him so much that he escaped the lash in the Dismal. There he hid out for three months. The first few weeks were hard living, but after a month, he said that he had become "as hard as a litewood knot, and nothing could hurt me." His absence, it seems, weighed heavily on his enslaver, who sent another enslaved person into the Dismal to negotiate with Pompey, promising better treatment if he returned. Pompey, petit maroon, returned to an enslaved but more bearable environment.[66] "Runaway Jim" used a similar "unseen telegraph communication" to negotiate from the Dismal Swamp over many weeks with his enslaver a pledge not to sell him away to a speculator.[67]

As Pompey's and Jim's experiences demonstrated, petit marronage often initiated a negotiation between enslaved and enslaver that resulted in improved conditions (or accommodations) in bondage. And though fear of marronage sometimes made enslavers more brutal in their attempts to suppress it, it was just as likely to cause whites to employ a lighter approach with those remaining enslaved for fear that they might join the ranks of the self-emancipators. In times of heightened maroon activity and marronage, enslaved people were emboldened to do less work and be more openly vocal in their discontent. Residents of several eastern North Carolina counties petitioned the state legislature in December 1830 for relief from the influence of maroons. Enslaved people in the region had "become almost uncontroulable. They go and come when and where they please, and if an attempt is made to correct them they immediately fly to the woods and there continue for months and years Committing grievous depredations on our Cattle hogs and Sheep."[68]

When the threat of marronage seemed highest, transgressions that might have otherwise been punished with a whipping or other corporal means might be allowed to slide. Moreover, an explicit threat to escape to the Dismal

Swamp might exact concessions as well.[69] It was well known that once a self-emancipator reached the swamp, that person was all but irretrievable, leading some enslavers to be proactive in their concessions. Rather than risk completely losing his sizeable investment in enslaved property, one enslaver conceded to sell a man who had previously marooned in the Dismal for three years to the enslaver of his wife.[70] Even the potential of marronage, then, was a weapon in the hands of the enslaved and reduced the power of enslavers.[71]

Life as a maroon was still hard. Closeness to the edge of the swamp (and from the other perspective, the edge of the slave society) meant higher likelihood of detection and capture. Maroons were almost entirely reliant on what they could hunt, were given by their enslaved friends, or could gather in the immediate vicinity of their camp. Most movement had to be undertaken at night, as did the setting of fires for cooking, since smoke plumes could draw attention to and identify the location of a maroon camp. When fires absolutely had to be lit while the sun was up, maroons would burn dry hardwood (oak, maple, hickory), or oak or hickory bark, as these fuels were known to produce the least smoke.[72] Noise, whether gunshots, cries from children, or even loud talking was kept to a minimum.[73]

A fourth group of Fringe Maroons (and there was likely some overlap with the other three) used the swamp's edge as a base of operations for guerrilla raids on outside settlements. These maroons had different motivations from those who remained mostly on the defensive. For one thing, their groups tended to be larger, and as such required more provisions that could easily be gathered from slave labor camp supporters or produced themselves. They were also limited in the extent to which they could produce their own foodstuffs. Often on the move by necessity, maroon raiders could not very well keep livestock, nor could they plant crops that might take months to grow. Vegetable gardening would have been far too risky, because of both the likelihood of discovery and the potential loss of labor spent in cultivation that would have to be abandoned if their group had to move to another swamp location. Farming was usually limited to what James C. Scott has called "escape agriculture." Maroons might plant crops that were "unobtrusive," such as root crops that could be left in the ground for some time and harvested when most convenient, and that could be quickly abandoned and revisited after a threat had passed. Such crops were, Scott points out, "nearly appropriation proof."[74]

Despite often-herculean efforts to provision themselves, these maroons were frequently described by hostile outsiders as "too lazy" to work, and reviled as thieves and raiders of nearby slave labor camps or towns who took what they needed "without leave asked or granted."[75] Theft held no particular stigma among maroons, especially since enslavers' goods had been produced by (stolen) enslaved labor. "I did not think it wrong to steal enough to eat," one former maroon remembered. "I thought I worked hard to raise it, and I had a right to it."[76] As another appropriator of enslavers' property remarked, "Roast pig is a wonderful delicacy, especially when stolen."[77] The swamp supplemented their provisions. Large game (bear, deer, boar) might be worth the expenditure of precious ammunition, and grapes, berries, roots, and edible cattails grew plentifully in season throughout the swamp.

Inevitably, forays out of the swamp could turn violent. Travelers near the swamp's edge were warned to exercise extreme caution against frequent maroon highway robberies. The Great Dismal was one of the "strong swamps" from which maroons "commit many daring outrages."[78] Of course, "outrages" could have simply included the audacious fact of their marronage, and violent confrontations were initiated not only by maroons but also by whites out of fear or desire to capture "runaways." Regardless of who started a fight, maroons were well prepared for battle. Their lives as hunters and woodsmen already required it, as would their very survival in a tenuous and hostile world. Military reports of raids from the swamp frequently cite firearms, swords, knives, clubs, and pikes possessed by maroons. The maroons also manufactured bows and arrows, useful to preserve powder and shot for emergencies.[79] When proper bullets could not be had, improvised projectiles like metal scraps, stones, or buttons might be loaded into the muzzle of a gun.[80] One armed maroon, an outlawed man from Suffolk, Virginia, with a $1,000 price on his head, was captured after several skirmishes in the 1850s. Though shot several times, the captive was unhurt, thanks to his swamp-made body armor, a coat thickly wadded with turkey feathers that was impervious to small shot.[81]

These most militant swamp-dwellers were the most visible and therefore triggered the most anxiety among the white population surrounding the Dismal. In some cases, this notoriety was well earned. The maroon campaigns highlighted in the previous chapter were led by representatives of this group of Fringe Maroons. Probably over a hundred whites were killed by Dismal Swamp maroons before the Civil War, many in the attempted insurrections, others in robberies gone wrong or targeted attacks. Even rebellions without direct connections to the Dismal, like Nat Turner's uprising, were initially assumed to have originated there.

Most often, though, the main concern of these maroons was simple survival. Food and shelter always took precedence over revenge or plunder. Hunger might drive a maroon or maroons to take a life if a person stood between sustenance and starvation, but survival and maintenance of freedom were their priorities. For every group of Fringe Maroons who ventured out of the swamp bent on outright revolt, many more maintained their seclusion as much as possible rather than invite confrontation that could always lead to their reenslavement or death. Although guerrilla movements from the swamp garnered the most attention, most (contrary to the assumptions of fearful whites) had not belligerence but a full belly as their goal.[82]

All four groups of Fringe Maroons, for their own reasons, strategically positioned themselves for quick access to worlds both inside and outside the swamp. In the seventeenth and eighteenth centuries, before significant tracts of swampland were drained and put to cultivation, this heavily wooded transitionary region from dry ground to swamp was several miles wide at places and offered maroons enough concealment without requiring the extreme commitment or exposing them to as many dangers as the deep swamp interior. If they had to retreat further into the swamp to avoid capture, they would generally return to the perimeter once a threat had passed. By the late eighteenth century, however, much of the higher and drier land of the Suffolk Scarp, the western boundary of the Great Dismal Swamp, had been developed and the perimeter transition zone largely eliminated. This significantly reduced the degree to which Fringe Maroons could hope to avoid detection and harassment from the outside world.

With a swamp edge that may have shrunk to a half mile at most from a clearly demarcated outside world, marronage on the fringe required even greater vigilance and caution. As a result, it gradually became limited to shorter stays and very small groups or individuals.[83] Their dwellings were necessarily temporary, and had to be as unnoticeable as possible. Fringe Maroons in the Dismal Swamp dug out shallow "caves," or holes in the ground, sheltered within hollow trees, assembled makeshift lean-tos of branches, leaves, and palms, or, in the case of at least one maroon, slept in trees far above the swamp floor in a bed he called his "cocoon."[84]

Deep Swamp Maroons

At the other extreme were maroons who did everything they could to remain concealed and inaccessible to outsiders. These Deep Swamp Maroons had decided to not just extricate themselves from enslavement but completely cut themselves off from the world outside the swamp. They were also the most settled of all Dismal Swamp maroons, and nearly every aspect of their lives reflects a desire for permanence and independence.

Settled on and around potentially dozens of mesic islands many miles into the swamp's interior, the life of Deep Swamp Maroons reflected their isolation and unique living environments. The available evidence suggests that many autonomous communities existed across the interior of the swamp, united by common purpose, trade, and the exchange of news and information. Although the limited documentary and archaeological record cannot support a full mapping of the social and political world of the swamp, it is possible to piece together a fascinating glimpse into maroon life deep in the Dismal.

Deep Swamp Maroons built structures with the expectation of permanence. On the fringe, even in the preindustrial decades of the seventeenth and early eighteenth centuries, maroons took great risks when they constructed any type of substantial shelter, or for that matter, remained in one swamp location for an extended period of time. A larger settlement on the fringe would have attracted unwanted attention, and for a group of maroons who took pains to keep their voices at a low whisper at all times and burned fires only at night to minimize chances of detection, anything more than a lean-to or brush arbor would have been impractical. Moreover, in a type of marronage that required constant vigilance, the effort required to build a structure of any permanence could not have been spared, especially considering the relative likelihood of discovery and resulting waste of energy and resources.

However, with a protective buffer of miles of nearly impenetrable swamp between themselves and the outside world, an expanse that might take an outsider unfamiliar with the terrain days to negotiate, Deep Swamp Maroons could afford the investment in time and labor to craft structures they fully intended to be permanent. Documentary sources as well as sections of architectural footprints excavated by the GDSLS bear this out. On dry "islands" Deep Swamp Maroons, consistent with other hemispheric maroon communities, built rectilinear post-in-ground-type living structures with logs and timbers set between posts for structural support. They laid out raised wooden floors upon horizontally laid floor joists or vertical posts. Wall construction varied. Archaeological and documentary evidence indicates that some dwellings were sealed off from the elements by wattle and daub walls or mud chinking between horizontal logs.[85]

The labor and planning required to construct a house like this would have been considerable. Large holes had to be dug to accommodate structural posts that were between twenty and thirty centimeters in diameter (approximately seven to twelve inches), posts which themselves had to be cut from hardwood trees. In at least one structure (dated by archaeologists to around 1730) there is evidence of rotted posts being replaced with fresher supports.[86] Maroons dug trenches around the perimeter of the houses, and gathered and prepared the plants and clay necessary to construct weathertight wattle and daub walls.

Burned clay discovered in soils associated with architectural features is also in-
dicative of intentional soil hardening for structural stability. Overall, the evidence suggests that Deep Swamp Maroon structures were erected, strengthened, repaired, and used throughout at least a two-century era.[87]

Certainly, level and dry ground was prioritized for housing, but in the
case that the most desirable areas of a swamp island were already occupied,
maroons utilized alternative architectural approaches. They often moved soil
from one location of an island to another, digging it from borrow pits located
on higher ground and then utilizing it at another location (such as the cabin
constructed near Lake Drummond described as being "built upon ground
artificially formed.")[88] On swampy ground or over water, maroons built houses
elevated on stilts or even in the trees.[89] One practice described by a contemporary as exhibiting "considerable ingenuity" involved locating four short trees
whose trunks were roughly in a square, and lashing horizontal beams to them
to form a platform for "solid flooring" several feet above the ground. Above
that was constructed "a cabin of light boards."[90] Even on higher knolls, elevated houses were not superfluous, and most were raised some distance above
the ground as a protection against occasional flooding and pests. The space
also helped circulate the air in the warm months, and when enclosed with
dirt around the edges, insulated the house when it was colder.[91] It was also the
case that maroons built homes on sloping terrain during the periods of densest
population when more desirable sites were already taken.[92]

Maroons' homes were but a part of a deep swamp village. Dotting the
landscape would have been pits, each around three feet deep, that may have
been used as water filters, collecting drinking water after it had been filtered
through the surrounding sands.[93] Although houses of varying construction
would have filled a great deal of available dry ground, there were other outbuildings here and there, and fences of wood and vines enclosing some spaces.
In some sections, houses were constructed so that their entranceways faced one
another across a twenty-five-foot common area. Archaeological features adjacent to these structures also suggest that some maroons constructed porches
adjacent to their houses, which also faced one another.[94] Many daily activities
took place outside, possibly in the shared space of the central courtyard. These
likely included socializing and community preparation of food.[95]

The Deep Swamp Maroon diet was nutritious and offered residents a great
variety of food options. Indeed, Abraham Lester said that his wife, Larinda
White, ate so well that she grew "so fat she could hardly walk."[96] With the
swamp itself doing much of the work of protection from outside intrusion,
food security could be privileged more than in most maroon settlements. They

raised small livestock in pens near their houses, most likely poultry, goats, or pigs. As with other large maroon communities, women would have most likely kept community gardens on the elevated drier land of their settlements.[97] These pursuits allowed them to live, as one observer noted, "in security and plenty."[98]

Swamp soils are generally deficient in nitrogen, but manure from their chickens or other animal waste would have been used as a fertilizer—absolutely nothing would have gone to waste. Wood ashes would have been added to counteract soil acidity as well.[99] An acre of land in a black gum section of the swamp planted with corn could yield thirty to forty bushels at harvest, and sown as it usually was along with peas and beans (further diversified with other crops like squashes, gourds, sunflowers, and melons at the margins), a small area could yield many calories over several months. Rice was grown in wetter areas of the swamp. Most of these foods could be dried and easily stored for the winter. Sweet potatoes were also harvested in the colder months.[100] Deep Swamp Maroons' remoteness allowed an extensive husbandry that would have been impossible to hide nearer the swamp's edge.[101]

Yet even Deep Swamp Maroons' extensive farming enterprises would not have rendered them entirely self-sufficient. The forty bushels of corn possible from an acre's harvest, for instance, would not have gone very far by itself. If the average corn ration per person on a slave labor camp was a peck of cornmeal per week (from approximately thirteen to fifteen pounds of dried corn), even if maroons managed two harvests per year as many Virginia farms did, that amount would have fed only seven individuals for a year.[102] Expanding the size of their fields was, of course, problematic in the middle of a swamp where dry land was at a premium. Livestock would have been only sparingly butchered, especially chickens, who were counted on for a protein-rich egg a day. Rather, it was the natural bounty of the Dismal Swamp that made complete scission possible.

Dismal Swamp beekeepers maintained hives throughout the swamp that produced not just honey but wax for candles.[103] The seeds of the blue lupine flower were edible, wild muscadine grapes were bountiful in season, persimmon trees thrived in drier areas, and flour and ultimately course bread could be produced from swamp flora, including the seeds of certain reeds that an outsider declared to have a "considerable resemblance to wheat, and which will make tolerably good bread."[104] Acorns could also be gathered, hot leached, and ground to produce a flour, as could the roots of the abundant cattails in the swamp. Cattails, in fact, likely occupied a prime place in the maroon diet, as some part of that plant can be eaten during every season: in spring, tender stalks of the young plant are edible; in summer, the immature flower spikes can be cooked and eaten like corn on the cob; roots may be cooked like potatoes in the fall and ground into flour during the winter. Even as standard garden vegetables withered in the cold months, an acre of cattails could, by itself, sustain a maroon community, and grew in saturated patches that did not displace other vital dry-land activities and usages. Cattail roots contain as much protein as corn or rice, and more carbohydrates than potatoes. One acre of cattails can yield more than three tons of roots.[105]

Also available to the Deep Swamp Maroon plate were deer, turkeys, wild boar, feral goats, duck and other waterfowl, squirrels, otter, beaver, bear, turtle, frogs, muskrat, snakes, fish, and beef—cattle in the Dismal were "small, dark and very wild."[106] Undoubtedly, some maroons in the southernmost parts of the swamp would have sought to obtain the delicious meat of *Alligator mississippiensis*, the American alligator. Game moved into the cooler and damper areas of the swamp in the summer, and the swamp's residents knew just where to find animals and when.[107]

Maroon hunters equipped themselves with bows and arrows and utilized an array of hunting methods that took advantage of the swamp environment. Precious firearms and ammunition would have likely been saved for defense unless absolutely necessary to bring down big game. Maroons commonly set deadfalls and log traps to kill smaller animals. Just after the Civil War, a former maroon who had lived near the Dismal Swamp Canal described such a trap where "a great log" was raised off the ground, "fenced in by shingles or palings" driven down on either side to create an open space underneath. In that hole, a bait of a scrap of meat might attract a racoon who, if it tripped the trigger, would be crushed.[108] Bears were trapped in the same way.[109] A line, hook, and frog as bait was the favored method for catching turtles, with best results achieved under a full moon.[110] Wild pigs were plentiful in the northwestern section of the Dismal. There, at sundown, maroons would chase a boar into a particularly mucky portion of the swamp "where their feet can't touch hard ground" and "knock them over." They caught wild cows in similar fashion.[111]

The dark waters of the swamp, especially Lake Drummond, "thronged with fish."[112] With a pole and a line, a good fisherman could feed his family with a few hours' work surreptitiously along a canal or swamp stream. Fishing parties also frequently traveled with their bark or dugout canoes across the swamp and to Drummond, for perch, bass, pickerel, sunfish, and other panfish.[113] Large quantities of game meat and fish could be preserved for months of storage by drying or smoking them. Salt was rare in the swamp but could be produced (as it was by maroons in Suriname) from the ashes of dwarf sabal palms.[114] Animal bones and turtle shell fragments showing evidence of cooking have also been discovered in the deep swamp archaeological digs.[115]

Despite what outsiders assumed, the Dismal Swamp was a surprisingly healthy place.[116] A maroon named Charlie declared it a "dreadful healthy place to live" on account of the drinking water ("Best water . . . ever tasted by man").[117] The swamp's dark water was believed by many to have medicinal qualities, and its acidity made it naturally antibiotic. Pirates and other seafarers reportedly prized Dismal Swamp water and would fill their casks with the "elixir of life," which would never spoil, even after long periods of storage.[118] Outsiders also described African Americans in the swamp as being "remarkably healthy, and almost entirely free from the autumnal fevers that so severely scourge all the surrounding country."[119] Moreover, the swamp was said to "abound[ ] with medicinal plants."[120] Disease was not unheard of, but swampers fought sickness "with the natural remedies the wilderness . . . so bounteously supplie[d]."[121]

The bounty of the swamp was sufficient to sustain large numbers of people, including multigenerational families within its isolated depths. A few maroons originally absconded with their families in tow, or may have retrieved their spouse and children from another slave labor camp before fleeing on to the Dismal.[122] Unlike Fringe Maroons, however, who established themselves near their former homes or family specifically to remain in contact with loved ones, Deep Swamp Maroons would have realized the impossibility of maintaining those close connections. As one commentator wrote, marronage in the depths of the swamp "was the same as being buried alive, and meant a final separation from their families."[123]

Maroons, though, often met and married spouses in the swamp, and they had children there as well.[124] As Alvin Thompson points out, maroon children were more likely to be raised by both of their parents in a wholesome, healthy environment where enslavement did not exist.[125] Eventually, there were residents of the inner swamp who had never been someone's property, never experienced life outside the Dismal, and indeed some who would reach the end of their days having never set foot on solid ground outside the swamp or seen a white face.[126]

There was much worth protecting. Even deep in the swamp, maroons took great pains to keep their villages inconspicuous. According to multiple accounts, maroons cut paths in the deepest parts of the swamp near their settlements, but not running too far toward the outside. The approach to the village was one of these paths, but it was nearly impossible to find and follow without guidance. As these trails came together closer to a village, there might be a more distinguishable "road" with logs laid over wetter portions.[127]

Like many Fringe Maroons, Deep Swamp Maroons were well armed, though for defensive rather than offensive purposes. Some arrived with weapons. One study of Virginia slave ads from the eighteenth and early nineteenth century found that about 1 percent of runaways had weapons with them. If they made it to the swamp, they might also acquire a weapon there, whether one "carelessly" left aside by white hunters, or through trade once established in the swamp.[128] Several sources place pistols, rifles, and long guns in the hands of Deep Swamp Maroons. Osman, one of the few interior maroons actually witnessed by a white observer, was armed with such a gun.[129] A former maroon in 1863 listed two guns among his possessions.[130] Another source remarked that "they, in different ways, not unfrequently, manage to obtain fire arms and ammunition, which places them in quite independent circumstances."[131]

To be sure, firearms were rare, and maintaining them in good working order was quite difficult. Access to powder, flint, and ammunition was likely even more problematic. The GDSLS has uncovered examples of British and French gunflints from Deep Swamp Maroon settlements. These were, however, few and far between, and had clearly been painstakingly retained down to their last possible sparks.[132] Though swamp-smelted lead shot has been discovered in deep swamp excavations, it is rare, and of course the lead would have had to have been brought into the settlement from outside. Some maroons, such as Benjamin Randolph, brought lead shot into the swamp embedded in their own bodies from being shot by whites as they attempted to escape.[133] It is fascinating to imagine shot being removed from beneath the skin of a maroon and then being added to an ammunition stockpile for the support and protection of the community.

There is also ample evidence of ancient, swamp-sourced Native American arrowheads being reused by maroons, as well as ceramic sherds and broken glass being refined on-site into tools and arrow or spear points.[134] It is also likely that Deep Swamp Maroons fashioned weapons and even loaded their firearms with whatever else was available when needed, just like the Fringe Maroons who had filled their muzzles with metal scraps, buttons, and small stones.[135] Though this would have been labor-intensive, maroons could have also produced small quantities of gunpowder by extracting saltpeter (potassium nitrate) from dried urine and chicken manure, and combining it with a small amount of ground charcoal.[136]

Excavation of "nameless" site, American University field school, 2013.
Courtesy of Daniel O. Sayers.

GDSLS archaeologists have found relatively high concentrations of these items in apparent ammunition caches at what is believed to be a maroon fort or defensive structure on a higher-elevation swamp site.[137] These include the only gunflints recovered from the "nameless" site (one only for use in a pistol, implying the existence of a weapon only meant for defense or attack), lead shot, iron objects, glass chips, and ceramic shards, although swamp-sourced materials still make up the majority of the artifact assemblage recovered.[138] Here ammunition was stored by the community. Documentary and archaeological evidence suggests precious firearms may have been maintained as community rather than individual property.[139] This is also where maroons manufactured their own projectile points from pottery sherds and glass fragments. The fort occupied the highest ground on the "nameless" island, and evidence suggests consistent occupation of the crest area from circa 1620 until the Civil War era.[140] This would mean that community defense was one of the first needs seen to by early maroons upon establishing the settlement, as well as a community priority for the next two and a half centuries.

Though their level of armament would have supported it, it seems most likely that Deep Swamp Maroons would seldom if ever have sent raiding parties to the outside. Oriented as these maroons were toward complete separation

from the external world, such forays would have presented far too great a risk
to the settled lives they had worked so hard to establish and maintain. Fringe
Maroons, whose exposure would have precluded any type of agriculture, depended on such raids for a great deal of their sustenance. Deep Swamp Maroons had the luxury of self-sufficiency. Moreover, any potential haul resulting
from such a raid could only have been brought back to their community with
considerable difficulty and at a steep cost. These communities were often miles
from the nearest point of contact with the outside, an expanse that might take
a day or more to cross. This worked to their advantage as a barrier to outside
intrusion, yet it would have made the transport of plunder quite onerous, requiring days of crucial labor-hours that could not easily be spared. The artifact
assemblage of the GDSLS deep swamp excavations shows a near-total absence
of mass-produced materials or others from the outside world; Deep Swamp
Maroons relied almost entirely on items sourced within the swamp itself.[141]
A very small number of firearms stand out as the notable exception, yet as
potentially the most precious items a community possessed, they would have
been treated with the utmost care, repaired whenever possible, and never lost
or discarded. The near microscopic remnants of gunflints themselves utilized
down to the last possible firing, in fact, represent a significant portion of the
materials from the outside world found in the deep swamp excavations.

    It is no wonder that these maroons went to great lengths to remain stead-
fast in their isolation. Entrance to the deep swamp settlements was strictly
controlled. Even the smallest bits of information about the settlements were
tightly guarded by maroons and their allies.[142] If an outsider was a "one of the
asking-question" types, they might be told to keep those inquiries to themselves "or the swamp will get angry!"[143] Maroons were careful to avoid being
followed to their communities if they encountered outsiders, and would go to
great lengths to throw a tracker off their trail.[144] Moreover, paths to and from
the deep swamp settlements were concealed as much as possible. Multiple
sources mention secretive pathways through the swamp and over boggy or wet
terrain marked only by "notches cut on trees" with false trails and dead ends
as added precautions. Often, paths were so narrow (across logs laid end to end
over the swamp) that only a single person could pass at a time.[145] These circu-
itous routes would have kept outsiders disoriented, and would have frustrated
newcomers seeking to return back from the swamp and potentially giving up
a settlement's location.[146] It was common knowledge that any attempt by an
outsider to venture near an interior maroon settlement would entail great danger if he were discovered in the attempt.[147] It is likely that, as in other maroon
communities, strategically placed sentries required a password or secret call of

anyone they encountered, sentries who could call an alarm if the person was deemed a threat. It was unlikely that any of the Deep Swamp Maroon communities would ever be taken by surprise.[148]

Dismal Swamp maroons also appear to have extensively "vetted" potential recruits. Questions would be asked of the newcomers without revealing the locations of the communities, or newcomers seeking entrance to the interior might be observed for days or weeks before they were invited to join a settled community.[149] Abolitionist Emily Pearson described a man seeking entry to a deep swamp community who was told that "if you should not see a human being as you go . . . into the swamp, remember that many eyes are watching every step you take. This is our home, and we have to guard it."[150] Another source even suggests that Dismal Swamp maroons built a "cabin" for newcomers to the swamp, a halfway house of sorts where potential new community members could be observed, but situated far from the actual maroon village.[151]

Deep Swamp Maroons also maintained connections with trusted men and women still enslaved on labor camps who would occasionally arrange introductions and vouch for a potential maroon's trustworthiness.[152] Conversely, the community needed to be tightly contained, and newcomers would have to clearly indicate that they intended to not only abide by the rules of the community but to stay there permanently.[153] Other large maroon communities in the Americas, with clear similarities to practices in some nineteenth-century African city-states, held newcomers to some sort of probationary period or assigned them a community mentor (and monitor) who might guide and assess their trustworthiness, loyalty, skills, and dedication to marronage.[154] There is little reason to think that the same practice would not have been followed in the Great Dismal Swamp.

Interior maroons so zealously guarded their isolation and secrecy that, with a very few exceptions, they would do without some outside-produced good or item rather than venture out of the deep swamp recesses to get it. Because of the scarcity of mass-produced goods from outside the swamp, maroons used prehistoric Indigenous tools and artifacts whenever they were available. The swamp had been a favored hunting ground of precontact Indigenous people, and artifacts from that occupation including the arrowheads, ceramics, and stone knives that occasionally surface at some deep swamp locations.[155] The immense care with which they were repaired and repurposed and their very longevity show that they were highly prized and not easy to replace. Moreover, the fact that more than 75 percent of all stone flakes recovered from deep swamp excavations were small tertiary and microdebitage flakes suggests a constant reworking of those ancient tools.[156] In fact, the majority of materials recovered from historical contexts by archaeologists have been very small, less than half a centimeter at their widest, suggesting a community ethos and normative requirement that materials stay in use. When such tools could be found in the ground, fashioned out of animal bones or wood, or obtained through risky contact with the outside world, maroons recycled them almost into disappearance.[157] Deep Swamp Maroons even incorporated pieces of Native American ceramics dated 1200–800 BCE into their home construction to strengthen and shore up organic materials.[158]

Complete scission from the outside world was the defining aspect of Deep Swamp Maroon life. How that translated into authority and/or governmental structure internally is harder to say. Many maroon communities in the Americas were structured based on the military systems of white enslavers. This was especially the case with regards to communities frequently at war with European governments. However, many of these also retained important African features such as councils of government. A primary leader or small ruling group still relied to a large extent on the assent of the community. In some cases, authority rested as much upon personal influence as any rank or office an individual held.[159]

Fringe Maroons often took on (or were attributed) titles of a figurehead: General Peter, Captain Bob Ferebee, or "The General." In some of these cases, it seems possible that fringe leaders eventually moved into a deep swamp community.[160] But there were others clearly of the deep swamp who earned titles of "king" or "chief." Osman, for example, appears as a leader of Deep Swamp Maroons in the 1850s. His name was remembered with reverence almost a half century later in the area, and by the turn of the century Osman's biography had been (perhaps romantically) fleshed out a bit.[161] Osman was eventually remembered as "a famous African chief . . . who sought refuge from blood-hounds and pursuers in the inner and unexplored reaches of the swamp . . . [and] led a reign of terror in the wilderness during the early fifties."[162] Decades later, writers described him as "the legendary protector of fugitive slaves in the swamp."[163]

The revered memory of Osman fits with Caleb Winslow's description of Dismal Swamp government from 1870. Winslow was an antislavery Quaker who very likely interacted with maroons as a young man at his home in Perquimans County, North Carolina, on the edge of the Dismal.[164] He said that the maroons developed "a rude system of government, bound themselves together by the severest penalties, and condemned the traitor and spy to inevitable death."[165] Certainly the governance of Deep Swamp Maroon communities would have been highly structured and often harsh, yet there would have

"Osman." From Strother, "The Dismal Swamp,"
Harper's New Monthly Magazine, September 1856.

also been a degree of community democracy. As in the descriptions of Osman, leaders of the deep swamp communities possessed significant authority, but always toward the end of community service and protection.

Archaeologist Daniel Sayers argues that scission leaders would have figured prominently in the maintenance of community organization and social expectations, division of labor, conflict and dispute resolution, and subsistence strategies. Such a leader would also have had a significant responsibility for maintaining the community's distance from the outside world, including monitoring any contacts with outsiders. Indeed, with no examples in the known documentary record of military engagements or militia raids on deep swamp settlements from the outside, energy that might have been put into waging a constant defensive campaign could be spent enriching and sustaining deep swamp community life.[166]

Community rank and status almost certainly did not function the same way deep in the swamp as in the world outside. As Alvin Thompson points out, maroon societies were not based upon the same value systems as white slave societies in the Americas. These communities were born out of quests for freedom, not material gain and accumulation. Indeed, the amount of material resources available to even the largest or best-connected maroon communities was so small that the development of any sort of elite class defined by its wealth or accumulation of property was unthinkable.[167] Instead, leadership roles, while simultaneously imbuing someone with some forms of power, more likely manifested as "social equivalents" to certain specializations within the community. "Military" leaders may not have wielded the rigid authority of a commanding officer, but they were responsible for and controlled materials necessary for defense. Others may have controlled the flow of additional materials within the community to maintain social cohesion and avoid conflicts among community members.[168]

The descriptions above are not incompatible with other evidence suggesting that kinship was also an organizational force in the Deep Swamp Maroon communities. Authority among maroons was most often earned over time through the development of strong kin affinities rather than just military prowess or premaroon status.[169] Kinship rules would have developed over generations of deep swamp family development. Sayers suggests that kinship may have determined who could marry or cohabitate, where family units lived in the maroon village, or what types and divisions of community labor went on at the kin-group level. Kinship rules determined whether men monopolized leadership roles or if, as the scholar Kathryn Golden suggests in the case of the Great Dismal Swamp, authority and lineage passed through the mothers' line.[170] Certain kin groups, and individuals within those groups, emerged from these processes as community-sanctioned leaders.[171]

Although cosmic order—that is, spirituality—also influenced Deep Swamp Maroon life, very little is known of the details. African influences were likely quite strong among early eighteenth-century settlements, cosmology included. Tynes Cowan suggests that the Dismal Swamp, besides offering a physical refuge, also allowed maroons to maintain elements of African spirituality. Forests and water are significant elements in many African religions. The swamp, literally a combination of the two, offered maroons access to "living" water (an element central to sacred ceremonies in Dahomey and among the Yoruba and Ashanti) as well as the forest "boundary" valued among people of the Central Guinea Coast, "joining yet keeping apart this visible world of human existence and the other invisible world of spirit beings." For Africans from many parts of the continent, personal, spiritual, and communal health depended on maintaining a balance between wildness and the cultivated landscape.[172] The Dismal Swamp provided that balance most thoroughly.

Over the next century, with the creolization of the outside enslaved population and addition into deep swamp communities of maroons of different ethnic and cultural backgrounds, these groups grew increasingly multicultural. By the nineteenth century, Christianity likely predominated among spiritual maroons, although there is evidence from the deep swamp that other influences such as Islam and Vodou endured to some degree as well.[173]

As with everything else, available sources do not give a very clear picture of day-to-day spiritual life among Deep Swamp Maroons. Freedom, as John Blassingame declares, was the "constant prayer" and "all-consuming hope" of the enslaved, and it seems likely that some maroon parents began each day's family worship with a prayer of thanks for their liberty and for its maintenance.[174] Swampers were known to end their days "as is most agreeable to them . . . in singing and prayers, in which they are very loud."[175] Some may have sung, as W. L. Bost's mother did to him as an enslaved boy in North Carolina, the song that ended

> We camp awhile in the wilderness, in the wilderness, in the wilderness.
> We camp awhile in the wilderness, where the Lord makes me happy,
> And then I'm a-goin' home.[176]

It is uncertain what if any regular religious services maroons organized in the swamp. However, there is some evidence that Deep Swamp Maroons sometimes traveled from their village to another deep swamp location, or closer to the edges of the swamp, to participate in Christian religious ceremonies, including camp meetings and weddings.[177]

Several African Americans, free and enslaved, ventured into the Dismal Swamp to minister to the maroons.[178] Mary Perth, a woman enslaved in Norfolk in the 1770s, would tie her baby to her back at night and walk ten miles from her enslaver's house into the northern Dismal Swamp to deliver messages of deliverance, preaching from the Book of Exodus and from Paul's letter to the Galatians: "Stand fast therefore in the liberty wherewith Christ has made us free and be not entangled again with the yoke of bondage." She continued her ministry to the Dismal until her "considerable" following could sustain services on their own.[179] In the 1850s, an unnamed man, called a "prophet," began preaching in the southeastern (North Carolina) section of the Dismal

Swamp. "The preacher," a white writer noted, "had no church connection" and expounded "strange ideas," although it was unlikely his African American audience of around 200 shared this observer's condescension.[180]

"Ole Man" Toby Fisher, himself a maroon, was another swamp preacher who commonly ministered to swamp communities during the antebellum years. Fisher preached "like he's 'n earnest" on the shore of Lake Drummond. Charlie, another maroon of Fisher's community, recalled that "many have been the exhortation I have experienced that resounded through the trees, and we would almost expect the judgment day was coming there would be such loud vibrations, as the preacher called them." "I believe God is no respecter of persons," Charlie went on of Fisher's teachings, "and he knows his children, and can hear them just as quick in the Juniper Swamp as in the great churches." He remembered fondly the "nice prayers" he had shared with Ole Man Fisher.[181]

Alexander Keeling, described by a white visitor to the swamp in 1856 as "a reverend gentleman of color who resides on the border of the swamp," was another friend of the maroons who appears in the documentary record across nearly a century. "Uncle Alek" believed that he had been born in 1776, and had become religious while a drummer boy in the War of 1812.[182] He lived in a "hut" in the northwestern quadrant of the Dismal, near where the Norfolk and Western Railroad crossed the swamp (the track, to his great consternation, had been laid through his sweet potato patch in 1853).[183] Alek was a close friend and confidant of the enslaved canal workers and maroons. Although it is hard to place the location of Alek's home in the swamp, it was likely nearby, or even part of, an interior island maroon community. The same railroad track that rumbled through Alek's sweet potato patch also passed less than 500 meters from the "Williamson-North" archaeological site, an intensely utilized maroon location near the eastern edge of the original Dismal Swamp Land Company tract in Virginia.[184]

Regardless of whether Alek lived with or near maroons, they were important parts of each other's lives. Alek facilitated their escapes and frustrated slavers' attempts to retake them, gave them food and supplies when he could, and instructed them in the Word of "God Almighty."[185] Once enslaved by Rev. Jacob Keeling, rector of the Episcopal churches in Nansemond County, Virginia, he was freed as a young man.[186] He was described by an enslaved canal worker as a "prayer book Episcopalian through and through," and had declared his own religion powerful enough to protect him from all the dangers of the swamp: "Alexander believed that his religion was more protection to him from the dead and from the living, from the wild and the

"Uncle Alick." From Strother, "The Dismal Swamp,"
Harper's New Monthly Magazine, September 1856.

tame, from conjure or from poison than the whole of Col. Willis Riddick's militia was."[187]

Alek was fond of leading his followers in song. "Happy Canyon," "Children Drop Your Nets and Follow Me," and "John Saw the Holy Number" were three of his favorite hymns.[188] He could recite scripture from memory and had at his disposal as much "as is usually found in the head of the most erudite."[189] He was known as "a preacher under the old slave dispensation," and had prepared sermons for any occasion.[190]

Whether ordered by figureheads, kin groups, the cosmos, or a combination

of them all, Deep Swamp Maroon communities were organized, intentionally functioning communities. Yet it is hard to say to what degree deep swamp
communities interacted with each other, or just how many distinct communities existed in the swamp at a given point in time. However, we do know
there were many, and that they spanned the swamp. Osman, for instance,
was most likely part of a maroon community in the vicinity of Jericho Ditch
in the 1850s, in the northwest sector of the swamp. Charlie lived in a maroon
community just north of Lake Drummond some time prior to 1859, most likely
concealed in the Dismal Swamp Canal Company's tract. Abraham Lester
and his wife, Larinda White, marooned in several different locations in the
swamp in the 1850s but spent most of their time with a community located
near the northwest shore of Lake Drummond. Abraham also identified another maroon village approximately eight miles south of where he and Larinda
made their home. That community, he said, was "where families live."[191] If
Abraham's estimation of distance was correct, the settlement of "families"
was almost certainly the "nameless" site in North Carolina, the location where
the most intensive archaeological work has been undertaken by the GDSLS.
William Byrd encountered maroons living together in 1729 near the North
Carolina/Virginia line at the Northwest River.[192] The Dismal Swamp Company's rice field, which sat on a forty-acre island about a mile into the swamp,
had likely been a maroon community field before the community had to abandon it for another site in the 1760s.[193]

It is clear, though, that deep swamp communities *did* interact with each
other. Fully isolated, these communities would have struggled to be self-
sufficient. Not all islands would have supported sizeable crop fields, and those
that comprised enough dry land to do so may have also been far from large
beds of essential cattails. Game would have been more or less common in different sections of the swamp, and even the available building materials would
have varied. The Dismal included many diverse forest types, including large
stands of Atlantic white cedar (most prized for shingles) directly north and
south of Lake Drummond, two different species of pine along the eastern edge
of the Suffolk Scarp and the eastern half of the swamp, cypress gum in the
western swamp, and patches of swamp marsh (pocosin) throughout.[194] Also,
artifacts left from ancient Indigenous people were not distributed evenly in the
ground across the swamp.

Occasionally at least, Deep Swamp Maroons ventured far afield of their
settlements, and the boundaries of their communities were somewhat porous.
Spiritual leaders entered and passed through the swamp to minister to maroons (although maroons most likely and more often came to them). Dismal

Swamp beekeepers followed bees throughout the swamp along narrow paths. Maroons such as Osman traveled near camps of enslaved workers and likely had contact with them (they certainly knew him). "Uncle" Bob Garry was born and raised in a deep swamp community but developed and maintained relationships with people still enslaved and even white Dismal Swamp Company overseers.[195]

Archaeologist Daniel Sayers describes a "metacommunity" of Dismal Swamp maroons, the aggregate of many diverse swamp communities. Similar to maroon networks elsewhere in the Americas, these communities depended on each other (and on other maroons living on other swamp islands) and did approach something close to self-sufficiency through these relationships. Individual maroon communities did not necessarily think of themselves as distinct from other communities, at least in terms of the goods and materials they needed to survive.[196]

A lively cross-swamp reciprocity network linked deep swamp communities. Besides the canals, log paths, and occasional high ground, barely perceptible waterways wove throughout the swamp, especially its southern half. Described by archaeologist Rebecca Peixotto as "intermittent watercourses," a series of small and slow streams flow from the Suffolk Scarp. These streams do not appear on most modern maps, but they are remarkably clear on a detailed set of maps produced by the US Army Corps of Engineers in 1940. Some of these creeks pass near the "nameless site" and might have been utilized to link this maroon community with others to the west and southwest. Others in the northern swamp pass nearby known locations of Deep Swamp Maroon settlements.[197]

Consider, for example, how the numerous recycled lithic tools and sherds of Indigenous ceramic arrived in the hands of a maroon at the "nameless" site. There, prehistoric soil strata have not been found to contain correspondingly high concentrations of those artifacts. This is likely because the site was so isolated that prehistoric Native Americans occupied it only irregularly and nonintensively. Thus the artifacts used by the maroons of the "nameless" site, including cutting tools and arrowheads, had to have been brought in from elsewhere. Sources suggest that at other deep swamp locations, including another site excavated by the GDSLS along the Cross Canal, such artifacts were more plentiful.[198] When the levels of Lake Drummond are lower than normal, Native American arrowheads, axe heads, and other artifacts are sometimes exposed on sandbars off the northern shore.[199] The maroons of the "nameless" site, then, could have "mined" other swamp locations for these artifacts themselves. However, considering the evidence of continuous dense habitation even at the lower (and less desirable) elevations of the "nameless" site, other locations in the swamp that had been suitable for intensive use by precontact Native Americans also would have likely been at a premium for maroon settlement later and thus not available for excavations by the "nameless" community. It seems more likely that these artifacts entered the "nameless" site through a trade network linking Deep Swamp Maroon communities. Reliance on other isolated communities would have been safer from a security standpoint and most consistent with the community ethos of Deep Swamp Maroons. Lacking access to useful inorganic materials on their own island, "nameless" community maroons would have likely offered what they did have in relative abundance, items of their own organic material culture.[200]

"Nameless" maroons and others across the swamp filled their own niche in the metacommunity. The documentary record suggests that certain maroons (and groups of maroons at specific locations) "specialized" in certain skills, trades, or craft production.[201] That is, production of certain items often comes across more as a specialization than a necessary activity among so many others: the man described specifically as a "fisherman" who lived on a high knoll deep in the swamp and traveled often to Lake Drummond to cast his lines, the boys who made bark canoes, the man who crafted chairs, tables, and musical instruments for trade, the crews who "mined" the swamp for ancient Indigenous artifacts.[202] A maroon like Bob Garry could pursue his hunting specialty of black bears, for example, knowing that someone else labored to watch over fermenting grains and grapes and to produce the draft of cider or wine to take the edge off after a long day's hunt.[203] The swamp's leather tanners sustained its farmers, who filled the bellies of artisans weaving baskets into which foragers piled cattail roots and acorns. Reliance among deep swamp communities spread labor across the swamp, sustained everyone, and reinforced the exilic ethos that was the basis of Deep Swamp Maroon life.[204]

Enslaved "Swampers"

Deep Swamp Maroons also undoubtedly appropriated the canals and towpaths industrialists had caused to be cut through the swamp. Some of these maroons may have once even labored in the mire to dig them out by hand. Yet Deep Swamp Maroons would have only risked exposure on these cross-swamp thoroughfares when they were certain not to be seen by canal traffic, for while the swamp canal system may have facilitated their own travel it also brought those who would do them harm closer to their swamp communities.

Indeed, the canals may have been the greatest danger of all to maroons' way of life deep in the swamp. The canals did not impose "a near death sentence" upon the swamp as Jack Temple Kirby suggests, but nothing was the same after.[205] The digging of canals by small armies of enslaved workers and the rise of the lumbering and shingling industries within the swamp forced a fundamental reconfiguration of the Dismal Swamp landscape and reorientation of life for many maroons at the end of the eighteenth century. The Great Dismal itself was the most faithful and diligent protector the maroons had. However, as canals cut into it and lumbering operations moved into the interior, what had been hidden might be exposed, and the deep recesses of the swamp could be transformed into the edge of the swamp alongside a very busy canal thoroughfare. Besides providing inroads into the swamp, the main Dismal Swamp Canal, or more specifically shell spoil left over from its digging, may have blocked the drainage of the swamp to the east, while simultaneously raising water levels to the west. This resulted in the drying out of former swampland east of the canal, the establishment of farms where maroon territory once extended, and significantly diminished amounts of higher ground west of the canal on which maroon communities might settle.[206] An "industrial revolution" within the swamp forced dramatic changes for many Great Dismal Swamp Maroons.

Almost as soon as the two sections of canal met east of Lake Drummond in 1805, a second phase of construction commenced to deepen and widen the waterway, such that eventually 200-ton vessels could ply the canal (when the canal halves were first joined, four miles of canal remained, half the proposed distance).[207] Maroons who had once felt secure settling at the edges of the swamp now found their refuge encroached upon. In 1802, Maj. William Farange constructed along the canal a hostelry, the "Brickhouse Plantation," that became a popular wedding venue.[208] Several years later, the Lake Drummond Hotel was built along the canal on a site straddling the North Carolina/Virginia line; it was appropriately nicknamed "The Halfway House."[209] In June 1814, a twenty-one-ton craft sailed from the Albemarle Sound, through the Dismal Swamp Canal, and into the Elizabeth River and Norfolk, the first "ship" to traverse the new Tidewater highway.[210]

From the moment the canal opened up easy access to the swamp's interior, the timber industry dominated Dismal Swamp business concerns. Barrel staves, fence rails, ship timbers, railroad crossties, and especially shingles were in high demand.[211] The Canal Company early on employed enslaved labor to harvest the wood products of the swamp, and in 1792, to expand its labor force, offered new shares in the company at $250 each or in exchange for "one able-bodied Negro who was not addicted to running away."[212] By the 1830s, at least 500 enslaved workers worked in the swamp to produce these products

"Carting Shingles." From Strother, "The Dismal Swamp,"
Harper's New Monthly Magazine, September 1856.

and to perform the backbreaking labor of digging canals to transport them through the swamp.[213]

Shingles might be riven from cypress or juniper in two- and three-foot lengths, loaded onto two-wheeled, mule-pulled carts that were driven back over split log roads back to camp by "carboys" (often grown men). The shingles were then loaded onto shallow-bottomed boats called lighters to be poled up or down the canal and out of the swamp.[214] It cost Dismal Swamp industrialists approximately four dollars (including enslaved labor, supplies, etc.) to produce a thousand three-foot juniper shingles that they would then usually sell for between twenty and thirty dollars. The Dismal Swamp Land Company sold approximately 1.5 million shingles per year in the four decades before the Civil War.[215]

The labor arrangement employed to harvest the rich timber of the swamp was quite unique. Enslaved workers would have to venture into the virgin swamp itself, far from their settlements adjacent the canal. These workers were called "shingle-gitters."[216] Every winter (generally in January or early February) and again in the summer (July or August) crews of enslaved men (and possibly some women) were led into the swamp by an enslaved driver. Their labor was only loosely directed. With several months of supplies (including pork, cornmeal, flour, and some clothing) groups of workers mostly labored independently and at their own pace. They built shelters for themselves (almost always out of swamp-collected lumber). One visitor to a Canal Company labor camp described some of these "huts" as "mere shanties or covers for five or six men to lie in, close-packed, like spoons, with heads to the back wall, and feet to the fire in front."[217] Sloping roofs were no higher than four feet off of the ground, which was covered with a layer of fine shingle shavings the workers used as a bed.[218] They also hunted, fished, and enjoyed a degree of "freedom" uncommon in other types of enslaved labor. So long as they completed their "task" of producing a certain quantity of shingles by the end of the season, nothing else was required of these enslaved shingle workers. If they brought in shingles in excess of their quota (or enough to offset their "hire" of around $100 a year), they might be compensated for the overage with cash and/or additional provisions.[219]

The arrangement was close enough to freedom on the broad continuum of enslavement that many swampers did not make a final break for it even when they knew freedom might be just beyond their camp. Moses Grandy, whose enslaver allowed him to hire out in the Dismal, and who knew the waterways of the swamp like the back of his hand, worked within the slave system and saved up enough money to purchase his own freedom.[220] Another man condescendingly described by a white swamp supervisor as possessing "good sense in a negro" did the same, with enough left over to fund his emigration to Liberia.[221] Frederick Law Olmsted noted that these enslaved workers were "quasi-free" and "live[d] measurably as a free man," with few instances of "rascality" to report.[222] "Swamp slaves," another observer wrote, "were the happy lords of the domain."[223]

Some enslaved workers, of course, found that they enjoyed these degrees of freedom so much that marronage, even in the Dismal, would be preferable to their enslavement. Many enslaved swampers thus slipped away to become maroons.[224] Ned, a man formerly enslaved in Isle of Wight County, Virginia, was representative of many others. He had been hired out to slave in the northeastern Dismal south of Norfolk. One day Ned set out with his work crew seeking timber in the swamp. When the gang found a likely looking place to begin their labors, Ned just kept on moving into the swamp, picking up speed, and never looking back. "I suspect," his enslaver reported, that "[he] has eloped from me." Perhaps his escape deeper into the Dismal was planned with the assistance of his uncle, who had "been runaway for some time."[225]

That a different and more permanent type of freedom existed deep inside the swamp was well known to both maroon and enslaved canal workers. Their work for Dismal Swamp industries had taken them deep into the undeveloped and isolated areas of the swamp, often a great distance from their camp and the canal. There, they would have come into contact with Deep Swamp Maroons.[226] It is hard to say just how closely the two groups interacted given the dedication to scission that the Deep Swamp Maroons held, but as archaeologist Daniel Sayers suggests, perhaps because of the relative freedom and mobility enslaved canal workers were offered under their task system and the nature of their tasks themselves, "shingle-gitters" may have been drawn to "enduring and fortified forms of marronage" deep in the swamp.[227]

Liminal Maroons

In addition to the "shingle-gitters" who might become maroons, there were also maroons who actually worked in the timber camps to sustain themselves in freedom. This third group, *Liminal Maroons*, were men and women who intentionally and regularly kept a foot in the outside world and settled into another form of permanent swamp life in which they had very little need to remain undetected. The enslaved workers and these maroons were, in the words of one former swamp slave, "quite intimate" with each other.[228] Evidence of a declining Deep Swamp Maroon population after 1800 suggests that many of these men and women had migrated from the swamp's interior.[229] Others marooned to the Great Dismal Swamp specifically to avail themselves of a life that avoided the terrors of both the plantation and life on the run. The lure of a life of relative freedom "hidden" in plain sight drew self-emancipators from Virginia, North Carolina, and beyond to the swamp.

An important aspect of the "intimate" relationships between maroons and enslaved workers is reflected in the description of the slaves as "shingle-gitters" instead of either shingle-makers or shingle-cutters. This title implies that the worker, rather than cutting his shingles in the camp and under the eyes of the company, went into the undeveloped swamp and "got" them.[230] Their "task" each week was to bring in approximately 400 shingles, and just as the task system functioned in the Carolina Lowcountry, the requirement was based on the productivity expected of a prime hand over a week.[231] In the Dismal Swamp, this quota was expected to offset expenses and recoup the price of the enslaved worker, who was often hired from his or her owner by the season.[232] A week's task generally took five days to complete.[233] However, when the shingles were counted, the number of shingles produced by a company of enslaved "gitters" often far exceeded the number of workers on the roll multiplied by a worker's maximum expected productivity.[234] In the official records of the Great Dismal Swamp Land Company, there is no commentary or conjecture about how this occurred; shingles are simply tallied for individual "gitters."[235]

The solution to the mystery is found in the testimony of maroons and other close observers. "Gitters" who were largely free to their own devices, whether motivated by personal gain or by goodwill toward fellow victims of oppression, often became the employers of Dismal Swamp maroons. On counting days, they brought in not only the shingles they had produced themselves but also those produced by maroon subcontractors. "In a word," one keen observer wrote in 1857, "more shingles are got out of the swamp, as illegally inhabited, than could be obtained by making it a perfect desert by rigorous legal measures."[236] The workers who brought in these enormous loads would be paid per piece for their overage (sometimes as many as 32,000 shingles, four times the amount necessary to offset their hire for the season), then return to their swamp camps to divide the earnings.[237] For his service and the danger to which he exposed himself, the "gitter" kept a part of his payment for the maroons' labor and paid the balance in cash or supplies to the hidden workers (who included both men and women). Maroons could expect to earn food, clothing, powder, and bullets, or as much as two dollars a month for their off-the-books labor.[238]

Tom Weston and Joe Seguine were remembered as master "swamp merchants" in this system. Seguine managed to amass so many shingles each four-month season that, after paying off his hire, store account, and other debts, he would clear $150. Weston was remembered as a slacker who, although he had a camp in the swamp, "generally idled fully half his time" in the swamp town of Deep Creek. Nonetheless, Tom was credited with enough shingles each settling-up day to always have a cash balance. White swamp agents at Deep Creek were fully aware that Tom subcontracted shingle work out to "runaways in the swamp" who would produce shingles at half price, minus the cost of corn and coffee that Tom procured for them at the canal store.[239] Settling up days at Deep Creek in July and December were festive occasions and often so lucrative for enslaved swampers like Seguine, Weston, and others that they would bring in their families to buy calico dresses, head scarfs, shoes, and other goods.[240]

The corporate interests would have undoubtedly been aware of these arrangements, otherwise tasks for enslaved workers would have been revised upward. The aiding and abetting of "fugitives" or knowingly using maroon labor was a crime that carried severe penalties, thus the company's silence regarding the maroons' presence in the swamp. The closest that company accountants come to acknowledging their very profitable arrangements are occasional and ambiguous notations such as "extra lightering & other work done by hands this month," and tabulations for anonymous workers alongside others who are named.[241] Regardless, everybody benefited from this arrangement. The workload of the "gitter" might be lightened, and maroons were able to earn an income without leaving the safety of the swamp.

Managers and foremen of the Land Company closed their eyes in accord with judiciously unwritten company policy, sometimes almost literally: company officials seldom recorded their enslaved workers names or physical descriptions, making it easier for maroons to slip back and forth between the swamp and company worlds. Dismal Swamp Land Company agents were also sometimes allowed to engage in "side work," that is, employing enslaved workers to produce shingles or other items from "old refused Timber" already worked over by company workers. This would have clearly incentivized directly hiring or allowing maroons to work these jobs for enslaved workers.[242] "So," one European observer noted, "the nearer advantage turns the scale against the majesty of the law, as it does in many portions of the earth besides the borders of the Dismal Swamp."[243]

Contractors freely acknowledged their past reliance on maroon labor after the Civil War. One man admitted that "it was none of his business to interfere and get the ill will of his workmen, especially as the runaways were the hardest workers of his gang." Why should he trouble himself? He was supposedly unaware of their existence and never had to pay them himself.[244] Thirty-five years after the war ended, former maroon Bob Garry could disclose his close relationship with a Dismal Swamp "overseer" who was well aware of his activities in the swamp.[245]

Although severe penalties in Virginia and North Carolina could befall white people found guilty of dealing with maroons, the biggest risks were taken by maroons themselves. The consequences of a deal gone bad could be catastrophic for them—capture and loss of freedom, torture, death, or discovery of their village. Trust was possibly the most precious resource for maroons in the Dismal. Newcomers to the deep swamp, if they were deemed faithful enough to be allowed entry to a settlement, had to build trust over weeks, months, or even years to become a permanent member of the community. Hardly any whites were accepted into the circle. Along the canal, maroons placed incredible trust in enslaved associates who did not always deserve it. "Swamp merchant" Tom Weston, for instance, would occasionally betray maroons if they fell behind on their tab, especially if their owners had advertised reward money for their return.[246] Joseph Church, an enslaved man who himself was on good terms with maroons, confirmed that maroons risked betrayal if they fell too deeply into the debt of an enslaved worker.[247] Maroons had to know with confidence whom to trust and whom not to trust, and how to retain the loyalty of their enslaved brethren. The maintenance of a loyal network of swampers, enslaved and marooned, required constant vigilance, especially as opportunities for contact between outsiders, enslaved and maroon canal workers, and Deep Swamp Maroons greatly increased as canals sliced into the swamp.[248]

Marronage Rerouted

The canals had fundamentally reoriented the swamp, although the reach of these waterways can easily be overstated—canals were still miles apart and many maroon islands could easily have remained isolated. The "nameless" site, for example, remained miles from the nearest canal, an expanse impassable on horseback or even a standard canoe, and one that would have taken days to traverse on foot, depending on the season and water levels. In other cases, however, islands that had once been hidden deep in the Dismal found themselves directly in the path of industrial development. In 1815, for example, the Cross Canal (aka Hamburg Ditch) project, which would run east-west across the swamp two and a half miles south of the Virginia/North Carolina line, reached a forty-acre island in the southeast quadrant of the swamp. This island had been home to a sizeable Deep Swamp Maroon community. Within the metacommunity of the swamp, this island had likely been a major source of mined Indigenous tools that circulated through the rest of the swamp.[249] The Cross Canal split the island in two, and what had once been an isolated interior location was brought fully into the outside world.

Deep swamp security would not have loosened; if anything the imperative for defensive vigilance would have increased. Yet the swamp *was* closing in on the isolated communities, and with Deep Swamp Maroons patrolling the swamp far beyond their villages and canal-based workers often ranging far into the deep swamp to extract timber, opportunities for encounters and interactions were undoubtedly frequent. Adapting to the new circumstances, some outsiders likely earned the trust of Deep Swamp Maroons as partners in trade and brokers of information. Osman, for instance, was well known among canal workers whom he would not have known if his deep swamp community was completely isolated. Bob Garry, who had been born to maroon parents in a deep swamp community and grew up there, eventually cultivated relationships with whites and nonmaroon African Americans along the canal and around the edge of the swamp.[250] Alek Keeling negotiated with ease the worlds of the Deep Swamp Maroons, canal settlements, white industrial agents, and populations outside the swamp, white and Black.[251]

The extent of these relationships may never be known, but the documentary and archaeological records both attest to their growth in the nineteenth century. Friendly "shingle-gitters" and canal maroons bartered what surplus goods they had for Deep Swamp Maroons' game or handiwork.[252] After around 1800, materials from the outside world began making their way more frequently deep in the swamp. There were no other potential trade partners for Deep Swamp Maroons if they desired to remain in the swamp, so the source of such goods was almost certainly maroon or enslaved canal workers.

Archaeologist Daniel Sayers has also discovered what he believes could have been a hoard of trade goods hidden beneath the floor of a canal worker's cabin, goods ultimately meant for the Deep Swamp Maroons. This cache of machine-cut nails, gunflints, clear glass bottles, and lithic and ceramic shards would have had little value among workers along the canal with regular access to mass-produced materials from the outside world, but they would have been especially prized among interior maroons.[253] Similarly, animal pelts, musical instruments, furniture, and surplus food from the interior would have been attractive to a struggling maroon on the fringe or to a sparsely supplied enslaved canal worker. At the Cross Canal site, Sayers has also recovered materials originating from the swamp, further evidence that a two-way exchange system existed between maroons of the deep swamp and those who lived near the canal.[254]

Sayers also argues that the diminishing isolation of Deep Swamp Maroons could have actually been a strategy to build alliances and protect their communities as the outside world encroached on the deep swamp. The circumstances that made trade between the groups of maroons more frequent would have also clearly demonstrated to Deep Swamp Maroons the increasing likelihood that they might come in contact with people connected to the outside. By establishing friendly trade relations with a limited and select group of outsiders, Deep Swamp Maroons could trade on their own terms with trusted partners who, because of their own self-interest in monopolizing deep swamp trade, would have had a significant motivation to keep deep swamp locations secret.[255] Some sources hint at the possibility that trade meetings even occurred at neutral locations between deep swamp communities and canal camps.[256]

The presence within deep swamp communities of materials produced outside the Dismal not only provides insight into maroon trade networks but also seems to show a dynamic deep swamp population. Although establishing a reliable population figure for maroons in the Dismal Swamp is impossible, in the nineteenth century, the Deep Swamp Maroon communities seem to have begun shrinking. White observers on the outside assumed the swamp population to be in decline.[257] One observer in the 1850s believed that only a small number of maroon communities could possibly eke out a tenuous existence in the swamp, and only then by reliance on work with shingle crews.[258] It is not clear on what evidence white outsiders based these statements. However, a European visitor rightly pointed out a major flaw in these arguments: the claim that swamp maroons found "both an asylum and the means of subsistence in it" "rather contradicts the statement that they are very keenly pursued and hunted out of it."[259]

The archaeological record does not support the contemporary suggestion that hardly any maroons were left deep in the swamp by the 1850s. There is clear evidence of continuous occupation of deep swamp locations from the seventeenth century through at least the Civil War. However, although materials produced outside the swamp increasingly appeared in deep swamp villages as the canal system worked its way through the swamp, these materials were not evenly distributed across such sites. No mass-produced nineteenth-century items have been recovered from lower-lying areas of deep swamp locations, and there is no evidence of permanent nineteenth-century architecture in those areas either. This suggests that less desirable locations had fallen out of use, and that the population density that had necessitated the full utilization of dry ground for living space had subsided.[260] Most communities remained intact, but they seem to have become smaller.[261]

This was not necessarily because fewer maroons were entering the swamp, however. Men and women still self-emancipated with the swamp as their goal, but their options once within the swamp included more modalities than they might have had previously. Simply put, canals brought more people deeper in the swamp than before, closer to deep swamp communities, and more regularly in contact with Deep Swamp Maroons. It is likely that the increased opportunity to work in the shadows of enslaved canal laborers made more maroons interested in "herd[ing] with the shingle getters."[262] These Liminal Maroons remained (and sought to be) partially connected to the outside world from which they had escaped. One more step removed, Deep Swamp Maroons were reestablishing links to the outside as well.

As a white-haired Deep Swamp Maroon sat on his porch smoking a pipe in August 1831 (with tobacco that had passed from a white resident of the swamp border to an enslaved shingle-cutter, and from him to his maroon friend whom he paid with a racoon's pelt and an ear of corn), and maybe his name was Abraham Turner, he could not have known that the outside world was in a panic, convinced that a thousand maroons were pouring forth from the swamp to cut whites' throats. They weren't, but mixed with the faint sound of a banjo being plucked on the far side of his village was the even fainter braying of a sorrel mule, possibly the one formerly ridden by Abraham's son at the head of a column of rebels fighting for their lives. Nat Turner had been thrown from the mule, and in the story that Uncle Alek Keeling told until he died, an enslaved mother and her child eventually found the wandering beast, climbed on its back, and rode it into the safety of the Dismal to escape the carnage unfolding just to the east.[263]

The outside world was coming to the Great Dismal Swamp.

CHAPTER FIVE

Dismal Swamp
Marronage Triumphant

I have been a wild man. Every man's hand against me—a companion
of the dragons and the owls this many a year. I have made my bed with the
leviathan, among the reeds and the rushes. I have found the alligators and
the snakes better neighbours than Christians. They let those alone that
let them alone, but Christians will hunt for the precious life.
—Harriet Beecher Stowe, *Dred*, 1856

The voice of Dred still crieth in the Dismal Swamp as some
prophet of the Lord, "Woe to the land polluted with blood."
—"The Peril of the South," 1859

IN THE AFTERMATH of the Nat Turner rebellion, the numbers of
self-emancipators able to make it into the Dismal Swamp shrank,
and the conduct of guerrilla warfare from within it was quieted for
a time. Over the next two decades, there were no reports of maroon
raids originating from the swamp. Slave catchers were emboldened to attempt
to penetrate the swamp in search of "fugitive property," and legislators in Virginia and North Carolina passed laws that they hoped would end the threat
of Dismal Swamp marronage once and for all. By the 1850s, outsiders assumed
that the Dismal's maroon population had dwindled to negligible numbers.

It had not. Rather, maroons continued to inhabit the Dismal in large numbers, and what outsiders interpreted as evidence of a dwindling presence there
actually obscured a period of retrenchment and growth under a new generation of leaders.

It was also during this last antebellum decade that the accumulated intellectual burden of more than two centuries of Dismal Swamp marronage became
unbearable for white supporters of slavery in the Tidewater and beyond. Even
as whites reassured themselves that the actual maroon threat was shrinking,
the symbolic shadow the Great Dismal Swamp cast over the South grew. As
enemies of slavery ramped up their attacks from without, the festering sore

from within that the maroons represented, and the South's inability to eradicate the actual and ideological threat therein contributed to the hysteria that ultimately led to disunion and civil war.

THE DEGREE OF the Upper South's panic at the Nat Turner revolt may be gauged by the military mobilization of the region in its immediate aftermath. Rather than the end of a rebellion quickly put down, many feared it was but the beginning of a devastating age of insurrection. The militia in both Virginia and North Carolina mustered and marched toward Southampton, three companies of the US Army with artillery mobilized from Fort Monroe, and the Norfolk Navy Yard sent a company of Marines and arms for a thousand soldiers. The governor of Virginia notified Washington of a state of emergency.

Three days later, Virginia militia Brig. Gen. Richard Eppes informed the governor that the rebellion had been crushed, that all its leaders (except Turner) were dead or captured, and that the killing of whites was over. The slaughter of those suspected of having participated in the uprising, however, was far from over. As militia units returned to their homes, they laid low any African Americans who crossed their paths. "The roads," one reporter wrote, "were strewn with the carcasses of negroes." One North Carolina militia unit captured and beheaded a group of African Americans they encountered near Cross Keys, stuck the heads on posts lining the road, and continued on their return march home.[1] Over a hundred free and enslaved African Americans were murdered in the immediate aftermath of the rebellion.[2]

It is noteworthy that most of the militia of the Virginia Dismal Swamp counties never marched off to Southampton. Augmented by the US Army, they had stayed put at the northern edge of the swamp.[3] The Southampton rebellion may have been over, but the potentially larger threat in their own backyards remained intact. Indeed, it was possibly even increased by fleeing followers of Nat Turner who remained at large and sought the shelter of the Dismal Swamp to protect their lives and regroup for further "offensive demonstrations."[4] The fire of the rebellion may have been extinguished, but the Great Dismal loomed like a volcano ready to blow. Residents in its shadow remained terrified because they knew "not when, or where, the flame will burst forth, but we know that death in the most horrid forms threatens us."[5]

The Dismal Swamp militias could not rest easy. If their estimates were correct—that between 2,000 and 3,000 maroons lived in the swamp—they were woefully outnumbered.[6] And if the actual numbers were even higher, as may have been the case, then they could imagine a fate no better than French armies had met in Haiti.

Initial reports were that Turner's surviving rebels were reaching the protection of the swamp from the northeast.[7] Whites attempted a raid into the swamp itself, but one report admitted that the "labyrinth proved an insurmountable obstacle, and prevented the pursuers from penetrating into its innermost recesses."[8] Defeated by the swamp as all others had been before them, they next undertook a sweep of areas adjacent to the dry swamp in pursuit of something to show for their efforts. There followed a general roundup of African Americans who were personally unknown to militiamen or who could not give a satisfactory account of themselves for the time of the rebellion, including forty in Nansemond County, Virginia, and a dozen each in Norfolk County, Virginia, and Gates County, North Carolina.[9] This show of force had little impact, and many of those arrested were quickly released.[10]

Antimaroon Measures in the Wake of the Rebellion

Yet the militia presence around the edges of the Dismal was not relaxed in the wake of the Turner revolt as it had been before once insurrection scares in the area had passed. Whites around the swamp had "magnified the menace of danger" of the Dismal to the "conscious desserts" of Turner's rebellion.[11] All able-bodied men in the region would be subject to militia duty going forward, even the six otherwise indispensable lock-keepers of the Dismal Swamp Canal, which would be closed to commerce and its keepers pressed into service in case of insurrection.[12] The patrol system was also fully revived around the swamp, and laws requiring free African Americans to produce papers on demand were more strictly enforced.[13] African Americans of any suspicion were watched closely, sometimes for many months, and those believed to have any knowledge of insurrectionary plots or marronage risked jail or torture.[14]

Professional slave catchers became bolder in their attempts to reclaim self-emancipators from the Dismal. By the 1840s, slave catchers had been accused of intentionally setting the swamp on fire to flush out maroons. This blunt technique was reported to have "driven from their hiding places a large number of runaway slaves, who have, in many cases, been secreted for years." One slave catcher's arson in 1845 resulted in the forced return of a family of twelve maroons to their former slave labor camp. "Where in the whole history of the human race," an abolitionist reader of the report asked, "is there an incident more full of horror than that revealed in the above cool-blooded paragraph?" These freedom-seekers, "*fearing tigers and hyenas less than their 'brother man' and 'sister woman'* . . . are not allowed to dwell even in that dismallest of 'dismal' swamps."[15]

In the late 1830s and early 1840s, "Dismal N— Hunting" developed as a distinct line of work in the area.[16] This could be a lucrative occupation for a man with luck, stamina, and the right skill set.[17] Some enslavers were willing to offer a significantly more substantial reward for self-emancipators who were captured in the Dismal for the extra danger to which catchers would expose themselves. An advertisement placed in Elizabeth City for Abram offered a fifty-dollar reward for his capture, and 50 percent more "if taken in or on the borders of the Dismal Swamp."[18] Prince's capture in the Dismal would earn a slave catcher double the prize than if he were detained elsewhere—$100.[19]

These bounty hunters employed specially trained dogs, although no specific breed was preferred over another: any of the "ordinary hounds of the South" could be trained for the job.[20] Joseph Church, an enslaved canal worker interviewed in 1853, described the training regimen: "They are shut up when puppies, and never allowed to see a negro except while training to catch him. A negro is made to run from them, and they are encouraged to follow him until he gets into a tree, when meat is given them. Afterward, they learn to follow any particular negro by scent, and then a shoe or a piece of clothing is taken off a negro, and they learn to find by scent who it belongs to, and to *tree* him, etc." If a "fugitive" was eventually treed by dogs, he would be ordered to surrender himself, and "if he did not stop they would shoot, and sometimes kill him."[21]

One such hunt in 1848 discovered "a company" of maroons in the Dismal and after a brief skirmish whites "shot them down like partridges." A witness reported that so many maroons had been recently hunted down that others abandoned the swamp "and returned to their former masters."[22] A mother with her children returned to her master in 1845 when slavers made her marronage too dangerous to maintain.[23] If they encountered maroons in the swamp, whites sometimes might shout out a warning or a command to stop before opening fire, but their default was to shoot. A farmer living at the edge of the swamp confirmed that he had known of four maroons being shot in a single day. However, most continued to value freedom above all else, and would surrender to no man. Joseph Church, an enslaved confidant of maroons, knew that *"some on 'em would rather be shot than be took."*[24]

Ultimately, few Dismal Swamp maroons were retaken, dead or alive. Most who were captured were snatched up on the fringes of the swamp by precision hunting parties looking for advertised individuals, that is, not through broad or general attempts to "scour" the swamp. The substantial rewards were seldom enough to entice slave hunters into the deep swamp, even if they could have navigated it. Even dogs lost their effectiveness the further into the swamp they plunged. Scent trails could not be maintained through the muck and the mire, and the deeper into the briars and thick swamp brush the dogs went, the more likely they were to bark or yelp when scratched, giving away any possibility of surprise.[25] Maroons also routinely killed hounds sent on their trail.[26] There is no evidence of a deep swamp settlement's discovery in raids upon the Dismal's deepest recesses.[27]

The once-tacit acknowledgment that enslaved people and free African Americans aided maroons was now fully in the open. Lawmen in the Dismal Swamp region ordered even stricter and more regular patrol and guard directives, including night and day patrols, and the quarters of enslaved families were more frequently searched. This was to be done on a routine basis and not only in response to "scares."[28] Religious meetings along the swamp edge where maroons and enslaved people might fellowship together were prohibited, and those who continued to meet in worship were subject to flogging. Moses Grandy's brother-in-law Isaac went "into the woods" at the edge of the Dismal to preach to a small group of enslaved people (and very possibly maroons). When the meetings were discovered, several enslaved participants were taken, flogged, and forced to reveal the identities of other participants, some of whom were then executed. For preaching, Isaac was flogged and his back "pickled," a process that was repeated "so on for some months." His wife and baby were sold, then four more of his children, one by one. Finally, for encouraging enslaved people to congregate near the Dismal, Isaac the "troublemaker" was sold away.[29] Such measures "alarmed" potential maroons and enslaved allies, and were reckoned to have been somewhat successful in frustrating maroon activity in and around the Dismal.[30]

By 1832, it was common for "obnoxious" free Black people (or anyone considered a "dangerous free n—") to be "visited" and abused by night riders.[31] Enslaved people were valuable personal property, but little stopped enraged and terrified whites from "[taking] revenge on the free people of color."[32] At the margins of the Great Dismal Swamp free Black people "suffered severely." "Nat Turner's War," one man so abused recalled, became "a pretext for the wholesale arrest of free people of color," especially those around the Dismal who could not easily provide free papers and who were by default assumed to be agitators or maroons planning to make "a bold blow for the liberty of all the slaves" in the region.[33]

This fear was not without merit. Willis Augustus Hodges, a free Black man working on the Dismal Swamp Canal with 500 enslaved laborers, hatched a plot in 1827 to attack his overseer and lead the army of workers to freedom.

Willis Augustus Hodges.
From Irvine Garland Penn, ed., *The Afro-American
Press and Its Editors* (Springfield, Mass.: Wiley, 1891).

Only a sober assessment of their lack of arms compared with those of the area's whites dissuaded him from carrying out the plan.[34] Again in 1833, Hodges was rumored to be "attempt[ing] to free all the slaves in Princess Anne County" and was described as "a second Nat Turner." This time, other free Blacks in the community were intimidated into putting pressure on Hodges, who soon left Virginia for New York. Hodges's plots never advanced to execution, but even the rumor of insurrection pushed whites to terrorize the free Black community of the Dismal Swamp region.[35]

By 1846, marronage to and in the Dismal had become (or, more accurately, had remained) such a problem that lawmakers in both Virginia and North Carolina, including both governors, considered draconian legislation to specifically deal with the problem.[36] That year the North Carolina General Assembly passed "An Act to Provide for the Apprehension of Runaway Slaves in the Great Dismal Swamp and for Other Purposes." Lamenting the growing incidence of marronage, especially that abetted by free African Americans and poor whites, lawmakers expressed their concern that Dismal Swamp maroons "remain setting at defiance the power of their masters, corrupting and seducing other slaves, and by their evil example and evil practices lessening the due subordination, and greatly impairing the value of slaves in the district of country bordering of the said great dismal swamp."[37]

Enslaved people laboring in the swamp would be required to go before the county clerk of court and have their detailed description recorded (very similar to the description that might accompany a runaway notice), a copy of which would be delivered to the employer's agent in the swamp to keep on hand. Free African Americans were subject to the same requirement, and they would be required to keep a copy of their official description on their person at all times employed. If any enslaved worker could be proved to "consort with, or work, or be employed in company with any runaway slave," that person would be subject to thirty-nine lashes laid on by a justice of the peace. Any white person found guilty of the same would be subject to a fine or imprisonment of at least three months. Free African Americans found guilty of the provisions of the act could be sold into slavery. Slave catchers stood to collect an additional twenty-five dollars above whatever reward might be offered by an enslaver if they took a Dismal Swamp maroon.[38] The next year, the act was extended to four counties adjacent to the Dismal Swamp: Tyrell, Washington, Beaufort, and Hyde.[39]

The increased emphasis on surveillance betrayed an increasing desire on the part of Tidewater slavers to exert some control, *any* control, over an institution that seemed to be slipping away from them. Everything about the Dismal Swamp seemed to undermine southern power structures. Of course, this had been the case for over a century, but the Turner rebellion and increasing public chatter regarding marronage were reminders that whites exerted far less mastery over their human property than they would like. The 1847 registry law may not have done anything to actually prevent marronage, but its passage might create an appearance of authority and control over the bodies of enslaved people.

The Spectral Threat of Maroons

Despite the unrest of the 1830s and 1840s, by most accounts the Dismal Swamp had finally become the economic engine that would have made George Washington proud, and industrial operations within it expanded through the late 1850s. The swamp was, in Frederick Law Olmsted's reckoning, "of considerable commercial importance." Houses and other buildings up and down the

Eastern Seaboard were constructed of Dismal Swamp lumber, its shingles covered the roofs of some of the finest homes in America, and its barrels filled the cargo holds of ships sailing between the United States, Europe, and the Caribbean. These items were all at "great demand at high prices."[40]

However, whatever order the 1847 registry law seemed to offer, and the riches obtaining to Dismal Swamp company investors, were but pieces of a facade covering an unstable structure. Not only were the principle corporate operations in the swamp overextended and poorly capitalized, the labor system most commonly used in the swamp had the potential to undermine the entire enslavement system. The Dismal Swamp companies' pursuit of profits at the expense of "appropriate" discipline of the enslaved was quite problematic. The arrangements between enslaver and enslaved (and by extension, with maroons) provided for an incentive-based task system and unprecedented degrees of freedom. Workers toiled under minimal supervision, were provided relatively generous rations, and might even enjoy some free time for hunting, fishing, or recreation once task(s) were completed. While this may have had the effect of encouraging accommodation to enslavement in some cases, only its profitability masked the real dangers of the practice. Once in the swamp, enslaved people were exposed to ideas about freedom, rebelliousness, and marronage that undermined the ideological underpinnings of slavery and its workability as a system of labor. They met those who had thrown off enslavement, and came to understand that their labor was a marketable commodity that they could claim as well.

The swamp continued to embarrass whites. It was coming to represent failure not just to "subdue" and control nature (which even a grid of canals across the swamp could only barely begin to do) but also to exert power over people who, according to proslavery orthodoxy, should have no power at all. The swamp absorbed their human property and refused to grant them entry apart from boats that plied the canals. African Americans, in contrast, were masters of the swamp, able to navigate it with ease. In fact, whites often required an African American guide if they wanted to enter the swamp proper. This power inversion, placing their hands in the lives of Black men, was disconcerting to say the least. African Americans were able to assert a "utilitarian proprietorship" over the Dismal that stood in stark relief to the powerlessness of whites.[41]

Maroons were not utilizing the Dismal much differently after 1831 than they had before. If anything, they were withdrawing further into the isolation of the swamp in response to crackdowns from without. What *had* changed was whites' fuller appreciation of the swamp's rebellious potential. To be sure, William Byrd had issued a warning in 1728 that a future maroon empire might be gathering in the Dismal. The parallels between the Dismal Swamp maroon campaigns of the early nineteenth century and Santo Domingo were there to see if observers were willing to make the connections. Some did. But Nat Turner's supposed connection to the Dismal had been made explicit, and widespread knowledge of West Indian slave rebellions in the 1830s further worried enslavers about the volcano slumbering at the edge of their civilized world.

Maroons were not just in the swamp; they circulated among the enslaved in secret late-night meetings, reunions, and even rebellion plots. Enslavers knew this and were powerless to stop maroons from "corrupting and seducing other slaves," and spreading the influence of "their evil example and evil practices."[42] Enslaved people still on the labor camps, slaveholders believed, remained content with their lot until taught otherwise. The initial explanation of Nat Turner's insurrection as a maroon campaign from the Dismal Swamp makes more sense in this light. It was at first "not believed" to be more than a "local and desperate effort of a few misguided beings, urged on to the deeds of blood, by the harpies from the Swamp, for the sake of booty."[43]

Related to maroons' "corruption" of the still-enslaved was their chipping away at "due" subordination to "masters." Certainly "due" subordination did not include supplying and provisioning maroons from slave labor camp stores, hiding maroons in their quarters at times, and facilitating communication across the countryside. These would have been crimes punishable by fine or imprisonment of at least three months if the offender was white but potentially torture or murder if the offender was enslaved. Often, not even the threat of death could break the "fidelity" of the enslaved to maroons.[44] For the enslaved, even knowing of maroons in their midst constituted resistance to the system. The behavior of maroons influenced acts of resistance by those still enslaved.[45]

Single self-emancipators whose marronage took them far from their slave labor camp had minimal influence on the still-enslaved, with the exception of possible inspiration. Similarly, petit maroons who "lurked" nearby but eventually returned were not major threats. To be sure, the woman who permanently escaped deprived her enslaver of her full value as property, and the "lurker" withheld the value of her labor while laying out, but the lone self-emancipator was no longer in a position to "corrupt" other enslaved people. An enslaver might even appreciate the opportunity to give the petit maroon a very public whipping upon her return as an example to others. However, committed maroons in the Dismal remained in the shadows, untouchable, influencing and inspiring the enslaved and in numbers large enough to potentially bring war down on slavery.[46]

Still, enslavers could not fully crack down with impunity upon aiders and abettors of maroons. Fear of maroon activity often led to the passage of harsh laws and extralegal suppression measures directed at potential self-emancipators, but slavers also had to tread lightly to avoid pushing their enslaved people into an embrace of the very marronage they hoped to curtail. As Harriet Beecher Stowe noted in her 1856 novel *Dred*, proximity to the Dismal Swamp had always been a considerable check on the power of enslavers and overseers.[47] Enslavers noted with frustration that in times of heightened maroon activity (real or imagined), still-enslaved people more frequently defied the power of and rejected full subordination to their "masters."[48] At one point when marronage had reached an alarming rate on the Virginia side of the swamp, an enslaver who "'bused" people on the labor camp discovered that he risked pushing them to "go an' live in the swamp first."[49]

Rather than whippings or threatened sale, enslavers near the Dismal often had to depend on fear of snakes and bears to deter potential Dismal Swamp maroons. Of course, fear, even that of potential death in the swamp, was often not as strong as a desire to be free. Maroons said as much. Harriet Jacobs, who marooned in a swamp near the Great Dismal, remembered the terrible swamp experience that was a part of her own self-emancipation:

> We were covered with hundreds of mosquitos. In an hour's time they had so poisoned my flesh that I was a pitiful sight to behold. As the light increased, I saw snake after snake crawling round us. I had been accustomed to the sight of snakes all my life, but these were larger than any I had ever seen. To this day I shudder when I remember that morning. As evening approached, the number of snakes increased so much that we were continually obliged to thrash them with sticks to keep them from crawling over us. The bamboos were so high and so thick that it was impossible to see beyond a very short distance . . . the heat of the swamp, the mosquitos, and the constant terror of snakes had brought on a burning fever. . . . I could scarcely summon courage to rise. But even those large, venomous snakes were less dreadful to my imagination than the white men in that community called civilized.[50]

For enslavers, marronage was also very expensive. When it loomed as a direct threat, the raising of militias and patrols wasted resources and labor. At the same time, the forced productivity of enslaved people declined. When the swamp attracted frustrated enslaved people like a magnet, it lessened the market value and reliability of those who remained on the slave labor camp. Enslavers refused to pay premium prices for property likely to disappear into a swamp. Enslaved property with a documented history of marronage lost value.[51] A man or woman marooned in the Dismal might be "sold running" or "sold in the woods" at a greatly reduced value (sometimes half or more—the speculator took the risk of recovering the maroon from the swamp).[52] Even if not sold, fees and rewards to be paid to slave catchers in the Dismal might cost an enslaver 25–50 percent of the market value of an enslaved person.[53] Thus the very act of marooning reduced the "value" of an enslaved person to his or her enslaver.[54] "The 'riches' of the slaveholder," abolitionist James M. McKim wrote in the context of the Great Dismal Swamp, "'make themselves *legs* and fly away.'"[55]

Maroons, unlike self-emancipators who escaped to a "free" territory or state, also continued to drain off food and supplies. More damaging and harder to distill into dollars and cents was enslavers' lost sense of security. They acutely felt the growing potential of rebelliousness among the still-enslaved who were influenced and inspired by maroons.[56] How much must enslaved property be discounted if "corrupted" by ideas of Black power, insubordination, and hope?

This was one of the main reasons enslavers struggled with competing desires to publicize marronage or bury it as much as they could. Enslaved people had keen ears, especially when empowering news was in the air. An entire slave labor camp might be aware of the activities of maroons nearby, especially if they had once been one of their own or maintained family relations. Whites believed that enslaved people did not need to be further encouraged by reports of marronage, whether through reading about them or hearing the news from someone who had read such accounts. Many southern newspaper editors shared a well-understood "code of silence" when it came to news of enslaved people's rebelliousness, including marronage.[57]

A great deal of effort was expended in attempting to suppress what was already well known among the enslaved. Moreover, enslavers did not want to advertise their powerlessness to keep maroons on the labor camps. When marronage does appear in enslavers' documents or newspapers, it is almost always in the context of maroon activity put down. In this way enslavers' might demonstrate their power, or flex their muscles publicly. For every runaway ad placed for an enslaved person assumed to have marooned in the Dismal, or newspaper account of a maroon campaign not yet put down, thousands of acts of maroon rebelliousness went unreported, the details of almost all of them unknown, deep in the swamp. Quite simply, there was nothing to be reported besides the power and tenacity of the enslaved and powerlessness of enslavers. Their impotence was closely connected to their ignorance.

Winning a War Not Waged

The existence of maroon communities within the Dismal Swamp was no secret. That enslaved people took refuge there was well known locally since the early eighteenth century, and scattered reports of their activities (Fringe Maroons) and sometimes worried romantic conjecture about their swamp lives (Deep Swamp Maroons) appeared in newspapers and travel accounts for the next century, rolling off presses both near and far-removed from the Tidewater region. Many whites assumed they knew something about the Dismal Swamp maroons from having read accounts of maroon activity in South and Central America and the Caribbean. The name of the swamp itself suggested something of its nature, topography, and character. Few questioned assertions that the swamp exuded poisonous gasses, that buzzards would not fly directly over it, and that in its depths lurked tigers, alligators, and wolves. Some recalled that George Washington, heroic father of the nation, had some connection with it.

But actual knowledge of the Dismal and its inhabitants was scarce through the 1840s. William Byrd's account of his 1728 survey of the dividing line was circulated among his friends but not actually edited and published until 1841, long after his death. Edmund Ruffin, an admirer of Byrd, published Byrd's "Proposal to Drain the Dismal Swamp" in his serial *The Farmer's Register* in 1837, but only because of its value to the developing field of agricultural science, Ruffin's hobbyhorse. In his introductory essay, "Observations Made during an Excursion to the Dismal Swamp," Ruffin pointed out that although few people had heard or read a description of the Dismal, "however slight and imperfect," even fewer "have made any personal observation of, or paid much attention to . . . its circumstances very remarkable." In the absence of "better digested and more accurate information," Ruffin offered an essay of some 10,000 words to satisfy his readers' curiosity, by far the most extensive report on the Dismal to that point.[58]

Notably, Ruffin, described by a biographer as "the archetype of the proslavery southerner," did not write a word about maroons.[59] "The only sign of life," he noted (human sign, it must be assumed), was the "'camp' of a pair of shingle-getters," who, as might be expected, were nowhere to be found. Only at the end of his visit to the swamp does he encounter "old Toby Fisher," whom he described as an aged shingle-getter. Fisher recounted some particulars of swamp life at the turn of the century. The enslaved workers of the swamp, Ruffin assured his readers, were (like Fisher appeared to be) happy, healthy, only lightly worked, and simple of mind.[60]

Consistent with his views on the character of the enslaved ("The negro is naturally timid, unenterprising, fearful of and averse to change to any new and untried condition"), Ruffin's Dismal Swamp could be no refuge of self-emancipators.[61] He made no mention in his essay of the clandestine economy of the "shingle-gitters" and their maroon associates, and never discovered (or more likely, was not informed by his subject) that Toby Fisher was not only a gray-haired "shingle-gitters" but also free (he was in fact a Liminal Maroon who had once emancipated himself and now lived "hidden in plain sight"), a revered minister to other maroons along the Dismal Swamp Canal.[62] Maybe Ruffin was naive; or maybe he believed that no good could come from drawing attention to the swamp's more revolutionary residents.

What Ruffin would not see, and what others dared not, was evident none-theless. The Dismal Swamp and its maroon inhabitants were winning a war most of them were not even actively waging. Developers were not measurably closer to "subduing" the swamp than they had been a century earlier, and maroons were salt in their wound. It was clear by now that the swamp was not as inaccessible as white outsiders made it out to be. As whites and industrialists whimpered about obstacles, African Americans in remarkable numbers had moved into and through the swamp. Moreover, the nimbleness with which maroons traversed the swamp was unnerving to enslavers. The inescapable conclusion many whites drew was that African Americans were somehow better at manipulating the swamp, that they could succeed in this case where whites had failed, and there was little that could be done about it. The terrain that white developers so desperately desired to conquer could only be navigated by escaped "property" over which they could exert no more power than they could over the swamp. The inability to control nature was at least possible for enslavers to wrap their brains around—hurricanes, droughts, tornadoes, and the like could not just be willed into submission, and harsh landscapes, admittedly, took time to subdue. The inferiority of the enslaved to the enslavers, however, was not meant to be something that needed to be forced or imposed. It was meant to be the natural order of things, acknowl-edged and even appreciated by the enslaved themselves. Enslavers were forced, if only privately, to acknowledge that their mastery of slave society was far from absolute, and that, at least in the Tidewater, it ultimately rested upon a shaky foundation of Dismal Swamp peat and mud.[63]

Outside of the swamp (just as in it), maroons were nearly indistinguishable by whites from enslaved people. For a population who might occasionally craft detailed and discrete descriptions of African Americans in the way of adver-tising for their "escaped property," whites seldom troubled themselves much with distinguishing one enslaved person from another, and in the antebellum years, around 40 percent of Virginians and 30 percent of North Carolinians were enslaved.[64] Enslaved people represented not only the workers who toiled to harvest the timber products of the swamp but also the labor used to transport those products. As historian Ryan Quintana suggests, the enslaved were the "circulating lifeblood" of slave society infrastructure and often the primary users and occupants of the region's roads and canals.[65] The maintenance and expansion of the Tidewater's economy, and by extension, the preservation of its social order, depended on whites' constantly being surrounded by enslaved African Americans and possibly even covert maroons. To preserve a fragile psychological comfort, whites could not imagine being thoroughly hemmed in by calculating, intelligent, independent thinkers eager to maroon at a moment's notice. North Carolina's registry law was but a superficial and minimally effective psychological balm, and in some ways magnified the paranoia by its tacit acknowledgement of marronage in enslavers' midst.

Real psychological comfort would thus come only from homogenization, not detail or distinction. Those hundreds of dark faces enslavers might encounter on a given day needed to merge into a faceless army of brutes. The mass of the enslaved had to be seen to lack intelligence and individual identities, apart from a harmless and generic one, and within this order whites constructed the "Sambo" trope to serve as the dominant personality of enslaved workers. Sambo was contented and devoted to his enslaver. Childlike in his simplicity, he required the influence and guidance of superior whites, without which he could not function on his own. Enslavers insisted on the happiness of their enslaved people. Enslavement, then, was the beneficent act of a generous enslaver for which the enslaved were grateful.

On Sambo's imagined shoulders were thus placed some of the most important ideological underpinnings of the "peculiar institution." Enslavers were eager to see Sambo in their enslaved people because the trope suggested uniform contentedness (which meant safety and productivity). The enslaved, for their part, often coopted Sambo for themselves, feigning fidelity and contentment to hide threats to white power and to protect themselves from jealous enslavers who demanded to be seen as benevolent paternal figures. Sambo allowed them to mask small or great acts of rebellion.[66]

Scholars have long concurred that Sambo was a white construct, a self-delusion adopted to deflect notice from abundant contradictory evidence (John Blassingame calls Sambo "almost mandatory for the Southerners' emotional security"), and also to offset the terror inherent in Sambo's counterpart, "Nat," the chronically rebellious personality on the slave labor camp.[67] Nat,

"Portrait of Wild Bill."
From Calvin Henderson Wiley, *Roanoke, or, "Where Is*
Utopia?" (Philadelphia: T. B. Peterson & Brothers, 1866).

of course, was derived from the name of Nat Turner, whose own history was entangled with that of the Dismal Swamp. The existence of maroons could not be squared with the image of Sambo; Nat "lurked" in the shadows just as maroons did, and instead of a single bad apple on the slave labor camp that might be conspicuously punished and made an example of, the threat of the "baaad negro" in the swamp was magnified by several orders of magnitude.

As Tynes Cowan suggests, white southerners' real fear was that "Nat" was hiding beneath a "Sambo" mask. Maroons had clearly not been content in their enslavement—they preferred living among snakes, alligators, and bears to life on a slave labor camp. They were master woodsmen, free by their own efforts and thriving, without white direction or support, in a swamp landscape whites could not enter into or surveil. They were violent when necessary, possessed secret knowledge inaccessible to enslavers, and utilized the swamp as a space of Black autonomy and power. They asserted control over their own bodies and self-definitions. For *ideological consistency*, maroons had to be eliminated.[68]

Most troubling, maroons forced enslavers to question the loyalty of those still enslaved. If the maroons of the Dismal were willing to risk their lives in an escape and to live out their lives in a swamp, were those remaining really loyal, truly content, or were they biding their time to follow a well-established example and maroon in the swamp? How long could their labor be counted upon? Were they secure property? Had they not appreciated the "blessings" of civilization their proximity to whites had bestowed upon them? Maroons, in fact, were the "actual embodiment of black insurrection," and there lurked a potential maroon in every enslaved person.[69] For *psychological comfort*, maroons had to be eliminated.

As with everything else (apart from maroons), proslavery mental acrobatics got even more tangled in the Dismal. Maroons should not have existed, yet they did. In attempting to answer why and how, enslavers predictably resorted to racist explanations. Maroons had once been feeble-minded slaves who were foolish enough to think they knew better than their enslavers. Their escape to the swamp took them beyond the reach of the beneficent paternalism so freely and generously offered. Separated from civilization in the swamp, maroons had become degraded and animal-like "wild negroes" (and dangerous). Hungry for and accustomed to following the command of an intellectually superior white leader, the Dismal maroons were ripe to be turned to the advantage of a remarkable opportunist-rebel like Nat Turner, Tom Copper, Bob Ricks, or even a white abolitionist. Unlike self-emancipators who fled the region for a free state or Canada, maroons' stubborn decision to stay concealed but nearby embodied the constant threat of insurrection. For the *safety* of whites, maroons had to be eliminated.

Abolitionists Embrace the Dismal Swamp Maroons

Ironically, enslavers' aggressive and sustained measures to crack down on maroons in the wake of the Nat Turner rebellion strengthened their adversaries by exposing and publicizing the conditions of maroon life in the Dismal and the heavy-handed abuses most likely to capture the attention of abolitionists. Besides genuine humanitarian concern for those being hunted in the swamp, reformers appreciated the propaganda value of the fact that victims of enslavement were willing to take their chances in the swamp rather than live in bondage. In attempting to demonstrate their power in the wake of a revolt, whites around the swamp unwittingly sparked the imagination of allies of the enslaved and handed them a remarkably powerful symbolic tool at a crucial moment in their development.

The Turner rebellion coincided with the birth of the modern abolitionist movement in the United States. Antislavery writers and their growing readership were hungry for evidence of the iniquities of slavery. William Lloyd Garrison's *Liberator* made frequent reference to the Dismal and its maroon inhabitants from its earliest issues. The swamp itself often metaphorically stood for the sordid South and the institution of slavery—"an ugly feature on the face of our fair country."[70] Garrison reprinted without comment theories connecting the swamp with Turner's rebellion, and likewise reprinted related estimates of the number of Dismal maroons "concealed" in its depths.[71]

Abolitionists understood that these maroons represented one of the clearest and most forceful indictments of slavery available. They did not hesitate to articulate conclusions enslavers strove to suppress. "That hundreds of slaves prefer the danger and darkness of the dismal swamps to the homes and plantations of their Christian masters," Frederick Douglass wrote to the readers of his *North Star*, "is proof that they dread the wolfish propensities of the slaveholder more than they dread the real wolf."[72] At another point, with the Dismal Swamp clearly still on his mind, Douglass presented an audience with "one of the most telling testimonies against the pretended kindness of slaveholders." The fact that "uncounted numbers of fugitives are now inhabiting the Dismal Swamp, preferring the untamed wilderness to their cultivated homes—choosing rather to encounter hunger and thirst, and to roam with the wild beasts of the forest, running the hazard of being hunted and shot down, than to submit to the authority of kind masters," should suggest all one needed to know about the brutality of enslavement. The Dismal Swamp maroon "prefers to encounter a life of trial, however bitter, or death, however terrible, to dragging out his existence under the dominion of these kind masters."[73] A correspondent for the antislavery *Zion's Herald* simply asked readers why, "if the slaves are happy in their present condition, would they prefer a residence in the Dismal Swamp?"[74]

It was through poetry that the maroons fully burst onto the US literary scene and into the national popular imagination. The poet Henry Wadsworth Longfellow, himself an opponent of slavery, dramatized the Dismal Swamp maroons in his 1842 collection *Poems on Slavery*. One of the most-read writers of the nineteenth century (nicknamed the "household poet of America"), Longfellow had seldom waded deeply into politically charged topics.[75] The cause of antislavery, however, was apparently worth alienating some readers.

He had earlier considered writing a drama centered on Toussaint Louverture as his attempt to "do something in my humble way for the great cause of Negro emancipation," yet it was his collection of eight antislavery poems that made him a darling of the antislavery movement. The fourth poem in the series, "The Slave in the Dismal Swamp," took readers to a place of which many had heard but few knew much about:

> In dark fens of the Dismal Swamp
>   The hunted Negro lay;
> He saw the fire of the midnight camp,
> And heard at times a horse's tramp
>   And a bloodhound's distant bay.
>
> Where will-o'-the-wisps and glow-worms shine,
>   In bulrush and in brake;
> Where waving mosses shroud the pine,
> And the cedar grows, and the poisonous vine
>   Is spotted like the snake;
>
> Where hardly a human foot could pass,
>   Or a human heart would dare,
> On the quaking turf of the green morass
> He crouched in the rank and tangled grass,
>   Like a wild beast in his lair.
>
> A poor old slave, infirm and lame;
>   Great scars deformed his face;
> On his forehead he bore the brand of shame,
> And the rags, that hid his mangled frame,
>   Were the livery of disgrace.
>
> All things above were bright and fair,
>   All things were glad and free;
> Lithe squirrels darted here and there,
> And wild birds filled the echoing air
>   With songs of Liberty!
>
> On him alone was the doom of pain,
>   From the morning of his birth;
> On him alone the curse of Cain
> Fell, like a flail on the garnered grain,
>   And struck him to the earth!

Longfellow hit upon several tropes sure to hold the continued interest of his readers: blithe wildlife seemingly freer than the hunted maroon, the harsh swamp threatening the subject at every step, and the inescapable paradox that dangerous refuge in a swamp was preferable to a life enslaved. Longfellow offers no resolution to his subject, who would have to keep going, plodding deeper into the Great Dismal Swamp, his fate, like that of those still enslaved, remaining uncertain. His ordeal against slavery, like the campaign required of abolitionist readers, was far from over.

Longfellow had shone a bright light on the Dismal Swamp maroons, and his national and international audience was hungry for more. Abolitionists called for the wide circulation of his pamphlet as "one of the most efficient means of spreading anti-slavery truth."[76] As much as any location in the South, the Dismal was coming to be known as a site of Black resistance and marronage, even if most of the particulars remained shrouded in mystery. In fact, it was the mystique of the swamp that made it such an appealing subject. Nearly impenetrable and the size of an entire state, the Dismal lay directly in many self-emancipators' route from enslavement to freedom in the North. Filled with potentially thousands of maroons, some of them freedom fighters who directly engaged enslavers, as well as others seeking the invisibility the swamp offered them, the swamp allowed writers significant creative license.

In April 1851, Henry "Box" Brown's *Mirror of Slavery* opened to rave reviews in Boston. Brown, who in 1849 had gained national fame in escaping his enslavement by mailing himself in a box from Richmond to Philadelphia, created *Mirror* as a panoramic series of forty-nine scenes of slavery and freedom, painted onto a canvas eight to ten feet tall, and advertised as being "designed and painted from the best and most authentic sources of information."[77] Described by the *Boston Daily Evening Traveler* as "one of the finest panoramas now on exhibition," the work centered on a vivid scene titled "View of the Lake of the Dismal Swamp." Here, the Dismal, with countless maroons concealed in the shadows, represented a transitional space between slavery and freedom. In the estimation of the scholar Daphne Brooks, the swamp scene transported viewers from "a trajectory of abject turmoil into one of intensified fugitive resistance."[78]

Brown may have taken his title from a speech given by Frederick Douglass at the 1849 annual meeting of the American Anti-Slavery Society. "As long as slavery exists in this country . . . ," Douglass said, "the mirror of slavery must be held up to the nation."[79] Douglass himself was well acquainted with the Dismal Swamp by 1852, having gazed into its depths through Brown's panorama and read about it in abolitionist newspapers and correspondence with other abolitionists who had visited the Dismal and recounted the circumstances of its maroon inhabitants. Some of this he published in his own newspaper, the *North Star*, and featured in his antislavery lectures. It is also highly likely that, in Douglass's extensive Underground Railroad work and interactions with self-emancipators in the North like himself, he had met former Dismal Swamp maroons and learned of their swamp experiences firsthand.

Like Brown, Douglass appreciated the symbolic power of the Dismal Swamp maroons in the antislavery struggle, and he set parts of his only published work of fiction in the Dismal. Madison Washington, the protagonist of Douglass's novella *The Heroic Slave*, escaped his slave labor camp in southern Virginia after a brutal whipping and marooned in the Dismal "with the wolf and the bear" for five years. His family remained enslaved, but his wife visited him weekly at the edge of the swamp. The great Dismal Swamp fire of 1841, however, destroyed his swamp home along with those of "many a wandering fugitive, who . . . had sought among the wild beasts the mercy denied by our fellow men." The "grand conflagration," set by slave hunters to flush out their human property, destroyed the maroons' "city of refuge." "I ran alike," Washington laments, "from fire and from slavery."[80]

The same year *The Heroic Slave* appeared in a collection of antislavery essays, William Wells Brown published *Clotel; or, The President's Daughter: A Narrative of Slave Life in the United States*, widely considered the first African American novel. Brown's historical novel was based on extensive research.[81] One of *Clotel*'s plot lines runs through southern Virginia in the wake of the Nat Turner rebellion. In Brown's telling, Turner and hundreds of his followers actually did maroon in the swamp, where "runaway negroes usually seek a hiding-place," following their defeat at Southampton. There, they were welcomed into a maroon community led by an African-born man named Picquilo. He had been a maroon for two years, others of the community even longer. Brown's maroons were militant freedom fighters who relished the opportunity to mete out revenge on Virginia enslavers.[82]

So too did the maroons who populated the pages of Harriet Beecher Stowe's 1856 novel *Dred: A Tale of the Great Dismal Swamp*, one of the most popular books of the nineteenth century. Published at the height of "Bleeding Kansas" and the highly charged presidential election of that year, *Dred* was much more militant than Stowe's first antislavery novel, *Uncle Tom's Cabin*. It is set in and around the Dismal in Chowan County, North Carolina. The title character is a maroon of the swamp, imagined by Stowe as a composite of Denmark Vesey and Nat Turner (she included Turner's "Confessions" as an appendix to her book). Like Turner, Dred was a precocious religious leader prone to visions

and supernatural communications. He is portrayed as a revolutionary, traversing the Virginia/North Carolina region of the Dismal recruiting men and
women of like mind into his Dismal Swamp maroon community. Although
Dred is killed before leading a maroon army out of the Dismal, Stowe's novel
suggests that violence and rebellion were a logical response to slavery by maroons, and that the potential for such righteous bloodshed would loom over
the nation until slavery was abolished.[83]

From the moment Dred walks out of the Dismal Swamp and into the pages
of Stowe's novel, his strength, leadership qualities, character, and intellect are
apparent. The same may be said of the other residents of his maroon community. These qualities had been uncommon in African American characters
in *Uncle Tom's Cabin*—in *Dred* it was the loyal slaves and passive victims who
were rare. *Dred* was remarkable in its time for forcing its readers to consider
slavery from the point of view of revolutionary maroons in the Dismal Swamp,
as humans—lovers of freedom, with human motivations.[84]

From the mid-1850s, the name "Dred" became a kind of shorthand to reference the Dismal Swamp maroons.[85] Every enslaved person was a potential
maroon, and every maroon now became a potential revolutionary. All the
while the population of the Great Dismal Swamp grew as people sought freedom there in increasing numbers.[86] Enslavers around the Dismal felt acutely
powerless to deal with the maroon threat. Harsh management and close supervision only pushed more people into the swamp.

Local laws did not stop the spike in marronage, and even the governor of
North Carolina admitted that he could do nothing about maroons. Governor
Thomas Bragg denied a petition begging for his support in hunting down
maroons in 1856. The petitioners lamented that professional "negro hunters"
demanded more of a premium than they could raise to pursue maroons into
swamps. The "bad and daring character" of the maroons and the danger to
everyone living near the swamp had made them almost untouchable. Bragg
lamented that his power only enabled him to offer rewards for those accused
of capital crimes who had fled the state.[87] The North Carolinians were stuck
with the maroons threatening from their frontier.

Less-frequent reports on maroons in and around the Dismal in the 1830s
and 1840s did not indicate the absence of maroons. The often-cited estimate
of 2,000 to 3,000 maroons in the Dismal posited in 1831 grew in one observer's
opinion to 40,000 by 1852.[88] A mother with her children in tow may have once
returned from the swamp to their former enslaver, and others here and there
may have been captured by slave hunters, but clearly hundreds if not thousands
remained. Even if movement into the swamp was curtailed (and that would

be difficult to determine), movement out was insignificant. That the Dismal Swamp maroon population was not decreasing, and may have actually be expanding, even through natural increase, was a truth that most whites could not speak. As the mystery of the swamp provided a foundation for abolitionist authors' heroic narratives, its dark stillness filled enslavers' nightmares. Even more than actual fringe raids from the swamp, the maroons' potential to mobilize into something devastating was what terrified whites. That abolitionist authors increasingly conjured just that image in their writings during this relatively quiet period only magnified and gave shape to enslavers' fears.

James Redpath hoped to help inflame this paranoia in 1859 when he published *The Roving Editor, or, Talks with Slaves in Southern States*. Redpath was a radical abolitionist who had been a reporter for Horace Greeley's *New York Tribune* in the 1850s. He had traveled through the South "to see slavery with my own eyes, and personally to learn what the bondmen said and thought of their condition." He also had a militant agenda to "aid the slave" by "disseminating discontentment" and preparing the way for a rebellion.[89] When warfare erupted in Kansas between pro- and antislavery forces, Redpath cut short his southern tour and went there. In the West he became a close confidant and publicist of John Brown.

Redpath's book was remarkable for several reasons in addition to his advocacy and insightful commentary on enslaved southerners. He privileged firsthand testimony by African Americans and went to great lengths to obtain it. In *The Roving Editor*, Redpath assures his readers that "the bondman has been enabled, in his own language . . . to 'define his position on the all-engrossing question of the day.' Almost everybody has done it. Why then, should not he?"[90] Redpath includes one of the most detailed firsthand accounts of Dismal Swamp maroon life known to exist, in a detailed interview with Charlie, a former maroon of five years.[91]

Redpath saves Charlie's singular story of Dismal Swamp life for the end of his book, where he includes his boldest condemnation of slavery. The abolitionist, perhaps as much as the paranoid southerners he mentions throughout, appreciated the revolutionary potential of maroons and marronage. "The hunted maroons," he wrote of those in the Dismal Swamp and the swamps of Florida, "hate slavery and the race that upholds it, and are longing for an opportunity to display that hatred."[92] The coming maroon war, which he hoped to foment by facilitating "extended combinations" among maroons and enslaved people, would stop American slavery dead in its tracks. In this they would be aided by the multitude of self-emancipated people then living in Canada, perhaps Charlie among them. Rather than expanding slavery's reach west as southerners desired, Redpath warned that "the South will soon find enough to do at home."[93]

Redpath was not just exploring the vague possibilities for the possible end of slavery. To his readers, he put the question directly: "Is insurrection possible? . . . Do you ask for a programme of action?" If so, the maroons had shown the way:

> The negroes and the Southrons have taught us. The slaves of the Dismal Swamp, the maroons of Florida, the free-state men of Kansas, have pointed out the method. The South committed suicide when it compelled the free squatters to resort to guerilla warfare, *and to study it both as a mode of subsistence and a science.* For the mountains, the swamps and morasses of the South, are peculiarly adapted to this mode of combat, and there are numbers of young men, trained to the art in the Kansas ravines, who are eager for an opportunity of avenging their slain comrades, on the real authors of their death, in the forests and plantations of the Carolinas and Georgia. *Will you aid them—will you sustain them? Are you in favor of a servile insurrection?*
>
> Tell God in acts.[94]

John Brown and the Great Dismal Swamp

Redpath dedicated *The Roving Editor* to another admirer of maroons—the most wanted man in America, John Brown. Brown had been a student of maroons and maroon warfare for decades (at least since his thirties).[95] His readings on maroons were, in the words of biographer David Reynolds, "deep," and he dreamed of someday creating a maroon community that would play a role in bringing down slavery in the United States. One of Brown's Kansas partisans remembered that the old man had studied every book on insurrectionary warfare available to him, with special attention to the guerrilla campaigns of maroons.[96] Thomas Wentworth Higginson, one of Brown's "Secret Six" supporters of the Harpers Ferry plot, recalled that Brown's original plan that he had laid out to him did not initially seek to raise enslaved people into revolt but rather "to get together bands and families of fugitive slaves" and to establish them in a maroon colony.[97]

Brown and Redpath shared a deep interest in the guerrilla tactics of the maroons of Haiti and Jamaica and the Seminoles in their wars against the United States. They also understood the Dismal Swamp to be both the greatest potential source of maroon guerrillas, a stronghold, and one of the best possible retreats on the Eastern Seaboard.[98] In fact, the timeline of their interactions

and development of a close relationship suggests that they may have spent considerable time discussing together the revolutionary potential of the Dismal
Swamp maroons.[99]

That the Dismal Swamp was at least a frequent topic of conversation for
Brown is evidenced by his sons' recollections of Brown's plans much later.[100]
Brown had also been a close friend of Willis Augustus Hodges, who had
worked alongside maroons and enslaved canal workers in the Dismal Swamp
in 1827, plotted his own Black rebellion in the Dismal Swamp that same year,
and later had been labeled "a second Nat Turner" for his agitation among
Dismal Swampers. After Hodges moved to New York in 1836, he published
some of Brown's antislavery writing in his newspaper *Ram's Horn*, and the
men were later neighbors in the New Elba community of the Adirondacks.[101]
It is hard to imagine that Brown's fascination with the Dismal Swamp never
came up in the conversations of these abolitionists. That Hodges burned all of
his correspondence with Brown following the failed raid on Harpers Ferry in
1859 suggests fascinating possibilities.[102]

For Harpers Ferry, Brown had considered using the Dismal Swamp as his
retreat after his first strike against the federal arsenal. His extensive knowledge of the swamp and its maroon inhabitants and reconnaissance he had done
while surveying in Virginia in 1840 convinced him that the swamp could be to
his forces what the Everglades had been to the Seminoles in their war against
the United States.[103] It is unclear if Brown really intended to retreat to the
Dismal after his initial strike at Harpers Ferry (Washington, Fredericksburg,
Richmond, and many days' march stood between it and the swamp), but there
were reports of a letter addressed (but mislaid and not delivered) to Brown
having been discovered in Suffolk, Virginia, just after the raid. The writer
assured Brown that "he had ninety armed men in the Dismal Swamp who
would be ready at any time to join him."[104] However, once Brown's raid began
to unravel and he shifted his strategy from building an army to antislavery
martyrdom, the Dismal obviously no longer figured in his plans. If an armed
force had awaited him there, it dispersed back into the swamp.

In the immediate aftermath of Brown's failed raid, editors north and south
brought up the swamp in their analysis of the event, and the Suffolk letter received wide coverage. Several papers published timelines of events leading up
to Harpers Ferry. In this coverage, the Dismal Swamp appeared over and over,
beginning with its rumored involvement in Nat Turner's uprising, serving as
a silent reminder of insurrection scares of the 1850s, the swamp's symbolism
and reputation in popular culture, and a partial explanation of John Brown
himself.[105] Even if Brown's retreat to the swamp seems unlikely to a modern

reader, white Virginians in the wake of Nat Turner had come to regard the swamp as a danger to the stability of their regime, to the point that in their estimation any abolitionist must have the Dismal as a target.

In April 1860, John Brown Jr. reminded the residents of the Dismal Swamp region how tenuous their lives and livelihoods were at the edge of the swamp. In a letter to the president of the Republic of Haiti that was republished in the United States, Brown's son expressed his thanks for the condolences Haitians had offered following his father's execution. For his part, Brown Jr. extended his sympathies at the death of their hero Toussaint Louverture in a French prison in 1803, and assured Haitians that the memory of both men would burn bright: "The mutilated body can disappear; but the soul survives it." Their legacy, he said, "visits the cabins of the slaves of the South when night is spread over the face of nature" and "finds an echo . . . among the pines of the Carolinas, in the Dismal Swamp, and upon the mountain tops, proclaiming that the despots of America shall yet know the strength of the toiler's arm, and that he who would be free must himself strike the first blow."[106]

White residents of the Dismal Swamp region knew that, as in 1831, they had dodged a bullet. In the wake of the Nat Turner rebellion, they could rest slightly easier in the knowledge that he had never intended to bring the Dismal Swamp maroons into his fight. That he *could have*, though, continued to strike terror in their hearts. Brown's intentions were less clear, yet his public statements and those of his supporters well in advance of the Harpers Ferry raid placed the Dismal within his potential insurrectionary plans.

The failure of Brown's revolt, like Turner's, only gave whites a brief respite. Three weeks after Harpers Ferry, a northern minister delivered a sermon, widely reprinted, that proclaimed Brown to have been a thoroughly rational tactician rather than, as others often accused him of being, a crazy fanatic: "It is no impossible feat to plant a permanent armed insurrection in Virginia. Within a few days' march of Harper's Ferry lies the Great Dismal Swamp, whose interior depths are for ever untrodden save by the feet of fugitive slaves. A few resolute white men, harbored in its deep recesses, raising the flag of slave revolt, would gather thousands to their standard, would convulse the whole State with panic, and make servile war one of the inseparable felicities of slavery." "Permanent and chronic" slave revolt, he knew, would cause slavery to "quickly bleed to death." Had Brown succeeded at Harpers Ferry, he could have "lodged" himself in the fastness of the Dismal while Tidewater slave society hemorrhaged.[107]

Of course, just as Brown did not need to have been successful to throw the South into a terror over the fate of slavery, neither did an army of Dismal

Swamp maroons need to pour forth from the swamp to help kill the institution. In the wake of John Brown's raid, abolitionist Edwin Wheelock came close to articulating the real power of the Dismal Swamp maroons in a historical parallel. Napoleon, he pointed out, when preparing for the invasion of England in 1808, did not expect to conquer his enemy solely on the battlefield. More than conquering, he would "ruin" England. "The mere presence of my troops on her coast," he quoted Napoleon as declaring, "whether defeated or not, will shake her government to the ground, and destroy her social system."[108] The maroons of the Dismal Swamp were helping to prosecute a war against slavery without even mounting a direct campaign to oppose it. Their very presence, existence, and resilience were eroding slavery from within.

Edmund Ruffin had long traded Dismal Swamp boosterism for secessionism by the time of John Brown's raid. As soon as he learned of the action at Harpers Ferry, Ruffin rushed to the site, obtained fifteen of the pikes with which Brown had intended to arm rebels, and mailed them to southern governors with the note "Sample of the favors designed for us by our Northern brethren."[109] Ruffin well knew what might have transpired if Brown had succeeded and taken his war to the Dismal Swamp. After all, he had written more extensively on the swamp than just about any other southerner, and had studied and republished William Byrd's eighteenth-century writings on it. The danger, as Byrd warned, that the Dismal would rise as a new Rome now seemed imminent. Although Ruffin did not specifically name the Dismal in his 1860 novel *Anticipations of the Future, to Serve as Lesson for the Present Time*, it would not have been hard for his readers to imagine the swamp playing a role in the future secession crisis of his story and as a source of "armies" of "fugitives" intent on bringing down slavery from within.[110] As he passed the Dismal by rail on his way to Charleston in 1861 to help start the Civil War and then again on his return to Virginia to take up arms and fight it, the swamp would likely have loomed large in his imagination.[111]

The Civil War

The Civil War was upon the Dismal Swamp region almost immediately, even before Ruffin had returned from Charleston. On April 20, 1861, US forces preemptively destroyed the Gosport (Norfolk) Navy Yard and eleven ships to prevent capture by Confederates, and reinforced the garrison at Fort Monroe (just north of Norfolk across Hampton Roads). Benjamin Ewell, commander of the Confederate forces in Norfolk, did not attempt to defend Hampton or take Fort Monroe but rather focused his attention on fortifying the peninsula. In early May, Confederates (including hundreds of enslaved laborers) began constructing batteries at Sewell's Point five miles north of the Dismal and directly south across the James River from Fort Monroe. Enslaved work crews were compelled to construct defensive batteries at no fewer than a dozen other Hampton Roads locations. Over a thousand African American workers performed the forced labor of sinking boats and small ships or constructing rafts across river mouths.[112]

As soon as US forces had a secure foothold in the Dismal region at Fort Monroe, some northern leaders urged policymakers to capitalize on the Dismal's at-the-ready maroon population. Samuel Gridley Howe, another of the "Secret Six" financial supporters of John Brown's Virginia operations, suggested to the governor of Massachusetts that he support an expedition made up predominantly of African Americans "to go into the Dismal and other swamps and raise the thousands of refugees there to go out and make sallies and onslaughts upon the enemy." At the very least, this might divert Confederate resources away from other campaigns, and possibly "cause a worse than Bull Run panic."[113]

Although Howe's proposals were not adopted, many from the enslaved and maroon populations he had hoped to engage were not waiting for an invitation to involve themselves in the war. In the flurry of activity in the first month of the conflict, enslaved people began seeking their freedom behind Union lines at Fort Monroe. When Confederate officers from Norfolk approached the fort under a flag of truce on May 11 and requested the return of their human property under the Fugitive Slave Law, the fort's commander ordered the enslaved people arrested and remanded to the officers. Less than two weeks later, though, Maj. Gen. Benjamin F. Butler assumed the command. When his troops brought him three men enslaved by Confederate officer Charles Mallory who had presented themselves to a reconnaissance expedition and testified that they were being forced to work for the Confederate military, Butler declared their return to Mallory as injurious to the US war effort. He refused to deliver them and declared the men "contraband of war." This would not be a one-off occurrence. Butler declared that he would "continue to receive and protect all negroes . . . who come to see [him]."[114]

News of Butler's novel policy spread quickly. One confidant of maroons in North Carolina remembered that "the declaration of emancipation echoed through the gloomy solitudes of the swamp."[115] By summer, nearly a thousand "contrabands" had made their way to Fort Monroe. One reporter wrote that "gangs of fugitive slaves in parties of twenty or thirty . . . have 'seceded' to Fortress Monroe, and General Butler has made the best possible use of an evil, and employed the able-bodied to work at the entrenchments while the women have been set to washing, cleaning, &c."[116] This was far from an emancipation proclamation, but it was a step closer to freedom, validated by Congress in the Confiscation Acts of 1861 and 1862 and ratified in fact by formerly enslaved people themselves, who continued to arrive at the fort by the thousands.

After the Confederate position at Hampton Roads became untenable in August (and after Confederate Brig. Gen. J. B. Magruder had determined it to be more and more "the harbor of runaway slaves and traitors"), their forces abandoned the area, burning much of it upon their retreat.[117] In Hampton's ruins, "contrabands" established the "Grand Contraband" (or "Slabtown") camp, which grew to house at least 10,000 formerly enslaved people by the end of the war.[118] Others gathered in Suffolk, including "a large number of negroes" whose origins, as described by US soldiers, were likely in the Dismal Swamp.[119] Still others marooned in place. Dismal Swamp Land Company managing agent Willis Riddick wrote with exasperation that "it is now impossible to employ hands at all. They are all free. Shall I continue to feed negros that will not work? We are in a terrible fix here."[120]

US forces were also consolidating their foothold south of the Dismal. By the second week of February 1862, they had retaken Roanoke Island, opening up their way into the Albemarle region. Three days later, they moved up the Pasquotank River toward the Dismal Swamp and took Elizabeth City. After learning that the Confederates were building ironclads in Norfolk, Maj. Gen. Ambrose E. Burnside dispatched an expedition to destroy the locks and cave in the banks of the Dismal Swamp Canal so the enemy could not reach the Albemarle Sound with these new ships.[121]

Confederates were able to turn back the Union advance at South Mills, the southern terminus of the Dismal Swamp Canal, and thus frustrated Burnside's objectives. However, the Battle of South Mills would be the last real Confederate victory of the war in the Dismal Swamp region. With Federal gunboats on the Pasquotank and North Landing Rivers (bottling up the other canal leading to Norfolk), and with US troops in control of Hampton Roads north of the swamp, Confederate forces abandoned Norfolk, Portsmouth, and Suffolk by the late spring of 1862.[122]

These engagements were the first time that many enslaved people on the North Carolina side of the swamp became aware that there was a war being fought around them. Fourteen-year-old John Nichols was enslaved at the foot of the Dismal in Pasquotank County by Dempsey Richardson. He was told by Richardson that the US soldiers were there to kidnap them to sell away to Cuban sugar plantations, but that "they would whip the Yankees in a very few weeks." John and other enslaved people had a different take on the imminent appearance of the US Army—"a chance to escape." News that passed through the Dismal grapevine telegraph that "great armies" were just on the other side of the swamp encouraged them "to make the attempt."[123]

Nearly 300 enslaved people were to meet a guide at the edge of the Dismal at midnight on the selected night "ready for the plunge into the swamp." When the guide did not show as planned (he had betrayed the group to whites in the vicinity who were then in pursuit), John's father, Jim Hinton, "who knew something about the swamp" assumed leadership, having already "planned the scheme to cross the great swamp." Hinton's intimate knowledge of paths through the area suggests that he may have been acquainted with maroons settled in that section of the swamp (which included the large "nameless" village). Starting in quickly at a "lumberman's trail," John's father led the group to an old canal that had fallen into misuse. They continued for another day alongside it.[124]

By the second day, the white patrol had nearly overtaken them, and many of the group decided to turn back, surrender themselves, and hopefully avoid the harshest punishment for their attempted escape. John, his father, and "a few of the boldest" continued on into the swamp. "Never did I run faster in my life," John would remember. For two more days they traversed the swamp northward, along the old canal until it joined with the Dismal Swamp Canal. They eventually emerged in Portsmouth, Virginia, presented themselves to Union pickets they encountered there, and "entered government service." The escape through the Dismal to Union lines was also a transition by which young John began to perceive himself "as a man and not as a slave."[125]

Although not all US troops were particularly sympathetic to the plight of self-emancipators they encountered, many were. Some, like S. Millett Thompson of the Thirteenth New Hampshire Volunteers, arrived at their posts in and around the Dismal Swamp as fully formed abolitionists with experience helping freedom-seekers along the Underground Railroad and a desire to continue such efforts in the swamp they had first encountered in the pages of Stowe's *Dred*.[126] Others upon embarking down the Dismal Swamp Canal for the first time could not help but reflect on "upon the sad fate of many an unfortunate slave who to avoid a master's lash had, in these dreary wilds passed many a long year." As maroons ventured out of the Dismal, trading animal-skin breeches for Union blues, D. J. Evans with the Third New York Cavalry took pleasure in the realization that "a more hospitable asylum is afforded them now within the Union."[127] Ohio soldier Billy Parr was eager to welcome Dismal

Swamp maroons into Union lines, especially since the latter had previously sheltered southern Virginia Unionists and Confederate draft-dodgers in the swamp prior to the arrival of US gunboats.[128]

With thousands of freedom-seekers converging on the Hampton Roads area, it was almost impossible for officers to keep an accurate count of "contrabands" in their retinue. Maroons, usually men, would occasionally approach Federal lines to take stock of conditions before returning with their families.[129] Others may have sent their families "to the fastness of the swamp for safety" before presenting themselves to US troops at Fort Monroe.[130] Gen. Edward Wild confirmed that maroons who came to him in his December 1863 operation through the Dismal were "impossible to count, as they were constantly coming and going."[131] It was just as hard to determine who was self-emancipating from nearby slave labor camps and who was emerging directly from the Dismal Swamp. At base, the distinction was not terribly important by 1861. Marronage was a process all new "contrabands" experienced and shared.

When records were kept, military officials took a census of incoming "contrabands" that recorded their places of birth, prior residence, occupation, physical description, and sometimes other details. Men and women who were known to have marooned for some time in the Dismal usually named their former place of enslavement, or place of birth, for identifying purposes.[132] In just one division of the United States Colored Troops Infantry (the Thirty-Sixth USCT), at least 401 African American soldiers claimed to have been from one of the North Carolina or Virginia counties that include parts of the Dismal Swamp.[133] A very few, like the remarkable Abraham Lester and his wife, Larinda White, actually named the swamp as their previous home.[134]

Large numbers of people who became "contrabands," including entire families, spent some amount of time marooned in and around the Dismal Swamp before presenting themselves to US troops at Fort Monroe, Roanoke Island, New Bern, and other Union-held camps.[135] Others, by their own testimony, had marooned in the swamp previously (some for years) before approaching the Union lines.[136] Abraham Lester's official acknowledgment that he had marooned nearly five years in the swamp was remarkable, but even more so was the experience of an unnamed maroon, described by a soldier of the Thirty-Ninth Illinois Volunteers as "a venerable negro sage, whose sands of life had nearly run out—whose locks were as white as the driven snow." This old man had marooned in the "safe haven" of the swamp since the Revolutionary War, at least eighty years. However, by January 1862, this swamp elder had entered Union lines in Suffolk. He had lived the life of a Dismal Swamp maroon longer than any other documented person, but, he said, "now that I have lived to see the freedom of my race, and to know that I am a free man, I am ready to quit this world and go up yonder." After a life of Dismal freedom, he would die on dry, free soil.[137]

Dismal Swamp maroons knew that contraband life was not easy, and they determined for themselves if continued life in the swamp or behind Union lines was preferable. They would seldom leave the swamp in large groups unless this was the recommendation of a community leader.[138] Contrabands were often put to hard work. "A large number of negroes" from the Dismal Swamp were described as "usefully employed on the works which were in process of construction," near Suffolk, including fortifications, roads, and other construction projects.[139] About fifty contrabands were put to work at the "famous Sylvester Farm" on the edge of the Dismal Swamp.[140] Lucy and Paul Wiggins, who, with their young daughter, Adeline, had been enslaved in Gates County, North Carolina, marooned in the swamp before coming out to join a contraband camp near Norfolk. Together, they worked on the confiscated Baker Farm just outside of the city.[141] If circumstances turned out worse than expected outside of the swamp (which often occurred), it was easy to disappear back into it (which many did).[142]

For some, another option was military service. Paul Wiggins, for example, transitioned from enslavement on a labor camp, to marronage in the Dismal, to a contraband farm, and eventually into the United States Colored Troops.[143] At Roanoke Island, contrabands were organized into the First North Carolina Colored Volunteer (NCCV) Regiment (and later, the Second and Third NCCV Regiments). In August 1863, the First and Second North Carolina were attached to the Fifty-Fifth Massachusetts and sent south, ultimately participating in coastal campaigns in South Carolina, Georgia, and Florida, where they fought with valor and distinction (even, and especially, when their white counterparts buckled under pressure).[144]

By December 1863, General Butler had organized 800 African American troops as the Tenth US Colored Volunteers and sent them south to North Carolina under abolitionist commander Edward Wild. This unit was tasked with engaging the enemy in and around the Great Dismal Swamp, and recruiting more local "contrabands," including ones from within the swamp, to join them.[145] When they returned at the end of the month they numbered 700 more soldiers than when they had left, and had freed approximately 2,500 enslaved people. Wild, with a soft nod to John Brown, believed that if he could control the Dismal, he might attract the full support of its occupants: "great numbers of blacks . . . yet undrained, almost untouched."[146] Companies

A–L of the First Colored Cavalry and A–M of the Second, and the Thirty-Sixth, Thirty-Seventh, and Thirty-Eighth Regiments Colored Infantry were also organized to include African American soldiers from the Dismal Swamp and surrounding region. All units distinguished themselves in combat and conduct.[147]

Many other maroons served the war effort in less official capacities. Many former Dismal Swamp maroons worked for the Commissary Department in and around Norfolk. Billy Parr recalled that of the 200 "escaped slaves" he employed at Portsmouth, many originated in the swamp. These workers unloaded supplies from incoming ships, sometimes until very late at night.[148] After the Confederate evacuation of Norfolk, 100 Dismal Swamp "contrabands," including at least several who had marooned for years in the swamp, served as a labor crew to clear the North River and Dismal Swamp Canal of impediments and vessels sunk by Confederates as well as to destroy abandoned Confederate fortifications. The completion of their efforts opened a direct link between Fort Monroe and New Bern, North Carolina, and finally linked Burnside's forces with those northward. It also connected large gathering places for contrabands.[149] Five other Dismal Swamp maroons "presented themselves fearlessly" to a detachment of the Ninth New York Volunteers also working to clear the Dismal Swamp Canal (and others, they noted, had done so previously). At least one of the maroons had lived in the swamp for seven years, having "succeeded in baffling the bloodhounds." They were immediately put to work as auxiliary laborers, but perhaps their greatest usefulness was their ability to channel "that unexplained and mysterious system used for spreading information, known only to themselves and which no white man has yet been able to discover."[150] Two maroons who had "been in the swamps for five years" presented themselves to Burnside in March 1862 and were tasked with a range of labors within the camp.[151] Several Dismal Swamp maroons attached themselves to a passing cavalry company from Iowa on the northwestern fringe of the swamp in the spring of 1862 and provided valuable information on the best methods and locations to hunt in the swamp, especially for "impudent" feral hogs that might be a tasty addition to standard hardtack fare.[152] Emmett Ruffin, who had been an enslaved swamp worker when the war broke out, marooned not long thereafter and eventually served the US forces in the swamp as a wagon driver along the canal road.[153]

Dismal Swampers were also some of the most skilled guides and scouts in the region. Willis Augustus Hodges, the former farmer and Dismal Swamp Canal worker who had concocted at least two plots for mass emancipations of enslaved people and been run out of Princess Anne County in 1842, returned to his Dismal Swamp home from New York in May 1862 and served as a Union scout.[154] Embittered white locals remembered Hodges as "one of the most incendiary negroes that has ever cursed this section."[155] However, historian Richard Lowe calls Hodges "an invaluable resource for Federal units stationed around Norfolk" and a man who "made life miserable for some of the same men who had persecuted his family when he was a teenager."[156] Whites may have once feared Willis's developing into a "second Nat Turner," but in his new capacity, the army at Hodges's back would, in fact, cripple slavery.[157] William Kinnegy served as a scout after having been a maroon for five years.[158] A Massachusetts regiment posted in Norfolk kept a "corps contraband" of five Dismal Swamp scouts at the ready for guidance when they had to venture into or through the swamp.[159] George, who had been marooned in the "woods" at the edge of the Dismal, declared white US soldiers to be not "enough for the business" of finding their way through the swamp. He swore a loyalty oath and offered himself as their scout into the Dismal to capture Confederate guerrillas hiding there.[160]

By the summer of 1862, the Dismal Swamp and its hinterland fringes were clear of organized Confederate forces. US troops now controlled the territory at the northern and southern ends of the Dismal (Norfolk and Roanoke Island). However, guerrilla fighting would continue in and around the Dismal, and for the rest of the conflict warfare in the region was "more irregular, less predictable, meaner."[161] In one former Confederate's words, it was "a war without armies . . . one long, weary, suspicious, frightful watch, surprise, and reality."[162] A young US soldier later remembered passing through the swamp on a ship outfitted with a Gatling gun in case of sniping from the swamp along the canal. "It is my impression," he wrote, "that the enemy that we had to consider in the swamp did not, at least at this time, include any regular troops."[163] A war correspondent from Richmond wrote that the irregular swamp forces comprised "from five to six hundred negroes, who are not in the regular military organization of the yankees, but who, outlawed and disowned by their masters, lead the lives of banditti, roving the country with fire and committing all sorts of horrible crimes upon the inhabitants."[164]

The loyalties of whites in the region were always uncertain, often shifting week to week and depending on who was doing the asking. One Elizabeth City man remembered that "your nearest neighbor was often your truest and cruelest enemy."[165] North Carolina's governor felt the need to shore up loyalty by officially encouraging Confederate guerrillas to harass Federal troops and African Americans in and around the swamp, and to assassinate Unionists, Black and white.[166] African Americans, though, understood the high stakes of the war and defended and retaliated against Confederate guerrillas with great energy. Outfits made up of Confederate deserters, white Unionists, and local Black fighters ("stray darkies," in one soldier's recollection), were called Buffaloes (or "Buffs"). These units undertook strategic guerrilla attacks on those they believed to be "secesh" and often engaged with local home guard units.[167]

One of the most active Buffalo units was led by a Confederate deserter named John A. "Jack" Fairless. After being publicly shamed and having half of his head shaved for stealing supplies from his unit, Fairless deserted the Confederates, fled to the Chowan, Gates, and Perquimans County area of the Dismal, and there recruited at least 100 people, including "a company of armed negroes" from the swamp that a white woman described as "deamons."[168] Fairless's band was organized officially as Company E of the North Carolina United States Infantry.[169] Their headquarters was Wingfield Plantation, on the banks of the Chowan River at the southern end of the Dismal, the former home of outspoken secessionist Richard Dillard.[170] From there, Fairless's Buffaloes harassed Confederates and their home guard, while also encouraging hundreds of "contrabands" to "find freedom" under his command and protection. Enslaved people in North Carolina flocked "boldly to them in large numbers."[171] Fairless announced his intention to "clear the county of every slave," and Company E apparently had made progress toward that goal when it had to abandon its stronghold before James Longstreet's advancing forces in the spring of 1863.[172] Still, Company E managed an escape on US gunboats and left the Confederates a taunting note: "A leetle too late."[173]

The Confederates were always "a leetle too late" in the Dismal. Everywhere regular or irregular US troops went in the Dismal they did what injury they could to the old order and cleared a way for a new one. Pro-Confederate North Carolinians of the Dismal Swamp region would long remember 1863, the height of Buffalo activity, as the year of "THE BLACK FLAG . . . the dark year in the history of the Civil War." Compared to the Dismal region, with its wrath of white Unionists, contrabands in Federal uniforms, and swamp maroons "ready to spring upon us from covert," one man declared "the battlefields of Northern Virginia [to be] havens of rest and happiness," and Gettysburg "child's play."[174] A North Carolina editor advised his readers that "the fiat seems to have gone forth for stern and terrible work on the North Carolina frontier, in this dark and melancholy country of swamps, overrun with negro banditti, and now the especial theatre of the war's vengeance."[175]

By 1864, Buffaloes, maroons, and contrabands had effectively brought the Civil War to an end in the Dismal Swamp region. Edward Wild had proclaimed to the citizens of Currituck, Pasquotank, Perquimans, Gates, and

Chowan Counties that "you will never have any rest from us so long as you keep guerillas within your borders. It will be for your interest, therefore, to exert yourselves actively in driving them out." Moreover, he pointed out that "all slaves are now at liberty to go where they please, or stay. By assisting them on their way with food and transportation, you can save yourselves the necessity of visitations from the colored troops."[176] Supplying maroons and contrabands may have been a step too far for many white residents of the Dismal Swamp region, but delegations from those five counties grudgingly drafted resolutions to resist Confederate conscription and to expel all irregular guerrilla troops in their vicinity. Another group of 523 Pasquotank County residents petitioned Governor Zebulon Vance to disband all guerrilla units operating inside of the Chowan River.[177] Secessionists in and around the Dismal had quite literally been "overrun with negro banditti," as one Virginian put it.[178]

With hostilities under control from the Suffolk Scarp to the east, Buffaloes looked out from the swamp to the west in 1864. The region beyond the Dismal was also one of the most important sources of meat and supplies for the Confederate army in its fighting around Richmond. A secessionist journalist lamented the frequent "negro raids" on beef stocks by maroons traversing out of the Dismal.[179] These were not small groups but reported to be armies of 500 to 600 maroons (along with some Confederate deserters) "roving the country with fire and committing all sorts of horrible crimes upon the inhabitants," including cutting off the supply of beef to Confederate troops.[180] Confederate desertions had been rising as the war entered its late stages, but in late 1864 and early 1865 they had become "amazingly numerous." A Confederate field officer in Virginia wrote to Gen. Joseph Finegan that "in my opinion, the controlling influence that prompts our men thus to desert—. . . is the insufficiency of rations. Our men do not get enough to eat."[181] Another Confederate soldier writing from the front lines in late January 1865 knew why his fellow soldiers were abandoning the cause: "The reason they don't feed us any better may be that thay can not getit. . . . Our men can not and will not stand it much longer."[182]

In fact, they did not have to stand it much longer. With the lifelines to Richmond cut off, due at least in some part to the efforts of maroon irregulars and Union forces besieging the city, President Jefferson Davis and his cabinet abandoned the capital on April 2.

In the final months of the war that was already long lost, Confederate leaders debated what would have seemed unthinkable earlier in the conflict: the arming and freeing of African Americans in a desperate measure to hold off defeat. Robert E. Lee announced, "We must decide whether slavery shall be extinguished by our enemies and the slaves be used against us, or use them ourselves." Jefferson Davis concurred in the necessity, though others disagreed. Gen. Howell Cobb asserted that "if slaves will make good soldiers, our whole theory of slavery is wrong."[183] Lee's view of the necessity of arming African Americans ultimately swayed the Confederate Congress, which voted in March to implement such a policy.[184]

Dismal Swamp maroons knew who their enemy was. There was little chance that they saw anything that could be gained from an alliance with their enslavers. Indeed, the maroons were already free, already armed, and had been pouring forth from the swamp for years to aid the cause of emancipation. Two hundred years of marronage in the Dismal had already given Howell Cobb his answer. Maroons *were* good soldiers, and whites' whole theory of slavery *was* wrong.

Interestingly, to the chorus of opposition ringing out in the South, a new northern voice fearful of the Dismal Swamp maroons emerged during this debate. Although Haiti had always haunted enslavers, northerners began to panic now at the thought of what a similar Black army might actually accomplish in the American South. The fear was not so much that Davis and Lee's plan might work but that the policy, "like an exploding shell, will scatter its dangers in various directions." Already, vocal northerners were expressing their doubts about the reconstruction of the nation that must follow the war. If the South freed its enslaved people and armed them, they would undoubtedly demand the rights of citizens. Whites would then flee the South to avoid looking African Americans in the eye as equals, leaving millions of formerly enslaved people in control of the former Confederacy. Faced with this possibility, the editors of the *Chicago Tribune*, among others, implored all northerners to "put their shoulders to the wheel" and unite in a final push to defeat the Confederacy before the South's radical plan could be implemented. If not, maroons, contrabands, Black men, women, and children—now all free—in addition to an actual southern Black army that could easily outnumber their white counterparts, might unite "in prophetic vision a BLACK REPUBLIC from the Dismal Swamp to the Gulf of Mexico."[185]

The Great American Maroon Army never formed in the crumbling South. A month after the Confederate Congress authorized Black enlistments, and before any steps could be taken to carry out the scheme, Lee surrendered his Army of Northern Virginia. The last cannon had thundered in the Dismal Swamp long before that. Those Tidewater enslavers who had whipped them, sold them "running," hunted them with dogs, and fought a fruitless war against marronage for generations had been routed in the swamp by many of those same maroons.

In the Civil War, the Dismal Swamp had finally become the source of power enslavers always feared it might. Thousands of formerly enslaved people became the maroons their enslavers always knew lurked beneath the surface. Maroons became the liberators outsiders always thought they were, fighting their enslavers face to face on battlefields from the Dismal to Louisiana, Florida, and places between.

It was bittersweet news when word reached the depths of the swamp that the war was over and that slavery was dead. Many maroons had lived their entire lives in the Dismal and wondered what their next steps would be. Some long-established maroon communities left the swamp all together as soon as they "heard the news that the n—s all belonged to themselves now." They began to actively look for work, sought out direction on how to use new technology that had been developed while they had marooned, and, in many cases, kept alive the memory of loved ones who had not lived to see freedom on the outside.[186] Many ventured out of the swamp only warily, having been "outlawed" during their enslavement and not knowing if prices were still set on their heads.[187]

Some maroons returned to their swamp communities triumphantly after having been mustered out of service. Maybe Osman or Bob Ricks returned to the Dismal with a blue kepi and government issue rifle. Perhaps George and Washington, who not only marooned together to the Virginia side of the Dismal but were linked by their names to a white enslaver defeated by the swamp long before, brought home stories of service in Edward Wild's "African Brigade."[188] John Nichols, who had marooned in the Dismal before his enlistment in Union service, wanted to return to his old slave labor camp to stand before those who had enslaved him with "a pride in showing myself to them as a man and not as a slave." Nichols declared his earnest desire "to go once more in the Dismal Swamp," where his free manhood had begun.[189]

In the fall of 1863, a young US soldier wrote a letter to his former professor back at Oberlin College. The soldier, who identified himself only as "G" in his letter, had been tasked with taking a census of the freedmen on Craney Island, near Norfolk, Virginia. As G related, the simple chore of tallying newcomers quickly transformed into a fascinating afternoon of storytelling when the soldier encountered a family of African Americans and the head of their household, the forty-six-year-old Abraham Lester.[190]

After quickly noting his subjects' names and ages, the student-soldier moved on to a more detailed set of queries, the answers to which, up until that point, had varied little among his respondents. Abraham, however, piqued his interest with his answer to the first of these questions.

"How long have you been from home?" the soldier asked. This was a variant on the question listed on G's tally sheet, "How long have you been in our lines?" Other census takers had often encountered "contrabands" who did not fully understand what was meant by the question, and this simplified version assumed that their presence among Union troops dated from approximately the time they left "home"—that is, their former enslavers.

Without hesitation, Lester replied, "Four years." This, however, predated the commencement of the war itself. G tried to clarify himself. "How long have you been with the Union Army?" "Ever since they came to Suffolk," Lester replied. "I was in the Dismal Swamp three years, and when I heard that the Army had come to Suffolk, I went to them, and have been with them ever since."

Abraham Lester had understood the question perfectly, and only slowly did G realize that the family before him were maroons. Hailing as he did from Oberlin, the soldier would have undoubtedly read about the Dismal Swamp maroons in one of the antislavery publications that circulated freely in that hotbed of abolitionism. This was a story his professors and classmates back home would want to hear about. G sat down with the maroon family and took careful notes.

Abraham had been enslaved by a Thomas Menkins, a brutal man whose enslaved people frequently marooned. Faced with a beating for a minor transgression, Lester followed their example and marooned in the Dismal around Christmas 1857. He lived on the bounty of the swamp with his wife, Larinda, whom he met and married there. They lived in several different parts of the swamp in "huts" or "cabins," worked with enslaved shingle workers for a share of their pay, traded fish for other supplies, and shared their surplus food with other maroons in their community who needed it. When slave hunters would "drive the swamp" looking for runaways, Abraham's community would take extra precautions to remain secure and hidden, so their settlement was never discovered. He was also aware that his was but one of many maroon settlements in the swamp. His community was well connected to a cross-swamp grapevine between maroon settlements and reaching to slave labor camps across the Tidewater.

Abraham and his wife had at least one child while together in the swamp. However, he also gave G a list of seven children then with him on Craney

Island, some of whom were far too old to be children of Larinda White. "O, I have two wives," he said candidly. His first wife and family, separated during slavery, had been reunited with him in the contraband camp, and Abraham said that he "had done the best I could to take care of them; it has been pretty hard scratching, but I have got along so far."

It became clear that the final agony of the Civil War was perhaps the least of the worries that would burden these now-former maroons and others like them. Still a bit skittish at the sight of whites with guns after so many years in the swamp, they would have to wrestle with uncertainties in addition to the still-ambiguous meaning of freedom: how to parent a "wild child" who had never seen a white face, how to retrain one's feet to tread upon solid dry ground, how to live alongside those who had once sent snarling bloodhounds into the swamp on their trail.

Dismal freedom for maroons in the swamp had come with few assurances. Their new freedom was in an unpredictable and unprecedented new world. The only certainties (at least for these former maroons) were the marks recorded in the young soldier's notebook before he continued his census of the island: Abraham Lester and family—Great Dismal Swamp—freedmen.

From Dismal Freedom
to the Free Dismal

TO MAROONS, freedom, even Dismal freedom in one of the most treacherous swamps in North America, was preferable to a life of enslavement. Over ten generations, thousands of them sought it relentlessly and defended it constantly. Their self-extrication from enslavement in favor of exile in the wilderness among snakes and bears was, by itself, a most powerful indictment of slavery and its ideological underpinnings.

They made Dismal freedom into whatever they wanted it to be, and refused to be limited by others' definitions of freedom. The swamp and marronage offered freedom to temporarily lay out for days or weeks, freedom to maintain family connections, freedom to plot and organize, freedom to continue along in a journey to a northern state or Canada, or freedom to permanently disappear into the deepest recesses of the Dismal.

When the Civil War ushered in legal freedom, Dismal Swampers continued to define freedom on their own terms. Many left the swamp (some for the first time in their lives) to see what possibilities the new world outside held for them. As they had previously, they made a way where no way had existed before. It is unlikely that many maroons had read Lord Byron's poetry or the writings of abolitionists who loved to quote him, but they would have understood the truth of his verse "Hereditary bondsmen! Know ye not / Who would be free themselves must strike the blow?" For them, there was no need to ask the question. Former residents of the swamp did not consider themselves rescued, or redeemed. Making a living, in the most literal sense, had been their all-encompassing task, and their wages in the swamp were hard-earned. They had become free in the swamp entirely through their own efforts, and despite great odds.

When they left the swamp, they knew that they had earned the *new* freedom awaiting them as well. A New York soldier posted at the Dismal during the Civil War seemed surprised when maroons from the swamp did not express what he believed was an appropriate level of gratitude for their reception into Union lines. Observing contrabands was usually "great fun" for John Habberton, but these particular Dismal Swampers who decided to cast their lot with the US Army were less entertaining. "There was nothing funny about these colored people unless it was their extreme gravity. They weren't even excitable," he remembered. If anything, they were rather solemn. Habberton was perplexed: "They didn't throw up their hands and thank the Lord that at last they were on freedom's soil."[1] But that thanksgiving had most likely already occurred, and they had been "on freedom's soil," or at least in freedom's swamp, by their own courageous efforts, for some time already.

After the war, most former residents of the Dismal Swamp remained nearby. Some had become so attached to swamp life that they never left it and continued to work, now on the books, for the forest industries on the swamp's edges. A 1900 interview with a former maroon noted that "hundreds of human beings . . . negroes, known locally as 'swampers,'" still lived in the swamp, "out of sight or sound of civilization . . . in the employ of the lumber operators."[2] In the 1880s, a naval expedition on the Dismal Swamp Canal reported encountering "families of Negroes completely isolated from the outer world, and evidently the descendants of runaway slaves, once so numerous in the wilds."[3] At the "nameless" site deep in the North Carolina swamp, archaeologists have found evidence of human presence dating from the Middle Woodland period (ca. 200 BCE–500 CE), through the Civil War, and into the twentieth century.[4] The *spirit* of marronage lived on in the Dismal as well. In 1900, the swamp was reported to still offer sanctuary to African Americans on the "wrong" side of the law: "Negro fugitives from justice find the isolation and solitude of the camps safe refuge, for, unless their offense is serious, they are seldom followed thither."[5]

"Uncle Alek" Keeling, one of the most trusted allies and a minister to countless maroons, delivered mail between Virginia and North Carolina along the Dismal Swamp Canal and continued to preach the Gospel. He had become a local celebrity of sorts after David Hunter Strother published his sketch portrait in *Harper's* in 1856. In 1876, he traveled to Philadelphia to attend the Centennial Exhibition, thinking it quite appropriate since he believed he had been born on July 4, 1776. By the time he "lay down and died" at the age of 104, he had "preached the gospel to thousands of his fellow men" and "carried with him the esteem of all who knew him, both white and colored."[6]

Even more famous was the sketch Strother had made of Osman, a maroon he encountered deep in the Dismal off the Jericho Canal. Postwar, Osman Hunter; his wife, Hester; and their family settled in the closest town to their former swamp home, Portsmouth, Virginia.[7] They may have known each other

"Uncle" Bob Garry as a young man hunting bear in the Dismal, and in his old age. From "The Dismal Swamp," *Monmouth Inquirer*, January 22, 1903.

in the swamp, but Osman's family and that of Abraham Lester undoubt-ably swapped stories of "Dismal freedom" as neighbors—their houses sat just blocks apart. Willis Augustus Hodges, former Dismal Swamp Canal digger and alleged "second Nat Turner," followed his service as a Union scout as a delegate to the 1867–68 Virginia Constitutional Convention, where an embit-tered former Confederate remembered he "held sway and lorded it over the good people of the commonwealth."[8] "Uncle" Bob Garry, born into marronage in the Virginia sector of the swamp in 1820, renowned for his bear-hunting skills and relationships across the swamp and beyond, married in 1870 and established his household on the North Carolina side of the Dismal. In his eighties, he was still active as a farmer. In 1907, he guessed that he was "the oldest swamper in the world."[9] He may well have been.

Others ended up far from where they began. Charlie, who marooned with enslaved shingle workers, hunted boar and cattle in the swamp, and had been ministered to there by maroon preacher Toby Fisher, eventually moved on to freedom in Canada. There, he dictated his remarkable story to an abolitionist, who in turn got it into the hands of a US publisher. Moses Grandy traded swamp life for residence in Rhode Island and later Massachusetts. Other former residents of the Dismal, unnamed in the sources unfortunately, eventually joined communities in Delaware, Pennsylvania, and New York, among other northern states.

Yet how many other Dismal Swamp maroons shared the experience of "Long Davy" Coston, who marooned in the Dismal for half a century? He had escaped to the swamp some time before 1817, shared it with Mingo, Pompey Little, Ned Downs, Bob Ferebee, Bob Ricks, Charlie, Osman, and countless others, successfully avoided "runaway ketchers," and enjoyed a life of freedom unimaginable back on the slave labor camp from which he had escaped.

Suffolk resident Robert Arnold met Davy on his way *back* into the Dismal not long after the war. Arnold had struck up a friendly conversation on the road with the old man and casually asked him where he called home. To Davy, though, it was a "hard question," and required a much more complicated answer than one might have anticipated. The old man paused, pondered the question some more, and invited Arnold to take a seat beside him so that he could give a good and thorough answer. It would take a while.

Davy asked for some tobacco, packed his old corn cob pipe, and began to smoke it while recounting to Arnold the circumstances of his marronage. He had killed a white man in a fight over some food, and on the recommendation of his father, he fled to the Dismal Swamp.

"'I tell you, boss,' he said, 'when you get in the desert, if nobody sees nothing, the runaway catchers can't catch you.'"

There he stayed for decades, making a new life as a free man disconnected from the outside world, where a hangman's noose awaited him.

"'I stayed there until the war was over,' he said. 'I came out and have been looking about this place to see if I knew anybody, but they are all gone dead, and nobody knows me . . . I am very old now, and my home folks are all dead and gone and I know nobody.'"[10]

Davy was heading *back* into the Great Dismal Swamp, the only real home he had ever known, to live out his remaining days in glorious Dismal freedom.

ACKNOWLEDGMENTS

I FIRST LEARNED of the maroons of the Great Dismal Swamp, oddly enough, as I wasted time in the undergraduate library when I should have been studying for my first semester of law school exams. Rebellious self-emancipating men and women were much more interesting to me than contracts, torts, civil procedure, and the like. I ended up doing quite well on the exams—won an award even—but immediately thereafter began drafting what would become my graduate school admissions essay. It was a ridiculous document, written in the purple prose of an English literature major, that laid out my desires to study maroons, pirates, swamps, borderlands, and other liminal spaces, people, and things (although I didn't use the word *liminal*—I didn't know it yet). Cornell University took a chance on me, and I packed up my Jeep, cat, and the couple dozen books that I owned at the time and left South Carolina for the cold north.

I took a directed readings course on the topic of marronage, wrote my first grad school essay on the maroons of the Great Dismal Swamp in Jon Parmenter's Early America seminar, and gave a version of that paper at a conference in Norfolk, Virginia. That paper became the first publication line on my CV when the conference's organizers edited a collection of papers from the symposium. When I first visited the Dismal Swamp the afternoon of the conference, I could feel the history all around me, hidden in the thick forest and black waters. I knew that I was standing in a sacred spot. I left the swamp that day still fascinated by the history of which I had only scratched the surface, and miserably certain that I did not yet possess the research skills to proceed much further in telling the story of people who endeavored to remain concealed, even to this ambitious but green researcher.

So I left the swamp and its maroon history behind. I moved on to a project with whole archives related to it, meticulous documentation, and, among those people whom I would research, an awareness (even enthusiasm) that their written record would inform their place in history.

But the swamp was not done with me. As I moved from office to office, book project to book project, I maintained an always-growing box of research notes marked with a bold "GDS" on the side. As I had many years before, I would frequently steal time from other projects to scan an index for "maroons" here, to run a text search for "Dismal" there. The circle of scholars who had done any work on the maroons of the Dismal remained very small, and we were often brought together to discuss the topic—in documentary films, conferences, and interviews—enough to keep the Dismal from falling off of my radar.

At one of these events, I first met Daniel Sayers, then a grad student at William and Mary, who asked if I'd be interested in being part of an NEH grant proposal he was putting together to support research and archaeological fieldwork on the Dismal Swamp maroons. I was, and the grant funded a team of researchers for the next four years. My box of research notes became two boxes, then three, then became a towering, overflowing pile in a corner of my office. My constant Dismal Swamp research slowed my progress on three other books that would have all been far better, and to press much faster, if the pull of the Dismal hadn't been so strong.

To Jon Parmenter, Imtiaz Habib, Richard Green, Dan Sayers, Cassandra Newby-Alexander, and others who kept bringing me back, thank you. Thanks also to others who read all or parts of this and much earlier drafts, or who offered their insight in discussions on the Dismal, marronage, and resistance. You've all made this final version better than I could have myself. In particular (and in addition to those already named), Karl Austin, Ed Baptist, Rich Bodek, Vernon Burton, Sylviane Diouf, Walter Edgar, Doug Egerton, Kori Green, Graham Hodges, Carolyn Finney, Kathryn Benjamin Golden, Joe Kelly, Jane Landers, Dan Littlefield, Ted Maris-Wolf, Daisy Martin, Marcus Nevius, Christy Hyman, Maggi Morehouse, Richard Price, Jordan Riccio, Manisha Sinha, James Spady, Darrell Stover, Sue Taylor, Margaret Washington, Peter H. Wood, and the students in my History of Slavery and African American History classes at USC Aiken and USC Beaufort helped shape this project in their own important ways. The frank assessments, critiques, and suggestions of the anonymous readers to whom UNC Press sent my various proposals and drafts were also invaluable.

The staffs of the North Carolina State Archives, the Albert and Shirley Small Special Collections at the University of Virginia, the David M. Rubenstein Rare Book and Manuscript Library at Duke University, the Southern Historical Collection at the University of North Carolina, the Special Collections Research Center at the College of William and Mary, the Norfolk Public Library, the Oberlin College Archives, and the Library of Virginia offered tremendous assistance in my endeavors, and helped make my short and scattered research trips over sixteen years as efficient as they could have possibly been. The interlibrary loan staffs at USCB, USCA, and Cornell University kept rare and hard-to-find books at my fingertips.

I am grateful for generous financial support from the National Endowment for the Humanities, the University of South Carolina Institute for African

American Research, the University of South Carolina Institute for Southern Studies, University of South Carolina (RISE), and the USCB faculty development committee.

The staff at UNC Press once again showed why they are the best in the university publishing business. My editor, Brandon Proia, was another one of those folks who kept bringing me back to this project over the years, and who intrepidly guided it through peer review and the publication process. Alex Martin's copyediting saved me from some embarrassing mistakes and helped tighten my prose throughout.

I've already mentioned some of Dan Sayers's contributions (and my intellectual debt to him should be apparent in the main body of this book), but I would be remiss if I did not make it clear that I could not have written this book without his assistance and guidance. By bringing me on as the historian in the Great Dismal Swamp Landscape Study, he gave me access to the archaeological work that allowed me to fill otherwise unbridgeable gaps in the documentary record. He brought me into the Dismal itself and directly to the site of one of the swamp's maroon settlements, allowed me to be a part of his 2012 field school, and helped me make this a truly interdisciplinary study. Satisfying the Press's anonymous readers and hopefully impressing book reviewers to come was and is very important to me, but Daniel O. Sayers's enthusiastic approval of the manuscript is the one thing I would not have proceeded to this point without.

In the Dismal Swamp, every footstep is uncertain. My family, however, has been my rock as I trudged through this project. My wife sent me off into the swamp several times certain that I would return snake-bitten and close to death. The yellow flies in June turned out to be the biggest danger for me, but I sincerely thank Kim for letting me do what I had to do to make this story more real. Her concern apparently rubbed off on my son, who has grown up hearing me tell stories about the Dismal. Before one trip to the swamp (Daegan may have been five or six?), he slipped a handwritten note into one of my pockets: *"don't evr go into a sawmp. They stinc an ar dangrs."* My daughter, Millie, was ten feet away from me as I drafted this manuscript during the COVID pandemic and lockdown of 2020. As it turns out, supervising remote learning for the kids while writing a book may not be the most efficient way to get things done, but there's a little bit of her in every page, and I love that.

JBM
Beaufort, SC
April 12, 2021

NOTES

INTRODUCTION

1. See Edmund Jackson, "The Effects of Slavery," in *The Liberty Bell* (Boston: Massachusetts Anti-slavery Fair, 1842), 39–43; Edmund Jackson, "The Fugitive," in *The Liberty Bell* (Boston: National Anti-slavery Bazaar, 1847), 5–15; Edmund Jackson, "Servile Insurrections," in *The Liberty Bell* (Boston: National Anti-slavery Bazaar, 1851), 158–64.

2. Edmund Jackson, "The Virginia Maroons," in *The Liberty Bell* (Boston: Prentiss and Sawyer, 1852), 146.

3. Fred Hardesty, "The Great Dismal Swamp," *Raleigh News and Observer*, September 11, 1966.

4. "Porte Crayon" (David Hunter Strother), "In the Dismal Swamp," *Harper's New Monthly Magazine* 13, no. 73 (June 1856): 453.

5. "An Account of the Great Dismal Swamp," *Philadelphia Literary Magazine*, March 1805, in *Merrimack Magazine and Ladies' Literary Cabinet*, May 31, 1806, 167.

6. "The Dismal Swamp," *Forest and Stream* 5, no. 23 (January 13, 1876): 353.

7. See Richard Bodek and Joseph Kelly, introduction to *Maroons and the Marooned: Runaways and Castaways in the Americas*, ed. Richard Bodek and Joseph Kelly, xi–xii (Jackson: University Press of Mississippi, 2000).

8. Marcus P. Nevius, "New Histories of Marronage in the Anglo-Atlantic World and Early North America," *History Compass* 18, no. 5 (May 2020), https://doi.org/10.1111/hic3.12613.

9. Richard Price, *Maroon Societies: Rebel Slave Communities in the Americas* (Baltimore: Johns Hopkins University Press, 1996), 3; Alvin O. Thompson, *Flight to Freedom: African Runaways and Maroons in the Americas* (Kingston, Jamaica: University of the West Indies Press, 2006), 53.

10. Price, *Maroon Societies*, 105.

11. Referenced in Thompson, *Flight to Freedom*, 56–57.

12. See Thompson, 54.

13. James Spady, "Belonging and Alienation: Gullah Jack and Some Maroon Dimensions of the 'Denmark Vesey Conspiracy,'" in Bodek and Kelly, *Maroons and the Marooned*, 31–32, 48–49.

14. Thompson, *Flight to Freedom*, 58.

15. Neil Roberts, *Freedom as Marronage* (Chicago: University of Chicago Press, 2015), 10–11.

16. Daniel O. Sayers, *A Desolate Place for a Defiant People: The Archaeology of Maroons, Indigenous Americans, and Enslaved Laborers in the Great Dismal Swamp* (Gainesville: University Press of Florida, 2014), 79–80, 105–10.

17. Sylviane A. Diouf, *Slavery's Exiles: The Story of the American Maroons* (New York: New York University Press, 2014), 11.

18. See, for example, Bland Simpson, *The Great Dismal: A Swamp Memoir* (Chapel Hill: University of North Carolina Press, 1990), 76. Simpson is representative of the skeptics. In an otherwise marvelous book about the Great Dismal Swamp, he reads the apparent dearth of documentation of marronage as evidence that maroons did not inhabit the swamp in any appreciable numbers. Instead, he suggests they almost always lived "in the horror of desperation in clawed-out camps, in lightning burnt patches." This leads him to assume maroons lived in scattered, disorganized, small groups (if even in groups—Simpson suggests that most Dismal Swamp maroons were lone refugees). Although "a few of them managed a little Swamp society . . . any notion of reconstructed African villages springing up whole and happy in the Great Dismal before the War—the dreamy vision of a recent scholar—seems fantasy run away." Simpson misunderstands intentional silences from the maroon perspective, and the resulting dearth of information from enslavers. This interpretation does not recognize the agency, resilience, and creativity of African American maroons, which, here in *Dismal Freedom* and through archaeology (especially Sayers, *A Desolate Place*) has been not only fully acknowledged but conclusively proved.

19. See, for example, Price, *Maroon Societies*; Richard Price, *The Guiana Maroons: A Historical and Bibliographical Introduction* (Baltimore: Johns Hopkins University Press, 1976); Wim Hoogbergen, *The Boni Maroon Wars in Suriname* (Leiden: E. J. Brill, 1990); Carla Lewis Gotlieb, *The Mother of Us All: A History of Queen Nanny, Leader of the Windward Jamaican Maroons* (Trenton, N.J.: Africa World, 2000); Mavis Campbell, *The Maroons of Jamaica, 1655–1796* (Trenton, N.J.: Africa World, 1988); Kenneth Bilby, *True Born Maroons* (Gainesville: University Press of Florida, 2008); Gad Heuman, ed., *Out of the House of Bondage: Runaways, Resistance, and Marronage in Africa and the New World* (London: Frank Cass, 1986).

20. See Thompson, *Flight to Freedom*, 1–2.

21. Herbert Aptheker, "Maroons within the Present Limits of the United States," *Journal of Negro History* 24, no. 2 (April 1939): 167–84; Herbert Aptheker, "Additional Data on American Maroons," *Journal of Negro History* 32, no. 4 (October 1947): 452–60.

22. Herbert Aptheker, *American Negro Slave Revolts* (New York: Columbia University Press, 1943).

23. See Michael Mullin, *Africa in America: Slave Acculturation and Resistance in the American South and the British Caribbean, 1736–1831* (Urbana: University of Illinois Press, 1992), 61, where the author proclaims an "absence of a maroon dimension in the South, a serious loss for Southern slaves." People certainly escaped their enslavement, but in Mullin's telling, almost all of them sought freedom in the North and Canada. "One can only surmise," he writes, what would have happened had these rebels had decided to remain in the South." John Hope Franklin and Loren Schweninger characterize North American marronage as an "ephemeral" phenomenon, and treat the subject in just three pages in *Runaway Slaves: Rebels on the Plantation* (New York: Oxford University Press, 2000), 86–88. Another important work on colonial slavery, Philip D. Morgan's *Slave Counterpoint: Black Culture in the Eighteenth-Century Chesapeake & Lowcountry* (Chapel Hill: University of North Carolina Press, 1998), relegates discussion of marronage to six short paragraphs and

concludes that when such fugitive communities did form, they were "short-lived," especially in the Chesapeake, a region "not particularly conductive to maroon settlements" (449).

24. Eugene D. Genovese, *From Rebellion to Revolution: Afro-American Slave Revolts in the Making of the Modern World* (Baton Rouge: Louisiana State University Press, 1979), 69, 77.

25. Diouf, *Slavery's Exiles*. See also Nevius, "New Histories of Marronage," for an in-depth literature review concerning marronage.

26. Timothy James Lockley, *Maroon Communities in South Carolina: A Documentary Record* (Columbia: University of South Carolina Press, 2009).

27. See Kevin Mulroy, *Freedom on the Border: The Seminole Maroons in Florida, the Indian Territory* (Lubbock: Texas Tech University Press, 1993); Nathaniel Millett, *The Maroons of Prospect Bluff and Their Quest for Freedom in the Atlantic World* (Gainesville: University Press of Florida, 2013); Matthew J. Clavin, *Aiming for Pensacola: Fugitive Slaves on the Atlantic and Southern Frontier* (Cambridge, Mass.: Harvard University Press, 2015).

28. Harriett Beecher Stowe, Henry Wadsworth Longfellow, Thomas Wentworth Higginson, Martin Delany, Frederick Douglass, and Robert Frost, among others, all published work on the swamp and its human visitors or residents. The only thorough general overview of marronage in North America is Sylviane Diouf's recent *Slavery's Exiles* (2014). This book is a welcome addition to a near-nonexistent historiography, and examines the lives of maroons across the South from the colonial period through the Civil War. Diouf structures her history upon what she terms "the maroon landscape" that takes specificity of place fully into account in examining marronage. This is also a largely synthetic work, though it does include some fascinating original research. It does not devote more than a single chapter to any one maroon group. Though not a monograph, Timothy James Lockley has published *Maroon Communities in South Carolina: A Documentary Record* (Columbia: University of South Carolina Press, 2009), an outstanding documentary reader on maroon communities in South Carolina. His brief introduction is a valuable historiographic overview of maroon scholarship in the New World, and his document collection offers a fascinating glimpse into the lives of South Carolina maroons. Other historians have produced fine studies of marronage in Spanish North American colonies. Specifically regarding the Dismal Swamp maroons, archivist Tommy Bogger published an eight-page review of the extant historiography as part of a local public library pamphlet: "Maroons and Laborers in the Great Dismal Swamp," in *Readings in Black and White: Lower Tidewater Virginia*, ed. Jane H. Kobelski (Portsmouth, Va.: Portsmouth Public Library, 1982), 1–8. I published the first extended historical essay on the Great Dismal Swamp Maroons in 2008, "'Running Servants and All Others': The Diverse and Elusive Maroons of the Great Dismal Swamp," in *Voices from within the Veil: African Americans and the Experience of Democracy*, ed. William H. Alexander, Cassandra Newby-Alexander, and Charles H. Ford (Newcastle-upon-Tyne, UK: Cambridge Scholars, 2008), 85–105. This was more of an exploratory piece, and it drew primarily on secondary sources. Edward

Maris-Wolf's "Hidden in Plain Sight: Maroon Life and Labor in Virginia's Dismal Swamp," *Slavery and Abolition* 34, no. 3 (2013): 446–64, looks only at one group of Dismal Swamp maroons, those most closely connected to the industrial logging and canal economy of the early 1820s—that is, the most visible to contemporaries and most easily accessible in the documentary record. However, great numbers of Dismal Swamp maroons lived at some remove from these areas. Most maroons were thoroughly committed to avoiding and eschewing the outside world. Their reliance on the deep swamp itself created a maroon life quite different than the "one foot in, one foot out" population Maris-Wolf analyzes. The maroon community on which he concentrates is an important one, but just one of many, and his article only scratches the surface of maroon life in the swamp. There is tantalizing yet only passing commentary on these communities in Thompson, *Flight to Freedom*; Jack Temple Kirby, *Poquosin: A Study of Rural Landscape and Society* (Chapel Hill: University of North Carolina Press, 1995), 126–97; Simpson, *The Great Dismal* (1990); and David Cecelski, *The Waterman's Song: Slavery and Freedom in Maritime North Carolina* (Chapel Hill: University of North Carolina Press, 2001), 52, 124. Though Diouf's chapter stands as an impressive historical treatment of the subject, she agrees that the story of this hidden society demands more than just twenty to thirty pages of analysis. Of course, her focus was not any specific maroon community, but her chapter devoted to the Dismal Swamp is at once the best and the shortest in her book. Diouf, *Slavery's Exiles*, 209–29.

Three books have been published that deal exclusively with the Dismal Swamp maroons. Hugo Prosper Leaming's 1979 doctoral dissertation was published posthumously fifteen years later with minimal revisions as *Hidden Americans: Maroons of Virginia and the Carolinas* (New York: Garland, 1995). Though Leaming is clearly passionate about his topic, the value of this work is limited by his flawed writing and research methods. Dozens of pages often pass between footnotes that sometimes cite completely unrelated sources, powerful assertions often lack any evidence at all, reliance in many cases on works of fiction and children's books, and significant portions of the narrative that get bogged down in puzzling and rambling discussions of twentieth-century spiritualism and the supernatural. The only published review of this book concludes that "Leaming lost his way as an historian." Peter C. Stewart, "Review of Hugo Prosper Leaming, *Hidden Americans: Maroons of Virginia and the Carolinas*," *William and Mary Quarterly* 53, no. 3 (July 1996): 666–67.

Great Dismal Swamp Landscape Study director Daniel O. Sayers has recently published the results of his archaeological fieldwork as *A Desolate Place for a Defiant People* (2014). As an archaeological study, this is a path breaking work. Not only is Sayers the first archaeologist to undertake extensive fieldwork in the Dismal, but his discoveries thoroughly debunk any scholars who still insisted on minimizing the degree to which maroons used the swamp as a refuge from the 1600s through the Civil War. He also develops here a predictive model that will be very useful for future archaeological investigations of resistance communities, especially those occupying landscapes like the Great Dismal Swamp. However, Sayers, as might be expected, focuses almost entirely on the archaeological record and field methods and experience, and his work is meant primarily for professional archaeologists. He offers only a cursory overview of a small portion of the documentary uncovered for the GDSLS, and relies much more heavily on anthropological and archaeological theory than most historians may be comfortable with.

Marcus P. Nevius, *City of Refuge: Slavery and Petit Marronage in the Great Dismal Swamp, 1763–1856* (Athens: University of Georgia Press, 2020), examines petit marronage and the informal economy of maroons and enslaved people in the swamp. It is a detailed account of the industrial development of the swamp in the eighteenth and early nineteenth century — lumbering and internal improvement projects — and touches on the interactions of maroons, enslaved workers, and white corporate agents in developing a community along the Dismal Swamp Canal and adjacent to slave lumber camps. However, while identifying the potential for carving a space for freedom in plain sight of industrialists, Nevius does not fill that space with the maroons themselves. Rather, *City of Refuge* focuses primarily on the enslaved people in the swamp and the tacit acceptance of marronage by whites rather than marronage and those who lived it. Nevius does not consider all maroons, all motivations for marronage, or all Dismal Swamp locations across their nearly three-century history.

29. The GDSLS artifact collection and document archive are housed in the lab of Daniel Sayers at American University, Washington, D.C. Select artifacts are also on permanent display at the Smithsonian National Museum of African American History and Culture.

30. See Price, *Maroon Societies*, 4. Price argues that "maroon societies form a class or type that can yield unique insights about the Afro-American experience. By juxtaposing a large number of particularistic case studies drawn from throughout the Americas, I . . . suggest that those rebels who attempted to create communities of their own faced largely similar problems and arrived at comparable solutions." Thompson echoes Price's assessment. Although there was little or no communication between hemispheric maroons in different nations or speaking different languages, "the similarities of these solutions suggests an inner logic to their actions that transcended spatial and linguistic barriers." Thompson, *Flight to Freedom*, 7.

31. Jessica Roitman and Karwan Fatah-Black, "'Being Speculative Is Better than to Not Do It at All': An Interview with Natalie Zemon Davis," *Itinerario* 39, no. 1 (2015): 3–15.

32. Sayers, *A Desolate Place*, 5.

33. "Letter of Spotswood to the L'ds Commr's of Trade," July 21, 1714, in *The Official Letters of Alexander Spotswood, Lieutenant-Governor of the Colony of Virginia, 1710–1722*, ed. R. A. Brock (Richmond: Virginia Historical Society, 1885), 2:71; Leaming, *Hidden Americans*, 224.

34. "For the Register," *Raleigh Register*, October 25, 1862.

CHAPTER ONE

1. Jack Temple Kirby, *Poquosin: A Study of Rural Landscape and Society* (Chapel Hill: University of North Carolina Press, 1995), 4; Fred L. Willard, "Coastal Scarps, Islands, and High-Water Events: Indian Village Location Models," *East Carolina*

University Directed Studies in Geology (2011): 4, https://www.lost-colony.com
/Coastal_Scarps_Islands_And_High-Water_Events-Indian_Village_Location
_Models.pdf.

2. "The Rate of Deposition of Coal Forming Materials," *Mining Science* 70, no.
1748 (November 1914): 48; Gerald F. Levy, "The Vegetation of the Great Dismal
Swamp: A Review and an Overview," *Virginia Journal of Science* 42, no. 4 (Winter
1991): 412.

3. Kirby, *Poquosin*, 6.

4. Hubert Davis, *The Great Dismal Swamp: Its History, Folklore, and Science* (Richmond, Va.: Cavalier, 1962), 31–39; William Henry Stewart, *History of Norfolk County,
Virginia, and Representative Citizens* (Chicago: Biographical Publishing, 1902),
166–69.

5. Alexander Hunter, *The Huntsman in the South* (New York: Neale, 1908), 61.

6. Currently red maple is the most common and widely distributed tree community due to the impacts of modern forest cutting, drainage, and forest fires. Tupelo
gum, bald cypress, and Atlantic white cedar formerly dominated, but their harvest
by forest industrialists beginning in the eighteenth century and continuing until
very recently reduced their coverage to less than 20 percent of the total swamp. US
Fish and Wildlife Service, "Great Dismal Swamp: Wildlife and Habitat," https://
www.fws.gov/refuge/Great_Dismal_Swamp/wildlife_and_habitat/index.html
(accessed August 19, 2020).

7. "Corn Pollen in Swamp Hints Early Agriculture," *Science News-Letter* 88, no.
23 (December 4, 1965): 359; Peter C. Stewart, "Man and the Swamp: The Historical
Dimension," in *The Great Dismal Swamp*, ed. Paul W. Kirk (Charlottesville: University of Virginia Press, 1979), 56.

8. Hugo Prosper Leaming, *Hidden Americans: The Maroons of Virginia and the
Carolinas* (New York: Garland, 1995), 223.

9. Milton Ready, *The Tar Heel State: A History of North Carolina* (Columbia:
University of South Carolina Press, 2005), 30–31; William A. Link, *North Carolina:
Change and Tradition in a Southern State* (Hoboken, N.J.: John Wiley & Sons, 2018),
26; Stewart, "Man and the Swamp," 57–58. See also Jordan Riccio, "The People of
the Lonely Place: An Archaeological Exploration of Community Structure within
the Great Dismal Swamp," MA thesis (American University, 2012), 22–30.

10. J. Brent Morris, *Yes, Lord, I Know the Road: A Documentary History of African
Americans in South Carolina, 1526–2008* (Columbia: University of South Carolina
Press, 2017), 1–2, 38–39.

11. See John Lawson, *A New Voyage to Carolina* (London: n.p., 1709).

12. See Riccio, "The People of the Lonely Place," 26–30.

13. Wesley Frank Craven, *The Southern Colonies in the Seventeenth Century, 1607–
1689* (Baton Rouge: Louisiana State University Press, 1970), 317.

14. George Percy, "'A Trewe Relacyon': Virginia from 1607 to 1612," *Tyler's Quarterly Historical and Genealogical Magazine* 3, no. 4 (April 1922): 266–67.

15. See Eric Wolf, *Europe and the People without History* (Berkeley: University of
California Press, 1997), 202.

16. Marion Gleason McDougall, *Fugitive Slaves (1619–1865)* (Boston: Ginn, 1891), 90.

17. John Spencer Bassett, *Slavery and Servitude in the Colony of North Carolina* (Baltimore: Johns Hopkins University Press, 1896), 79. See also John Hamilton Howard, *In the Shadow of the Pines* (New York: Easton and Mains, 1906), 17.

18. Link, *North Carolina*, 24–25.

19. See David Stick, *Graveyard of the Atlantic: Shipwrecks of the North Carolina Coast* (Chapel Hill: University of North Carolina Press, 1952), 1–9.

20. Charles M. Andrews, *Colonial Folkways: A Chronicle of American Life in the Reign of the Georges* (New Haven, Conn.: Yale University Press, 1920), 220.

21. Jonathan Edward Barth, "'The Sinke of America': Society in the Albemarle Borderlands of North Carolina, 1663–1729," MA thesis (University of North Carolina Charlotte, 2009), 15–16.

22. Barth, 14–15.

23. David La Vere, *The Tuscarora War: Indians, Settlers, and the Fight for the Carolina Colonies* (Chapel Hill: University of North Carolina Press, 2013), 5.

24. A. Leon Higginbotham, *In the Matter of Color: Race and the American Legal Process — The Colonial Period* (Oxford: Oxford University Press, 1980), 26–31; "A Rising on William Pierce's Plantation, 1640," in *The Old Dominion in the Seventeenth Century: A Documentary History of Virginia, 1606–1700*, ed. Warren M. Billings (Chapel Hill: University of North Carolina Press, 2007), 184–85.

25. "Against Runawayes," in *The Statutes at Large: Being a Collection of All the Laws of Virginia, from the First Session of the Legislature, in the Year 1619*, ed. William Waller Hening (New York: R&W&G Bartow, 1823), 2:273.

26. Noelene McIlvenna, *Early American Rebels: Pursuing Democracy from Maryland to Carolina, 1640–1700* (Chapel Hill: University of North Carolina Press, 2020), 54–74; Leaming, *Hidden Americans*, 44.

27. Hugh Williamson, *The History of North Carolina* (Philadelphia: Thomas Dobson, 1812), 1:92.

28. Lawson, *A New Voyage to Carolina*, 166–67.

29. "The Discovery of New Britaine, 1650," in *Narratives of Early Carolina, 1650–1708*, ed. Alexander S. Salley (New York: Charles Scribner's Sons, 1911), 11.

30. "Examination of Witnesses in Nansimund County," March 25, 1708 (1707?), in *The Colonial Records of North Carolina*, vol. 1, ed. William L. Saunders (Raleigh: P. M. Hale, 1886) (hereafter *CRNC*), 676.31. "The Discovery of New Britaine, 1650," 9.

32. Francis Yeardley to John Farrar, May 8, 1654, in Salley, *Narratives of Early Carolina*, 27.

33. William S. Powell, *North Carolina through Four Centuries* (Chapel Hill: University of North Carolina Press, 1989), 52; William P. Cumming, *The Southeast in Early Maps* (Princeton, N.J.: Princeton University Press, 1958), 21–23. Batts's name also appears in some sources as "Batz." See F. Roy Johnson, *Tales from Old Carolina* (Murfreesboro, N.C.: Johnson, 1965), 23–24.

34. Elizabeth A. Fenn and Peter H. Wood, *Natives & Newcomers: The Way We*

Lived in North Carolina before 1770 (Chapel Hill: University of North Carolina Press, 1983), 24–25.

35. Catherine Albertson, *In Ancient Albemarle* (Raleigh: Commercial Printing, 1914), 7–8; "Instructions to William Berkeley Concerning the Settlement of Carolina," in *CRNC*, 1:51.

36. George Fox, *George Fox's "Book of Miracles,"* ed. Henry J. Cadbury (Cambridge: Cambridge University Press, 1948), 101.

37. Bland Simpson, *The Inner Islands: A Carolinian's Sound Country Chronicle* (Chapel Hill: University of North Carolina Press, 2006), 26.

38. Leaming, *Hidden Americans*, 51; George Fox, *George Fox's "Book of Miracles,"* ed. Henry J. Cadbury (Cambridge: Cambridge University Press, 1948), 101. Sources vary in their identification of Batts's closest Indigenous companions. The Chowanoke and Yeopim were close neighbors and closely related.

39. Donald Batchelor, *Becoming Americans* (Raleigh: Boson, 1996), 246; Leaming, *Hidden Americans*, 49–51.

40. *The WPA Guide to North Carolina: The Tar Heel State* (San Antonio: Trinity University Press, 2013), 281; Simpson, *The Inner Islands*, 26.

41. Jeffrey J. Crow, Paul D. Escott, and Flora J. Hatley, *A History of African Americans in North Carolina* (Raleigh: North Carolina Division of Archives & History, 1992), 1; Elizabeth A. Fenn and Peter H. Wood, "Natives and Newcomers," in *The Way We Lived in North Carolina*, ed. Joe A. Mobley (Raleigh: North Carolina Department of Cultural Resources, 2003), 27–28.

42. "The Second Charter Granted by Charles II, to the Proprietors of Carolina," in *Laws of the State of North-Carolina*, ed. Hen. Potter, J. L. Taylor, and Bart. Yancey (Raleigh: J. Gales, 1821), 1:4; Walter Edgar, *South Carolina: A History* (Columbia: University of South Carolina Press, 1997), 39.

43. Francis L. Hawks, *History of North Carolina from 1663 to 1729* (Fayetteville: E. J. Hale & Son, 1859), 2:148.

44. John Bennett Boddie, *Seventeenth Century Isle of Wight County, Virginia* (Chicago: Chicago Law Printing, 1938), 1:128–29; Thomas Woodward to John Colleton, June 2, 1665, in "Public Archives of the Original Thirteen States," *Annual Report of the American Historical Association for the Year 1906* (Washington, D.C.: Government Printing Office, 1908), 2:511.

45. Woodward to John Colleton, June 2, 1665.

46. Boddie, *Seventeenth Century Isle of Wight County*, 128–29; Larry Eldridge, *A Distant Heritage: The Growth of Free Speech in Early America* (New York: New York University Press, 1994), 7.

47. George Monck to William Berkeley, September 8, 1663, in *CRNC*, 1:54.

48. Thomas Woodward to John Colleton, June 2,1665, in "Public Archives of the Original Thirteen States," 511.

49. Noelene McIlvenna, *A Very Mutinous People: The Struggle for North Carolina, 1660–1713* (Chapel Hill: University of North Carolina Press, 2009), 31.

50. Nancy Isenberg, *White Trash: The 400-Year Untold History of Class in America* (New York: Penguin, 2016), 47.

51. "Affidavit of Thomas Miller Concerning Rebellion in Albemarle County," January 31, 1680, in *CRNC*, 1:283.

52. See *Shaping North America: From Exploration to the American Revolution*, ed. James E. Seelye Jr. and Shawn Selby (Santa Barbara, Calif.: ABC-CLIO, 2018), 293–95.

53. "Petition from Thomas Miller Concerning Rebellion in Albemarle County," June 29, 1680, in *CRNC*, 1:303–4; "Petition from the Inhabitants of Albemarle County Concerning Rebellion in Albemarle County," June 30, 1680, in *CRNC*, 1:305.

54. "Petition from Thomas Miller Concerning Rebellion in Albemarle County," June 29, 1680, in *CRNC*, 1:304.

55. "Affidavit of Thomas Miller Concerning Rebellion in Albemarle County," January 31, 1680, in *CRNC*, 1:283.

56. "Lord Culpeper to Lords of Trade and Plantations," December 12, 1681, in *CRNC*, 1:153–57.

57. "Report by Edward Randolph Concerning Illegal Trade in Proprietary Colonies, Including a Related Petition from the Proprietors," November 10, 1696, in *CRNC*, 1:467.

58. "An Act Prohibiting Suing of Any Persons within Five Yeares," January 20, 1670, in *CRNC*, 1:183–84.

59. "Memorandum from the Virginia Governor's Council to the Board of Trade of Great Britain Concerning Trade and Emigration to Carolina," October 19, 1708, in *CRNC*, 1:691.

60. Leaming, *Hidden Americans*, 91; Hawks, *History of North Carolina*, 590; Peter J. Coleman, *Debtors and Creditors in America: Insolvency, Imprisonment for Debt, and Bankruptcy, 1607–1900* (Washington, D.C.: Beard, 1999), 215–17; Sally E. Hadden, *Slave Patrols: Law and Violence in Virginia and the Carolinas* (Cambridge, Mass.: Harvard University Press, 2001), 33.

61. Kirsten Fischer, *Suspect Relations: Sex, Race, and Resistance in Colonial North Carolina* (Ithaca, N.Y.: Cornell University Press, 2002), 27; Crow, Escott, and Hatiey, *A History of African Americans in North Carolina*, 1.

62. See Thos. Holt et al. to Honbl. Sr—, March 24, 1709, in *Calendar of Virginia State Papers and Other Manuscripts, 1652–1781*, vol. 1, ed. Wm. P. Palmer (Richmond: R. F. Walker, 1875), 129. To be sure, racial boundaries did exist that separated Africans from Europeans in proprietary North Carolina, but they were much more porous than in other southern colonies in the late seventeenth and early eighteenth century. See Barth, "'The Sinke of America,'" 8.

63. Barth, "'The Sinke of America,'" 8.

64. Ira Berlin, "Time, Space, and the Evolution of Afro-American Society on British Mainland North America," *American Historical Review* 85, no. 1 (February 1980): 55; Peter H. Wood, *Black Majority: Negroes in Colonial South Carolina from 1670 through the Stono Rebellion* (New York: Alfred A. Knopf, 1974), 13–24, 94–97.

65. See "Prefatory Notes," in *CRNC*, 1:ix–x; Charles M. Andrews, *The Colonial Period of American History* (New Haven, Conn.: Yale University Press, 1937), 252.

66. Francis Veale, "The Manner of Living of the North Carolinians, December 19, 1730," ed. Edmund and Dorothy S. Berkeley, *North Carolina Historical Review* 41, no. 1 (Winter 1964): 242.

67. "Letter from John Urmston to the Society for the Propagation of the Gospel," July 7, 1711, in *CRNC*, 1:767; Jacqueline A. Martin, "The Maroons of the Great Dismal Swamp" (PhD diss., Western Washington University, 2004), 41–42.

68. "Proposal by the Board of Trade of England Concerning the Revocation of Proprietary Charters," March 26, 1701, in *CRNC*, 1:536–37.

69. "Memorandum Concerning the Governments of Proprietary Colonies," 1701, in *CRNC*, 1:541.

70. McIlvenna, *A Very Mutinous People*, 70.

71. Christine Ann Styrna, "The Winds of War and Change: The Impact of the Tuscarora War on Proprietary North Carolina, 1690–1729," MA thesis (College of William and Mary, 1990), 43.

72. McIlvenna, *A Very Mutinous People*, 89–90.

73. McIlvenna, 95.

74. "Address by Parliament to Anne, Queen of Great Britain," March 13, 1706, in *CRNC*, 1:639.

75. "Letter from Henderson Walker to Henry Compton," October 21, 1703, in *CRNC*, 1:572.

76. "Letter from William Gordon to John Chamberlain," May 13, 1709, in *CRNC*, 1:709; Styrna, "The Winds of War and Change," 61.

77. "Letter from Alexander Spotswood to Thomas Cary," June 21, 1711, in *CRNC*, 1:759.

78. "Narrative by Christoph von Graffenried Concerning His Voyage to North Carolina and the Founding of New Bern," in *CRNC*, 1:912; McIlvenna, *A Very Mutinous People*, 135.

79. "Letter from John Urmston to the Society for the Propagation of the Gospel," July 7, 1711, in Saunders, *CRNC*, 1:768.

80. McIlvenna, *A Very Mutinous People*, 135–36.

81. McIlvenna, 140.

82. "Letter from Alexander Spotswood to the Board of Trade of Great Britain," 92.

83. See Thos. Holt et al. to Honbl. Sr—, March 24, 1709, in Palmer, *Calendar of Virginia State Papers*, 1:129; "Lt. Governor Jenings to the Council of Trade," April 24, 1710, in *Calendar of State Papers, Colonial Series: America and West Indies, 1710–June 1711*, ed. Cecil Headlam (London: H.M. Stationary Office, 1924), 83.

84. *Journals of the House of Burgesses of Virginia, 1702/3–1705, 1705–1706, 1710–1712*, ed. H. R. McIlwaine (Richmond: E. Waddey, 1912), 4:240.

85. "Minutes of the Virginia Governor's Council," June 13, 1711, in *CRNC*, 1:757.

86. "Hyde, Edward," in *Dictionary of North Carolina Biography*, ed. William S. Powell (Chapel Hill: University of North Carolina Press, 1988), 3:247–48; McIlvenna, *A Very Mutinous People*, 142–43.

87. "Letter from John Urmston to John Chamberlain," July 17, 1711, in *CRNC*, 1:773; Styrna, "The Winds of War and Change," 77; McIlvenna, *A Very Mutinous People*, 143–45; Leaming, *Hidden Americans*, 187.

88. McIlvenna, *A Very Mutinous People*, 145.

89. "Minutes of the North Carolina Governor's Council," July 31, 1712, in *CRNC*, 1:864.

90. La Vere, *The Tuscarora War*, 74–76, 199.

91. "Narrative by Christoph von Graffenried Concerning His Voyage to North Carolina and the Founding of New Bern," in *CRNC*, 1:928–33.

92. Eugenia Burney, *Colonial North Carolina* (Nashville: Thomas Nelson, 1975), 68–70; McIlvenna, *A Very Mutinous People*, 148–50.

93. Leaming, *Hidden Americans*, 197.

94. McIlvenna, *A Very Mutinous People*, 150.

95. "Letter from Edward Hyde to the Lords Proprietors of Carolina," August 22, 1711, in *CRNC*, 1:802.

96. "Proclamation by Alexander Spotswood Concerning the Arrest of Thomas Cary et al.," July 24, 1711, in *CRNC*, 1:776–77.

97. "Narrative by Christoph von Graffenried," in *CRNC*, 1:920.

98. "Letter from Alexander Spotswood to the Board of Trade of Great Britain," October 15, 1711, and "Letter from Alexander Spotswood to William Legge," October 15, 1711, "Letter from Alexander Spotswood to the Board of Trade of Great Britain," July 26, 1712, in *CRNC*, 1:812, 814, 862.

99. McIlvenna, *A Very Mutinous People*, 150.

100. "Letter from Thomas Pollock to John Carteret," September 20, 1712, in *CRNC*, 1:876–77.

101. "Letter of Spotswood to Pollock," March —, 1713, in Palmer, *Calendar of Virginia State Papers*, 1:164.

102. "The Tuscarora Conspiracy in Carolina," *National Magazine* 19, nos. 2–3 (December 1893–January 1894): 148; Leaming, *Hidden Americans*, 225.

103. François-Xavier Martin, *The History of North Carolina from the Earliest Period* (New Orleans: A. T. Penniman, 1829), 1:265.

104. McIlvenna, *A Very Mutinous People*, 159–60.

105. Bassett, *Slavery and Servitude*, 19–20.

106. James Sprunt, *Chronicles of the Cape Fear River, 1660–1916* (Raleigh: Edwards & Broughton, 1916), 38–39; Philip Gerard, *Down the Wild Cape Fear: A River Journey through the Heart of North Carolina* (Chapel Hill: University of North Carolina Press, 2013), 167–68; Fenn and Wood, *Natives & Newcomers*, 49.

107. William S. Powell, *North Carolina through Four Centuries* (Chapel Hill: University of North Carolina Press, 2010), 133.

108. William S. Powell, *The North Carolina Colony* (New York: Macmillan, 1969), 61–62; Albert Edward McKinley, *The Suffrage Franchise in the Thirteen English Colonies in America* (Philadelphia: Ginn, 1905), 92.

109. McIlvenna, *A Very Mutinous People*, 159.

110. Quoted in John Clark Ridpath, *The New Complete History of the United States*

of America: Colonies to the Struggle with France (Washington, D.C.: Ridpath History, 1905), 5:1759.

111. "Letter of Spotswood to the L'ds Commr's of Trade," July 21, 1714, in *The Official Letters of Alexander Spotswood, Lieutenant-Governor of the Colony of Virginia, 1710–1722*, ed. R. A. Brock (Richmond: Virginia Historical Society, 1885), 2:71.

CHAPTER TWO

1. Daniel O. Sayers, *A Desolate Place for a Defiant People: The Archaeology of Maroons, Indigenous Americans, and Enslaved Laborers in the Great Dismal Swamp* (Gainesville: University Press of Florida, 2014), 82.

2. Charles Royster, *The Fabulous History of the Great Dismal Swamp Company: A Story of George Washington's Times* (New York: Vintage, 1999), 49.

3. J. F. D. Smyth, *A Tour in the United States of America* (London: G. Robinson, 1784), 237.

4. William Byrd, *The Westover Manuscripts: Containing the History of the Dividing Line betwixt Virginia and North Carolina; A Journey to the Land of Eden, A.D. 1733; and A Progress to the Mines. Written from 1728 to 1736* (Petersburg, Va.: Edmund and Julian Ruffin, 1841), 17, 26; Samuel Warner, *Authentic and Impartial Narrative of the Tragical Scene* (New York: Warner and West, 1831), 33.

5. Robin Marantz Henig, *The People's Health: A Memoir of Public Health and Its Evolution at Harvard* (Washington, D.C.: National Academies Press, 1997), 20; Megan Kate Nelson, *Trembling Earth: A Cultural History of the Okefenokee Swamp* (Athens: University of Georgia Press, 2009), 14; Lois N. Magner, *A History of Medicine* (New York: Marcel Decker, 1992), 305.

6. Byrd, *The Westover Manuscripts*, 24.

7. Byrd, 26.

8. Nelson, *Trembling Earth*, 14.

9. See Bland Simpson, *The Great Dismal: A Carolina Swamp Memoir* (Chapel Hill, University of North Carolina Press, 1990), 10.

10. Waverly Traylor, *The Great Dismal Swamp in Myth and Legend* (Pittsburgh: RoseDog, 2010), 2; "The Dismal Swamp of North America," in *The Terrific Register, or, Record of Crimes, Judgments, Providences, and Calamities* (London, 1825), 2:129–31.

11. Daniel O. Sayers, P. Brendan Burke, and Aaron M. Henry, "The Political Economy of Exile in the Great Dismal Swamp," *International Journal of Historical Archaeology* 11, no. 1 (March 2007): 69.

12. Sayers, *A Desolate Place*, 82.

13. See Rhys Isaac, *The Transformation of Virginia, 1740–1790* (Chapel Hill: University of North Carolina Pres, 1982), chap. 1; Owen O'Reilly, "The Power of Squares: Ideology in Landscape Archaeology and the Rectangular Land Survey of the United States of America," *Nebraska Anthropologist* 26 (2011): 30–45; Gregory H. Nobles, "Straight Lines and Stability: Mapping the Political Order of the Anglo-American Frontier," *Journal of American History* 80, no. 1 (June 1993): 9–35.

14. Daniel Miller and Christopher Tilley, *Ideology, Power and Prehistory* (Cambridge: Cambridge University Press, 1984), 27.

15. Sayers, *A Desolate Place*, 82.

16. Quoted in Catherine Bates, *Masculinity, Gender and Identity in the English Renaissance Lyric* (Cambridge: Cambridge University Press, 1997), 171.

17. Anthony Wilson, *Shadow and Shelter: The Swamp in Southern Culture* (Jackson: University Press of Mississippi, 2006), xiii.

18. Smyth, *A Tour in the United States of America*, 239.

19. Alvin O. Thompson, *Flight to Freedom: African Runaways and Maroons in the Americas* (Kingston, Jamaica: University of the West Indies Press, 2006), 36.

20. Wilson, *Shadow and Shelter*, 14–15.

21. Wilson, 53; Megan Kate Nelson, "Hidden Away in the Woods and Swamps: Slavery, Fugitive Slaves, and Swamplands in the Southeastern Borderlands, 1739–1845," in *"We Shall Independent Be": African American Place Making and the Struggle to Claim Space in the United States*, ed. Angela David Nieves and Leslie M. Alexander (Boulder: University Press of Colorado, 2008), 266.

22. See T. H. Breen and Stephen Innes, *"Myne Owne Ground": Race and Freedom on Virginia's Eastern Shore, 1640–1676* (New York: Oxford University Press, 1980), 30n38; Herbert Aptheker, *American Negro Slave Revolts* (New York: Columbia University Press, 1943), 166.

23. Breen and Innes, *"Myne Own Ground,"* 30; *The Statutes at Large: Being a Collection of All the Laws of Virginia, from the First Session of the Legislature, in the Year 1619*, ed. William Waller Hening (Richmond: Samuel Pleasants, 1810), 2:299.

24. See Edmund Morgan, *American Slavery, American Freedom: The Ordeal of Colonial Virginia* (New York: W. W. Norton, 1975), 213–92; Jeffrey R. Kerr-Ritchie, "'Their Hoped for Liberty': Slaves and Bacon's 1676 Rebellion," in *Voices from within the Veil: African Americans and the Experience of Democracy*, ed. William H. Alexander, Cassandra Newby-Alexander, and Charles H. Ford (Newcastle-upon-Tyne, UK: Cambridge Scholars Press, 2008), 75–84.

25. Aptheker, *American Negro Slave Revolts*, 169–71.

26. Thos. Holt et al. to Honbl. Sr—, March 24, 1709, in *Calendar of Virginia State Papers and Other Manuscripts, 1652–1781*, vol. 1, ed. Wm. P. Palmer (Richmond: R. F. Walker, 1875), 129; "Lt. Governor Jenings to the Council of Trade," April 24, 1710, in *Calendar of State Papers, Colonial Series: America and West Indies, 1710–June 1711*, ed. Cecil Headlam (London: H.M. Stationary Office, 1924), 83; Aptheker, *American Negro Slave Revolts*, 170.

27. *The Statutes at Large: Being a Collection of All the Laws of Virginia, from the First Session of the Legislature, in the Year 1619*, ed. William Waller Hening (Philadelphia: Thomas Desilver, 1823), 3:537–38; Anthony Parent, *Foul Means: The Formation of a Slave Society in Virginia, 1660–1740* (Chapel Hill: University of North Carolina Press, 2003), 151–53. See also Kathryn Elise Benjamin Golden, "'Through the Muck and Mire': Marronage, Representation, and Memory in the Great Dismal Swamp," PhD diss. (University of California, Berkeley, 2018), 64. Will would not be the last enslaved person to betray the trust of maroons. The relationship between maroons and those enslaved people remaining on labor camps could be complex, especially if and when maroons' activities resulted in a loss of goods intended for the enslaved

people or were followed by a crackdown upon some freedoms the enslaved had enjoyed. However, those Dismal Swamp maroons who settled isolated deep within the swamp enjoyed considerably more security against betrayal. See my discussions in chapter 4, as well as Timothy James Lockley and David Doddington's consideration of these complex relationships in their "Maroon and Slave Communities in South Carolina before 1865," *South Carolina Historical Magazine* 113, no. 2 (April 2012): 125–45.

28. F. Roy Johnson, *Tales from Old Carolina* (Murfreesboro, N.C.: Johnson, 1965), 19; Martha W. McCartney, *A Study of the Africans and African Americans on Jamestown Island and at Green Spring, 1619–1803* (Williamsburg, Va.: Colonial Williamsburg Foundation, 2003), 112.

29. Jedidiah Morse, *Geography Made Easy: Being an Abridgement of the American Geography* (Troy, N.Y.: Parker and Bliss, 1814), 201–2; *The New Encyclopedia of Southern Culture: Environment*, ed. Martin V. Melosi (Chapel Hill: University of North Carolina Press, 2014), 8:172; Benjamin Davies, *A New System of Modern Geography* (Philadelphia: J. Downing, 1813), 293; Isaac Weld, *Travels through the States of North America and the Provinces of Upper and Lower Canada during the Years 1795, 1796, and 1797* (London: John Stockdale, 1807), 1:135; Johnson, *Tales from Old Carolina*, 13–15, 18–20.

30. "Secret History of the Line" was not published until the twentieth century, when it was included in *William Byrd's Histories of the Dividing Line betwixt Virginia and North Carolina* (Raleigh: North Carolina Historical Commission, 1929).

31. Byrd, *The Westover Manuscripts*, 9.

32. Byrd, *The Dividing Line Histories of William Byrd II of Westover* (Chapel Hill: University of North Carolina Press, 2013), 352.

33. Byrd, *The Westover Manuscripts*, 13.

34. Byrd, 13–14.

35. Byrd, 17.

36. "Lord Culpeper to Lords of Trade and Plantations," December 12, 1681, in *Colonial Records of North Carolina*, ed. William L. Saunders (Raleigh: P. M. Hale, 1886), 1:153–57.

37. Byrd, *The Westover Manuscripts*, 17.

38. Byrd, 15.

39. Byrd, 19–20.

40. Byrd, 22.

41. Byrd, *The Dividing Line Histories*, 366.

42. See Emily C. Pearson, "In the Swamp," *The Liberator*, January 22, 1863; Thompson, *Flight to Freedom*, 192–93; Sylviane A. Diouf, *Slavery's Exiles: The Story of the American Maroons* (New York: New York University Press, 2014), 134–36. The Pearson source was part of a serialized novella titled *Plantation Pictures* published during the Civil War in the abolitionist newspaper *The Liberator*. Pearson had spent two years living as a governess in Virginia, where she had "ample time for writing and study" as well as "opportunity . . . for studying character" of enslaved people. She apparently kept "voluminous notebooks" of her studies and research. In writings

based upon that research, Pearson, her biographer concludes, portrayed enslaved characters "as individuals with recognizable, non-racialized personalities and full capacity for self-support." Moreover, Pearson's characters were often inspired by actual people she knew personally or had extensively researched (and appear in multiple writings—some of the characters in *Plantation Pictures* also appear in *The Poor White, or the Rebel Conscript*). Although presented as fiction, I have found much in Pearson's writings relating to maroons entirely plausible (and even confirmed in other nonfiction sources) and therefore will occasionally cite her work as supportive of other evidence. See Catherine E. Saunders, "Legacy Profile: Emily Clemons Pearson, 1818–1900," *Legacy* 29, no. 2 (2012): 300–317.

43. Byrd, *The Westover Manuscripts*, 25.

44. Byrd, 27.

45. Byrd, 29–30.

46. "An Act for Preventing Negroes Insurrections," in *The Law of Freedom and Bondage in the United States*, ed. John C. Hurd (Boston: Little, Brown, 1852), 1:234.

47. "An Act for Suppressing Outlying Slaves," in Hurd, 236.

48. "An Act Concerning Servants and Slaves," in *American Views: Documents in American History*, ed. Robert Aland Goldberg, Eric Hinderaker, and Dean L. May (Boston: Pearson, 2003), 62–66.

49. "An Act Concerning Servants and Slaves," in *The State Records of North Carolina: Laws, 1715–1776*, ed. Walter Clark (Goldsboro, N.C.: Nash Brothers, 1904), 23:62.

50. "An Act Concerning Servants and Slaves," 23:201–2.

51. *The State Records of North Carolina: Laws, 1715–1776*, ed. Walter Clark (Goldsboro, N.C.: Nash Brothers, 1904), 23:388, 488, 656; Marcus P. Nevius, *City of Refuge: Slavery and Petit Marronage in the Great Dismal Swamp, 1763–1856* (Athens: University of Georgia Press, 2020), 17; Jeffrey J. Crow, Paul D. Escott, and Flora J. Hatley, *A History of African Americans in North Carolina* (Raleigh: North Carolina Division of Archives & History, 1992), 4–6. Eventually, so many enslaved people were executed under the terms of the colony's slave code that lawmakers allowed castration as a substitute: compensation to masters for executed slaves took up too large a portion of the assembly's yearly expenditures.

52. Eric Nellis, *An Empire of Regions: A Brief History of Colonial British America* (Toronto: University of Toronto Press, 2010), 150.

53. Diouf, *Slavery's Exiles*, 26.

54. Sayers, *A Desolate Place*, 87–89.

55. "Letter of Spotswood to the L'ds Commr's of Trade," July 21, 1714, in *The Official Letters of Alexander Spotswood, Lieutenant-Governor of the Colony of Virginia, 1710–1722*, ed. R. A. Brock (Richmond: Virginia Historical Society, 1885), 2:71.

56. "Letter from Alexander Spotswood to Laurence Hyde," July 30, 1711, in Saunders, *Colonial Records of North Carolina*, 1:798.

57. See runaway ads for Spotswood's servants in *Genealogical Data from Colonial New York Newspapers: A Consolidation of Articles from the New York Genealogical and Biographical Record*, ed. Kenneth Scott (Baltimore: Genealogical Publishing, 1977),

11, 20; and *Abstracts from Ben Franklin's Pennsylvania Gazette, 1728–1748*, ed. Kenneth Scott (Baltimore: Genealogical Publishing, 1975), 190.

58. See Thos. Holt et al. to Honbl. Sr—, March 24, 1709, in Palmer, *Calendar of Virginia State Papers*, 1:129.

59. Thomson, *Flight to Freedom*, 127–28.

60. "Lt. Governor Gooch to the Council of Trade and Plantations," September 14, 1730, in *Calendar of State Papers, Colonial Series: America and West Indies, 1730*, ed. Cecil Headlam (London: H.M. Stationary Office, 1937), 276–77.

61. "Lt. Governor Gooch to the Council of Trade and Plantations," February 12, 1731, in *Calendar of State Papers, Colonial Series: America and West Indies, 1731*, ed. Cecil Headlam (London: H.M. Stationary Office, 1938), 41. See also Parent, *Foul Means*, 161.

62. John Brickell, *The Natural History of North-Carolina* (Dublin: James Carson, 1737), 357.

63. See Rebecca Anne Goetz, *The Baptism of Early Virginia: How Christianity Created Race* (Baltimore: Johns Hopkins University Press, 2016), 164–66.

64. "America and West Indies: March 1729, 16–31," *British History Online*, https://www.british-history.ac.uk/cal-state-papers/colonial/america-west-indies/vol36/pp327-342 (accessed February 26, 2020).

65. Diouf, *Slavery's Exiles*, 40, 49, 59. See also Marvin L. Michael Kay and Lorin Lee Cary, *Slavery in North Carolina, 1748–1775* (Chapel Hill: University of North Carolina Press, 1995), 127, 263–65; Richard Price, *Maroon Societies: Rebel Slave Communities in the Americas* (Baltimore: Johns Hopkins University Press, 1996), 20; and Eugene D. Genovese, *From Rebellion to Revolution: Afro-American Slave Revolts in the Making of the Modern World* (Baton Rouge: Louisiana State University Press, 1979), 53–54.

66. William Byrd to Lord Egmont, July 12, 1736, in *Virginia's Attitude toward Slavery and Secession*, ed. B. Munford, 20 (Frankfurt am Main: Outlook, 2020).

67. William Byrd, "A Southern Criticism of Slavery," in *Source-Book of American History*, ed. Alfred Bushnell Hart (New York: Macmillan, 1899), 119–21.

68. See Kenneth A. Lockridge, *The Diary and Life of William Byrd II of Virginia, 1674–1744* (Chapel Hill: University of North Carolina Press, 1987), 67–69.

69. Parent, *Foul Means*, 154; Kenneth A. Lockridge, *On the Sources of Patriarchal Rage: The Commonplace Books of William Byrd II and Thomas Jefferson and the Gendering of Power in the Eighteenth Century* (New York: New York University Press, 1994), 41–42.

70. William Byrd, *Description of the Dismal Swamp and Proposal to Drain the Swamp*, ed. Earl Gregg Swem (Metuchen, N.J.: Charles F. Heartman, 1922), 19.

71. Byrd, *The Westover Manuscripts*, 26.

72. Byrd, *Description of the Dismal Swamp*, 21–31.

73. Sayers, *A Desolate Place*, 155.

74. Smyth, *A Tour in the United States of America*, 64–65; Thomas C. Parramore, *Launching the Craft: The First Half-Century of Freemasonry in North Carolina* (Raleigh: Grand Lodge of North Carolina, 1975), 60–62. Although Smyth's popular

travel narrative was published in 1784, his presence near the Dismal Swamp dated back to at least 1763. If his knowledge of Dismal Swamp maroons living in the swamp for "twelve, twenty, or thirty years and upwards" was gained when he first came under shady circumstances to North Carolina from Virginia as an indentured servant, the maroons of his account might have lived in the swamp contemporaneously with Byrd's expedition.

75. Aitchison and Parker Account Book, 1763–1804, Accession #12992, Special Collections, University of Virginia Library, 51.

76. *A Century of Population Growth, From the First Census of the United States to the Twelfth, 1790–1900* (Washington, D.C.: Government Printing Office, 1909), 7.

77. Royster, *The Fabulous History of the Great Dismal Swamp Company*, 49.

78. "15 Octobr. 1763," Founders Online, National Archives, https://founders.archives.gov/documents/Washington/01-01-02-0009-0002 (accessed February 27, 2020); "[Diary entry: 28 October 1768]," Founders Online, National Archives, https://founders.archives.gov/documents/Washington/01-02-02-0003-0028-0028acc 2/27/2020 (accessed February 27, 2020); Royster, *The Fabulous History of the Great Dismal Swamp Company*, 82.

79. Royster, *The Fabulous History of the Great Dismal Swamp Company*, 83.

80. "Dismal Swamp Land Company Minutes of Meeting, 3 November 1763," Founders Online, National Archives, https://founders.archives.gov/documents/Washington/02-07-02-0164 (accessed February 27, 2020). See inventory and valuation of the enslaved workers at "Appraisement of Dismal Swamp Slaves, 4 July 1764," Founders Online, National Archives, https://founders.archives.gov/documents/Washington/02-07-02-0191 (accessed February 27, 2020).

81. Adventurers for Draining the Dismal Swamp, "Ledger A, 1750–1772: pg.194," George Washington Financial Papers Project, http://financial.gwpapers.org/?q=content/ledger-1750-1772-pg194 (accessed February 27, 2020).

82. Simpson, *The Great Dismal*, 42–44; Royster, *The Fabulous History of the Great Dismal Swamp Company*, 98.

83. "Cash Accounts, April 1764," Founders Online, National Archives, https://founders.archives.gov/documents/Washington/02-07-02-0179 (accessed February 27, 2020); "Appraisement of Dismal Swamp Slaves, 4 July 1764," Founders Online, National Archives, ttps://founders.archives.gov/documents/Washington/02-07-02-0191 (accessed February 27, 2020).

84. Nevius, *City of Refuge*, 26.

85. Nevius, 26.

86. Moses Grandy, *Narrative of the Life of Moses Grandy; Late a Slave in the United States of America* (London: G. Gilpin, 1843), 35.

87. Nevius, *City of Refuge*, 26.

88. Royster, *The Fabulous History of the Great Dismal Swamp Company*, 89.

89. Royster, 98; Nevius, *City of Refuge*, 26.

90. *Virginia Gazette*, April 2, 1772; "Appraisement of Dismal Swamp Slaves, 4 July 1764," Founders Online, National Archives, https://founders.archives.gov/documents/Washington/02-07-02-0191 (accessed February 27, 2020).

91. *Virginia Gazette*, February 18, 1773, July 10, 1773.

92. *Virginia Gazette*, June 23, 1768.

93. *Virginia Gazette*, October 6, 1768.

94. *Virginia Gazette*, April 13, 1769.

95. *Virginia Gazette*, July 10, 1778.

96. Royster, *The Fabulous History of the Great Dismal Swamp Company*, 117.

97. Royster, 147.

98. Royster, 217; Bland Simpson, *The Great Dismal: A Swamp Memoir* (Chapel Hill: University of North Carolina Press, 1990), 44.

CHAPTER THREE

1. "From George Washington to Richard Henry Lee, 26 December 1775," Founders Online, National Archives, https://founders.archives.gov/documents/Washington /03-02-02-0568 (accessed September 15, 2020).

2. *Diary of the American Revolution: From Newspapers and Original Documents*, ed. Frank Moore (New York: Charles Scribner, 1860), 1:160–61; "From George Washington to Richard Henry Lee, 26 December 1775," Founders Online, National Archives, https://founders.archives.gov/documents/Washington/03-02-02-0568 (accessed September 15, 2020).

3. Woody Holton, *Forced Founders: Indians, Debtors, Slaves, and the Making of the American Revolution in Virginia* (Chapel Hill: University of North Carolina Press, 1999), 148.

4. James Corbett David, *Dunmore's New World: The Extraordinary Life of a Royal Governor in Revolutionary America—with Jacobites, Counterfeiters, Land Schemes, Shipwrecks, Scalping, Indian Politics, Runaway Slaves, and Two Illegal Royal Weddings* (Charlottesville: University of Virginia Press, 2013), xliii.

5. *The Proceedings of the Convention of Delegates for the Counties and Corporations in the Colony of Virginia: Held at Richmond Town, in the County of Henrico, on the 20th of March, 1775* (Richmond: Ritchie, Trueheart, & Du-Val, 1816), 63.

6. David, *Dunmore's New World*, xlv.

7. David, xlvi, liii; Benjamin Quarles, *The Negro in the American Revolution* (Chapel Hill: University of North Carolina Press, 1961), 26; Thomas J. Wertenbaker, *Norfolk: Historic Southern Port* (Durham, N.C.: Duke University Press, 1962), 61–65.

8. Douglas R. Egerton, *Death or Liberty: African Americans and Revolutionary America* (New York: Oxford University Press, 2009), 89; Jill Lepore, *These Truths: A History of the United States* (New York: Norton, 2018), 94; Graham Russell Hodges, ed., *The Black Loyalist Directory: African Americans in Exile after the American Revolution* (New York: Garland, 1996), 111–12.

9. George Washington to Richard Henry Lee, December 26, 1775, in *Memoir of the Life of Richard H. Lee, and His Correspondence*, ed. Richard H. Lee (Philadelphia: H. C. Carey and I. Lea, 1825), 1:8–10.

10. Quarles, *The Negro in the American Revolution*, 21, 28–29.

11. Edmund Ruffin, "Observations Made during an Excursion to the Dismal Swamp," *Farmer's Register* 4 (January 1837): 516; Bland Simpson, *The Great Dismal:*

A Swamp Memoir (Chapel Hill: University of North Carolina Press, 1990), 44; Isaac Weld, *Travels through the States of North America and the Provinces of Upper and Lower Canada during the Years 1795, 1796, and 1797* (London: John Stockdale, 1807), 1:137.

12. Harry M. Ward, *The War for Independence and the Transformation of American Society: War and Society in the United States, 1775–83* (London: Routledge, 1999), 75.

13. William Wirt Henry, *Patrick Henry: Life, Correspondence and Speeches* (New York: Charles Scribner's Sons, 1891), 1:611.

14. Henry, 611.

15. William Tyree, "The Case of Josiah Phillips: How Virginia Came to Pass a Bill of Attainder," *Virginia Law Register* 16, no. 9 (January 1911), https://www.google.com/books/edition/The_Virginia_Law_Register/DDM1AQAAMAAJ?hl=en&gbpv=1&dq=%22josiah+phillips%22+%22dismal+swamp%22&pg=PA649&printsec=frontcover 650.

16. Ward, *The War for Independence*, 75; Tyree, "The Case of Josiah Phillips," 654–58.

17. Gen. Wm. Caswell to Gov. Burke, September 4, 1781, in *The State Records of North Carolina*, ed. Walter Clark (Goldsboro: Nash Brothers, 1907), 22:593.

18. Wertenbaker, *Norfolk*, 97; Thomas C. Parramore, Peter C. Stewart, and Tommy L. Bogger, *Norfolk: The First Four Centuries* (Charlottesville: University of Virginia Press, 1994), 99.

19. Hodges, *The Black Loyalist Directory*, 183–84; Charles Royster, *The Fabulous History of the Great Dismal Swamp Company: A Story of George Washington's Times* (New York: Vintage, 1999), 273.

20. Sylviane Diouf does not consider wartime escapees to be maroons, arguing that "wars did not have a major impact on marronage because more appealing options were or seemed available." These included possibility of legal freedom through service in the Revolution or, in the case of the Civil War, the potential for a general emancipation. Yet fighting for their freedom, on either side of the revolution, was part of self-emancipators' marronage. That they wore a uniform does not remove them from the process. Many more took advantage of wartime disruptions to maroon. A general emancipation during the Civil War seemed unlikely, and more immediate options to strike out for freedom, just as during the Revolution, were readily available for maroons (see chapter 5). See Sylviane A. Diouf, *Slavery's Exiles: The Story of the American Maroons* (New York: New York University Press, 2014), 36–37.

21. Marcus P. Nevius, *City of Refuge: Slavery and Petit Marronage in the Great Dismal Swamp, 1763–1856* (Athens: University of Georgia Press, 2020), 19.

22. Egerton, *Death or Liberty*, 88–89; Wertenbaker, *Norfolk*, 79.

23. J. F. D. Smyth, *A Tour in the United States of America* (London: G. Robinson, 1784), 101.

24. Smyth, 101; Weld, *Travels through the States of North America*, 104.

25. "The Great Dismal," *The New York Magazine; or, Literary Repository*, April 1791, 195.

26. Royster, *The Fabulous History of the Great Dismal Swamp Company*, 290.

27. John B. Scott to the Governor, April 23, 1802, in *Calendar of Virginia State*

Papers and Other Manuscripts: From January 1, 1799 to December 31, 1807, vol. 9, ed. H. W. Flournoy (Richmond: James E. Goode, 1890), 294 (hereafter Flournoy, *CVSP*, 9).

28. Bradford J. Wood and Larry E. Tise, "The Conundrum of Unfree Labor," in *New Voyages to Carolina: Reinterpreting North Carolina History*, ed. Larry E. Tise and Jeffrey J. Crow (Chapel Hill: University of North Carolina Press, 2017), 94.

29. Mohamed B. Taleb-Khyar, "Jean Fouchard," *Callaloo* 15, no. 2 (Spring 1992): 322.

30. "Liberty. Equality. Army of St. Domingo," *Balance and Columbian Repository*, June 29, 1802.

31. Joseph Cephas Carroll, *Slave Insurrections in the United States, 1800–1865* (Boston: Chapman & Grimes, 1938), 42.

32. Carroll, 44.

33. Herbert Aptheker, *American Negro Slave Revolts* (New York: Columbia University Press, 1943), 211–12; Thomas Newton to the Governor, May 10, 1792, in *Calendar of Virginia State Papers and Other Manuscripts*, vol. 5, ed. Wm. P. Palmer and Sherwin McRae (Richmond: Rush U. Durr, 1885), 540; W. Wilson to the Governor, May 10, 1792, in Palmer and McRae, *Calendar of Virginia State Papers*, 542.

34. Thomas Newton to the Governor, May 19, 1792, in Palmer and McRae, *Calendar of Virginia State Papers*, 5:552.

35. In Aptheker, *American Negro Slave Revolts*, 211.

36. This was not the planter and politician John Randolph of Roanoke. Aptheker, 213–14; Benjamin Campbell, *Richmond's Unhealed History* (Richmond: Brandylane, 2012), 83–84.

37. "A Letter to and from Slave Rebels," in Herbert Aptheker, *A Documentary History of the Negro People in the United States* (New York: Citadel, 1951), 1:28.

38. See Julius S. Scott, *The Common Wind: Afro-American Currents in the Age of the Haitian Revolution* (London: Verso, 2018).

39. See Timothy M. Matthewson, "George Washington's Policy toward the Haitian Revolution," *Diplomatic History* 3, no. 3 (Summer 1979): 321–22.

40. Nevius, *City of Refuge*, 32–33.

41. Royster, *The Fabulous History of the Great Dismal Swamp Company*, 290.

42. Royster, 341.

43. Edmund Ruffin, *Agricultural, Geological, and Descriptive Sketches of Lower North Carolina, and the Similar Adjacent Lands* (Raleigh: Institution for the Deaf & Dumb & Blind, 1861), 143, 211. Ruffin's first published description of the canal described its digging in the passive voice ("The canal was dug . . .") with no mention whatsoever of the laborers who dug it. Ruffin, "Observations," 517.

44. David S. Cecelski, *The Waterman's Song: Slavery and Freedom in Maritime North Carolina* (Chapel Hill: University of North Carolina Press, 2001), 109. See also Moses Grandy, *Narrative of the Life of Moses Grandy; Late a Slave in the United States of America* (London: G. Gilpin, 1843), 35.

45. Royster, *The Fabulous History of the Great Dismal Swamp Company*, 342.

46. Parramore, Stewart, and Bogger, *Norfolk*, 147; Royster, *The Fabulous History of the Great Dismal Swamp Company*, 343; Grandy, *Narrative*, 35.

47. Kathryn Elise Benjamin Golden, "'Through the Muck and Mire': Marronage, Representation, and Memory in the Great Dismal Swamp," PhD diss. (University of California, Berkeley, 2018), 66; Egerton, *Death or Liberty*, 279.

48. The best treatment of the Gabriel Rebellion is Douglas R. Egerton, *Gabriel's Rebellion: The Virginia Slave Conspiracies of 1800 and 1802* (Chapel Hill: University of North Carolina Press, 1993).

49. James Sidbury, *Ploughshares into Swords: Race, Rebellion, and Identity in Gabriel's Virginia, 1730–1810* (Cambridge: Cambridge University Press, 1997), 265–66.

50. Martin R. Delany, *Blake, or, The Huts of America: A Novel* (Boston: Beacon, 1970), 113–14.

51. Sidbury, *Ploughshares*, 265.

52. Hugo Prosper Leaming, *Hidden Americans: The Maroons of Virginia and the Carolinas* (New York: Garland, 1995), 252.

53. Douglas R. Egerton, "'Fly across the River': The Easter Slave Conspiracy of 1802," *North Carolina Historical Review* 68, no. 2 (April 1991): 88–98.

54. John Cowper to the Governor, April 17, 1802, in Flournoy, *CVSP*, 9:293.

55. "Baltimore," *Norfolk Herald*, n.d., in *North-Carolina Journal*, March 15, 1802.

56. Thos. Mathews to the Governor, March 10, 1802, in Flournoy, *CVSP*, 9:287. This may or may not have been the same "travelling friend" mentioned in an intercepted letter and said to have thousands of weapons at the ready north of the swamp (east of Petersburg). See Frank Goode to Roling Pointer, January 18, 1802, in Flournoy, *CVSP*, 9:274.

57. Thos. Mathews to the Governor, March 13, 1802, in Flournoy, *CVSP*, 9:288–89.

58. Egerton, "Fly across the River," 98.

59. *Balance and Columbian Repository*, June 8, 1802.

60. "Halifax County Court," April 23, 1802, in Flournoy, *CVSP*, 9:294.

61. *Balance and Columbian Repository*, June 8, 1802; John Cowper to the Governor, May 18, 1802, in Flournoy, *CVSP*, 9:301.

62. George Goosley to the Governor, June 5, 1802, in Flournoy, *CVSP*, 9:305–6.

63. "Extract from a Letter from Elizabeth City, North Carolina, Dated May 12, 1802," *Green Mountain Patriot* (Peacham, Vt.), June 9, 1802.

64. Aptheker, *American Negro Slave Revolts*, 229; John Scott et al. to The Citizens of Nansemond County, June 5, 1802, in Flournoy, *CVSP*, 9:307.

65. "Extract from a Letter from Elizabeth City, North Carolina, Dated May 12, 1802," *Green Mountain Patriot*, June 9, 1802.

66. *Weekly Raleigh Register*, June 1, 1802; *Norfolk Herald*, June 2, 1802; Aptheker, *American Negro Slave Revolts*, 231. Six conspirators arrested on the testimony of Mingo were later found not guilty, and Mingo had his ears cut from his head for his "perjury." See William A. Griffin, *Antebellum Elizabeth City: The History of a Canal Town* (Elizabeth City, N.C.: Roanoke Press, 1970), 124.

67. Aptheker, *American Negro Slave Revolts*, 230; Leaming, *Hidden Americans*, 250; Diouf, *Slavery's Exiles*, 259; "Extract from a Letter from Elizabeth City, North Carolina, Dated May 12, 1802," *Green Mountain Patriot*, June 9, 1802.

68. *Weekly Raleigh Register*, June 1, 1802.

69. "Extract from a Letter from Elizabeth City, North Carolina, Dated May 12, 1802," *Green Mountain Patriot*, June 9, 1802.

70. *Balance and Columbian Repository*, June 8, 1802; "Extract from a Letter from Elizabeth City, North Carolina, Dated May 12, 1802," *Green Mountain Patriot*, June 9, 1802.

71. Thomas Matthews to the Governor, June 15, 1802, in Flournoy, *CVSP*, 9:308–9.

72. William Wilkerson to the Governor, June 8, 1802, in Flournoy, *CVSP*, 9:306–7; "Negroes again Troublesome!!," *Norfolk Herald*, June 15, 1802, in *Lancaster Intelligencer*, June 23, 1802.

73. Benjamin Overman to Capt. Grice, June 10, 1802, in Flournoy, *CVSP*, 9:308.

74. See Aptheker, *American Negro Slave Revolts*, 230–32.

75. Thomas Newton to the Governor, August 28, 1802, in Flournoy, *CVSP*, 9:318.

76. Kemp P. Battle, "Sketches of the History of North Carolina in 1802," *Wachovia Moravian* 11, no. 122 (April 1903): n.p.

77. John Cowper to the Governor, March 11, 1802, in Flournoy, *CVSP*, 9:287.

78. See Bland Simpson, *Two Captains from Carolina: Moses Grandy, John Newland Maffitt, and the Coming of the Civil War* (Chapel Hill: University of North Carolina Press, 2012), 5, 169.

79. Aptheker, *American Negro Slave Revolts*, 145, 241, 243.

80. *Edenton (N.C.) Gazette*, November 18, 1807.

81. *Edenton Gazette*, October 5, 1808.

82. Richard W. Byrd to the Governor, May 30, 1810, in *Calendar of Virginia State Papers and Other Manuscripts, From January 1, 1808 to December 31, 1835*, vol. 10, ed. H. W. Flournoy (Richmond: James E. Goode, 1892), 82–83 (hereafter Flournoy, *CVSP*, 10).

83. Flournoy, *CVSP*, 10:82–83.

84. LaSalle Corbell Pickett, *Kunnoo Sperits and Others* (Washington, D.C.: Neale, 1900), 69–74. Pickett is a problematic source, she being best known for her tendentious "historical" writings promoting the ideology of the Lost Cause and attempting to resurrect the military reputation of her husband, former Confederate general George E. Pickett. *Kunnoo Sperits* is presented as the true, "phonetically genuine" record of African American stories she had heard over the course of her life. That there are exaggerations therein and most likely outright fabrications is quite likely. However, much of her writing in *Kunnoo Sperits* on the Great Dismal Swamp and the people who inhabited it is corroborated in other reliable sources, and suggests either true firsthand knowledge or extensive background research by the author. I at least find most of her writings regarding "Uncle Alek," a well-known and otherwise well-documented friend of maroons, believable. He numbered among the "Black preachers" who frequented the Dismal. See also Sayers, *A Desolate Place*, 91–92; Nevius, *City of Refuge*, 57; and Simpson, *The Great Dismal*, 105.

85. Richard W. Byrd to the Governor, May 30, 1810, in Flournoy, *CVSP*, 10:82–83.

86. Aptheker, *American Negro Slave Revolts*, 246n6.

87. Richard W. Byrd to the Governor, May 30, 1810, in Flournoy, *CVSP*, 10:82–83.

88. F. Roy Johnson, *Tales from Old Carolina* (Murfreesboro, N.C.: Johnson, 1965), 155–56; Golden, "'Through the Muck and Mire,'" 68–69.

89. *Norfolk Herald*, June 29, 1818, in *New York Herald*, July 7, 1818.

90. "Negro Hunt," *Norfolk Herald*, December 16, 1818, in *Pittsburgh Weekly Gazette*, January 5, 1819; William S. Forrest, *Historical and Descriptive Sketches of Norfolk and Vicinity: Including Portsmouth and the Adjacent Counties, during a Period of Two Hundred Years* (Norfolk: Lindsay and Blakiston, 1853), 445–46; *Norfolk Herald*, n.d., in *Clarion and Tennessee State Gazette*, December 29, 1818.

91. "Murder and Robbery," *Norfolk Herald*, December 4, 1818, in *Charleston Daily Courier*, December 12, 1818; "Negro Hunt," *Norfolk Herald*, December 16, 1818, in *Pittsburgh Weekly Gazette*, January 5, 1819; *Norfolk Herald*, n.d., in *Clarion and Tennessee State Gazette*, December 29, 1818; Christopher H. Bouton, *Setting Slavery's Limits: Physical Confrontations in Antebellum Virginia, 1801–1860* (Lanham, Md.: Lexington, 2019), 123.

92. "Murder and Robbery," *Norfolk Herald*, December 4, 1818, in *Charleston Daily Courier*, December 12, 1818; Bouton, *Setting Slavery's Limits*, 123.

93. Bouton, *Setting Slavery's Limits*, 123.

94. "Negro Hunt," *Norfolk Herald*, December 16, 1818, in *Pittsburgh Weekly Gazette*, January 5, 1819.

95. "Negro Hunt"; Bouton, *Setting Slavery's Limits*, 126.

96. Christopher H. Bouton, "Against the Peace and Dignity of the Commonwealth: Physical Confrontations between Slaves and Whites in Antebellum Virginia, 1801–1860," PhD diss. (University of Delaware, 2016), 249–51.

97. Forrest, *Historical and Descriptive Sketches*, 446. See also "Negro Man Mingo," *Norfolk Herald*, n.d., in *Edenton Gazette*, March 2, 1819.

98. Bouton, *Setting Slavery's Limits*, 125; "Negro Hunt," *Norfolk Herald*, December 16, 1818, in *Pittsburgh Weekly Gazette*, January 5, 1819.

99. *Norfolk Herald*, n.d., in *Clarion and Tennessee State Gazette*, December 29, 1818.

100. *Norfolk Herald*, December 16, 1818, in *Pittsburgh Weekly Gazette*, January 5, 1819; *North Carolina Star*, July 4, 1823.

101. "A Serious Subject," *Norfolk Herald*, May 12, 1823, in *New York Evening Post*, May 15, 1823.

102. *Raleigh Weekly Register*, June 6, 1823; *Norfolk Herald*, May 12, 1823, in *New York Evening Post*, May 15, 1823; *Norfolk Herald*, n.d., in *Clarion and Tennessee State Gazette*, December 29, 1818; William Henry Stewart, *History of Norfolk County, Virginia, and Representative Citizens* (Chicago: Biographical Publishing, 1902); "Norfolk," *Niles Weekly Register* (Baltimore), June 7, 1823, 217.

103. *Vermont Journal*, June 2, 1823; *Raleigh Weekly Register*, June 6, 1823.

104. *North Carolina Star*, July 4, 1823.

105. *North Carolina Star*, July 4, 1823; *Raleigh Weekly Register*, June 6, 1823.

106. See Johnson, *Tales from Old Carolina*, 156–58.

107. *The Laws of North Carolina, Enacted in the Year 1822* (Raleigh: Bell & Lawrence, 1823), 28–29.

108. Diouf, *Slavery's Exiles*, 227. This bill was repealed in December 1823, but another version was passed in 1846. See *A Revisal of the Laws of the State of North-Carolina Passed from 1821–1825* (Raleigh: J. Gales & Son, 1827), 82.

109. *Norfolk Herald*, December 16, 1818, in *Pittsburgh Weekly Gazette*, January 5, 1819.

110. *Argus of Western America*, March 10, 1824; *National Gazette*, June 15, 1824; *Weekly Raleigh Register*, February 13, 1824; *American Beacon*, June 16, 1823.

111. *Weekly Raleigh Register*, June 27, 1823; Simpson, *The Great Dismal*, 115.

112. *Elizabeth City Star*, n.d., in *Fayetteville Weekly Observer*, May 20, 1824; *North-Carolina Free Press*, June 11, 1824; *National Gazette*, June 15, 1824; Jack Temple Kirby, *Poquosin: A Study of Rural Landscape and Society* (Chapel Hill: University of North Carolina Press, 1995), 181; Diouf, *Slavery's Exiles*, 240–42.

113. *North-Carolina Free Press*, June 25, 1824;

114. *Weekly Raleigh Register*, November 19, 1824.

115. *North-Carolina Free Press*, June 11, 1824; *National Gazette*, June 15, 1824; Kirby, *Poquosin*, 181.

116. Thomas R. Gray, *The Confessions of Nat Turner* (Baltimore: Thomas R. Gray, 1831), 9; Kenneth S. Greenberg, "Name, Face, Body," in *Nat Turner: A Slave Rebellion in History and Memory*, ed. Kenneth S. Greenberg (New York: Oxford University Press, 2003), 18; David F. Allmendinger, *Nat Turner and the Rising in Southampton County* (Baltimore: Johns Hopkins University Press, 2014), 33–34, 315n45; Kirby, *Poquosin*, 181.

117. Gray, *The Confessions of Nat Turner*, 7.

118. *Richmond Constitutional Whig*, August 23, 1831, in David Brion Davis and Steven Mintz, eds., *The Boisterous Sea of Liberty: A Documentary History of America from Discovery through the Civil War* (New York: Oxford University Press, 1998), 387.

119. *Norfolk Herald*, August 24, 1831, in *National Gazette*, August 27, 1831.

120. *Evening Post*, August 29, 1831.

121. "Negro Insurrection in Virginia," *Gazette*, n.d., in *Danville (Vt.) North Star*, September 13, 1831.

122. *Norfolk Herald*, August 26, 1831, in *National Gazette*, August 29, 1831.

123. "The Late Insurrection in Virginia," *Norfolk Herald*, August 29, 1831, in *National Gazette*, September 1, 1831.

124. Samuel Warner, *Authentic and Impartial Narrative of the Tragical Scene* (New York: Warner and West, 1831), 30–31.

125. *New York Gazette*, n.d., in *The Liberator*, September 17, 1831; Higginson, "Nat Turner's Insurrection," *Atlantic* 8, no. 46 (August 1861): 173; Leaming, *Hidden Americans*, 260.

126. *The Negro's Flight from American Slavery to British Freedom*, prefatory remarks by George Thompson (London: John Snow, 1849), 14; Warner, *Authentic and Impartial Narrative*, 12; Robert Arnold, *The Dismal Swamp and Lake Drummond: Early Recollections. Vivid Portrayal of Amusing Scenes* (Norfolk: Green, Burke, & Gregory,

1888), 23–27; *Proceedings of the General Anti-slavery Convention* (London: John Snow, 1843), 78; Leaming, *Hidden Americans*, 260.

127. *Norfolk Herald*, August 26, 1831, in *National Gazette*, August 29, 1831; Aptheker, *American Negro Slave Revolts*, 301.

128. "Insurrection of the Blacks," *Niles Weekly Register* (Baltimore), September 3, 1831.

129. Warner, *Authentic and Impartial Narrative*, 31; Sayers, *A Desolate Place*, 104.

130. Warner, *Authentic and Impartial Narrative*, 12, 31; *Weekly Raleigh Register*, September 29, 1831. See also Charles E. Morris, "Panic and Reprisal: Reaction in North Carolina to the Nat Turner Insurrection, 1831," *North Carolina Historical Review* 72, no. 1 (January 1985): 37.

131. See Sayers, *A Desolate Place*, 104; Golden, "'Through the Muck and Mire,'" 71; Sally E. Hadden, *Slave Patrols: Law and Violence in Virginia and the Carolinas* (Cambridge, Mass.: Harvard University Press, 2001), 142.

132. Gray, *The Confessions of Nat Turner*, 17.

133. Warner, *Authentic and Impartial Narrative*, 35.

134. *New York Gazette*, n.d., in *The Liberator*, September 17, 1831.

135. Edmund Jackson, "The Virginia Maroons," in *The Liberty Bell* (Boston: National Anti-slavery Bazaar, 1852), 149.

136. *Petersburg Index*, October 1, 1869.

CHAPTER FOUR

1. In this and most cases that follow, I have reworked dialect as it appeared in the original document. This not only makes the passages easier to read but also avoids replicating the preconceptions and stereotypes of white authors who originally recorded the passages. I will provide the original language in footnotes. See George P. Rawick, *From Sundown to Sunup: The Making of the Black Community* (Westport, Conn.: Greenwood, 1972), 176–78. This quote is from "When Boys Were Men," *Montour American* (Danville, Pa.), July 31, 1902, and reads in the original: "de woods was full of 'em."

2. Meel R. Eppes, *The Negro, Too, in American History* (Chicago: National Educational, 1939), 159; Thomas J. Wertenbaker, *Norfolk: Historic Southern Port* (Durham, N.C.: Duke University Press, 1962), 30; Edmund Jackson, "The Virginia Maroons," in *The Liberty Bell* (Boston: National Anti-slavery Bazaar, 1852), 149.

3. J. F. D. Smyth, *A Tour in the United States of America* (London: G. Robinson, 1784), 239.

4. Jackson, "The Virginia Maroons," 146.

5. John Boyle O'Reilly, *Athletics and Manly Sport* (Boston: Pilot, 1890), 393.

6. O'Reilly, 23.

7. Frederick Douglass, *My Bondage and My Freedom* (New York: Miller, Orton, 1855), 435–36.

8. See Herbert Aptheker, *American Negro Slave Revolts* (New York: Columbia University Press, 1943), 152.

9. Daniel O. Sayers, *A Desolate Place for a Defiant People: The Archaeology of Maroons, Indigenous Americans, and Enslaved Laborers in the Great Dismal Swamp* (Gainesville: University Press of Florida, 2014), 22–23.

10. Sayers, 25, 118–20, 131. GDSLS director Daniel Sayers chose to call it the "nameless site" (no capitalization) in the event a historically used name comes to light. The site sits approximately two miles into the swamp from the Nansemond Scarp and three and a half miles from the Cross Canal in the North Carolina Dismal Swamp.

11. Daniel O. Sayers, "The Underground Railroad Reconsidered," *Western Journal of Black Studies* 28, no. 3 (2004): 440.

12. As political scientist Neil Roberts argues, as important as it is to understand slavery as freedom's opposite, one should always consider "the equally important liminal and transitional social space *between* slavery and freedom . . . the process by which people emerge *from* slavery *to* freedom." Neil Roberts, *Freedom as Marronage* (Chicago: University of Chicago Press, 2015), 4.

13. James Redpath, *The Roving Editor, or, Talks with Slaves in the Southern States* (New York: A. B. Burdick, 1859), 288.

14. *Edenton Gazette and North Carolina General Advertiser*, May 8, 1827, in Freddie Parker, *Stealing a Little Freedom: Advertisements for Slave Runaways in North Carolina, 1791–1840* (London: Routledge, 1994), 382.

15. Parker, 382.

16. J. Brent Morris, "'Running Servants and All Others': The Diverse and Elusive Maroons of the Great Dismal Swamp," in *Voices from within the Veil: African Americans and the Experience of Democracy*, ed. William H. Alexander, Cassandra Newby-Alexander, and Charles H. Ford (Newcastle-upon-Tyne, UK: Cambridge Scholars, 2008), 133, 144.

17. *State Gazette of North Carolina*, January 3, 1789.

18. *Edenton Gazette and North Carolina General Advertiser*, December 14, 1818. See also David Griffith, *The Estuary's Gift: An Atlantic Coast Cultural Biography* (University Park: Pennsylvania State University Press, 1999), 1–3.

19. Daniel Drayton, *Personal Memoir of Daniel Drayton* (Boston: Bela Marsh, 1855), 20–22. See also H. Cowles Atwater, *Incidents of a Southern Tour, or, The South, as Seen with Northern Eyes* (Boston: J. P. Magee, 1857), 45.

20. Fountain's ship could accommodate forty to fifty passengers. See Gary Collison, *Shadrach Minkins: From Fugitive Slave to Citizen* (Cambridge, Mass.: Harvard University Press, 1997), 49; Mary Ellen Snodgrass, ed., *The Underground Railroad: An Encyclopedia of People, Places, and Operations* (London: Routledge, 2015), xxxi, 197, 214; William Still, *Still's Underground Railroad Record* (Philadelphia: William Still, 1886), 165–72; Tom Colarco, *People of the Underground Railroad: A Biographical Dictionary* (New York: ABC-CLIO, 2008), 130.

21. Collison, *Shadrach Minkins*, 124–25. See also *The Youth's Political Instructor*, part 2, *Exhibiting the Horrors of Slavery* (Belfast: Henry Greer, 1852), 47.

22. "Fifty Dollars Reward," *Richmond Enquirer*, October 19, 1858.

23. Peter Randolph, *Sketches of Slave Life, or, Illustrations of the Peculiar Institution* (Boston: Peter Randolph, 1855), 17.

24. "New York Committee on Vigilance Agent's Record, 1846–1847," in Irving H. Bartlett, "Abolitionists, Fugitives, and Imposters in Boston, 1846–1847," *New England Quarterly* 55, no. 1 (1982), 103.

25. William Still, *The Underground Railroad* (Philadelphia: Porter & Coates, 1872), 169.

26. Atwater, *Incidents of a Southern Tour*, 57; LaSalle Corbell Pickett, *Kunnoo Sperits and Others* (Washington, D.C.: Neale, 1900), 72.

27. David S. Cecelski, *The Waterman's Song: Slavery and Freedom in Maritime North Carolina* (Chapel Hill: University of North Carolina Press, 2001), 123–33.

28. Still, *Still's Underground Railroad Record*, 424.

29. Redpath, *The Roving Editor*, 295. Quote in original: "'Spect I better not tell de way I comed: for dar's lots more boys comin' same way I did."

30. Isaac Candler, *A Summary View of America* (London: T. Cadell, 1824), 137–39; Walter Prichard Eaton, *Barn Doors and Byways* (Boston: Small, Maynard, 1913), 191; Walter Prichard Eaton, "The Real Dismal Swamp," *Harper's Monthly Magazine* 122, no. 727 (December 1910): 24, 26–27.

31. "In the Swamp," *The Liberator*, January 22, 1864.

32. "Life in the Swamp [continued]," *Lorain County (Ohio) News*, September 23, 1864.

33. See Emily Clemens Pearson, *The Poor White, or, The Rebel Conscript* (Boston: Graves and Young, 1864), 131–32; John R. Winslow to Caleb Winslow, August 27, 1845, transcript in Winslow Family Papers, 1712–1945, North Carolina State Archives, PL90.18.

34. William Byrd, *The Westover Manuscripts: Containing the History of the Dividing Line betwixt Virginia and North Carolina; A Journey to the Land of Eden, A.D. 1733; and A Progress to the Mines. Written from 1728 to 1736* (Petersburg, Va.: Edmund and Julian Ruffin, 1841), 18.

35. Jackson, "The Virginia Maroons," 146.

36. Willis Augustus Hodges, *Free Man of Color: The Autobiography of Willis Augustus Hodges*, ed. Willard B. Gatewood (Knoxville: University of Tennessee Press, 1982), 10–17.

37. Pickett, *Kunnoo Sperits*, 72.

38. *Edenton Gazette and North Carolina General Advertiser*, December 25, 1820.

39. "$20 Reward," *Democratic Pioneer*, January 5, 1858.

40. "25 Dollars Reward," *Edenton Gazette and North Carolina General Advertiser*, June 16, 1808.

41. Marisa Kelly, "Runaway Jim," *The Ladies' Repository: A Monthly Periodical* 33 (August 1873): 123.

42. Samuel Warner, *Authentic and Impartial Narrative of the Tragical Scene* (New York: Warner and West, 1831), 34–35. See also Atwater, *Incidents of a Southern Tour*, 49–50.

43. Alvin O. Thompson, *Flight to Freedom: African Runaways and Maroons in the Americas* (Kingston, Jamaica: University of the West Indies Press, 2006), 139; Sylviane A. Diouf, *Slavery's Exiles: The Story of the American Maroons* (New York: New York University Press, 2014), 115–16.

44. Redpath, *The Roving Editor*, 290; Diouf, *Slavery's Exiles*, 115–16.

45. Redpath, *The Roving Editor*, 292; "Life in the Swamp [continued]," *Lorain County News*, September 23, 1864.

46. See James Spady, "Belonging and Alienation: Gullah Jack and Some Maroon Dimensions of the 'Denmark Vesey Conspiracy,'" in *Maroons and the Marooned: Runaways and Castaways in the Americas*, ed. Richard Bodek and Joseph Kelly, 30–54 (Jackson: University Press of Mississippi, 2000).

47. Samuel Huntington Perkins, "A Yankee Tutor in the Old South," ed. Robert C. McLean, *North Carolina Historical Review* 47, no. 1 (January 1970): 62; Frederick Law Olmsted, *A Journey in the Seaboard Slave States* (New York: Mason Brothers, 1861), 101.

48. Diouf, *Slavery's Exiles*, 123; Redpath, *The Roving Editor*, 291.

49. Diouf, *Slavery's Exiles*, 117, 129.

50. Charles L. Perdue, Thomas E. Barden, and Robert K. Phillips, eds., *Weevils in the Wheat: Interviews with Virginia Ex-slaves* (Charlottesville: University of Virginia Press, 1976), 117. Quote in original: "runned away an' didn' never come back. Didn' go no place neither. Stayed right roun' de plantation."

51. Perdue, Barden, and Phillips, 252.

52. William H. Robinson, *From Log Cabin to the Pulpit, or, Fifteen Years in Slavery* (Eau Claire, Wisc.: James H. Tifft, 1913), 32.

53. "In the Swamp," *The Liberator*, January 22, 1864.

54. Vincent Harding, *There Is a River: The Black Struggle for Freedom in America* (New York: Harcourt Brace, 1981), 48–49.

55. John W. Blassingame, *The Slave Community: Plantation Life in the Antebellum South* (New York: Oxford University Press, 1979), 192–93.

56. See Kathryn Elise Benjamin Golden, "'Through the Muck and Mire': Marronage, Representation, and Memory in the Great Dismal Swamp," PhD diss. (University of California, Berkeley, 2018), 74; J. M. McKim, "The Slave's Ultima Ratio," *The Liberator*, February 5, 1858.

57. *Edenton Gazette and North Carolina General Advertiser*, May 9, 1820.

58. Golden, "'Through the Muck and Mire,'" 127–28.

59. John R. Winslow to Caleb Winslow, August 27, 1845, in Winslow Family Papers, 1712–1941, North Carolina State Archives, PC 90.18.

60. Pickett, *Kunnoo Sperits*, 72. Quote in original: "de all knowed dat de whippin' pos' ner jail, ner nuttin'couldn' mek him tell on 'em, en dat he allers gin 'em sump'n t'eat, en gin em' matches, en vided his backer wid 'em."

61. See Olmsted, *A Journey in the Seaboard Slave States*, 100; and Pickett, *Kunnoo Sperits*, 65.

62. Pickett, *Kunnoo Sperits*, 65. Quote in original: "w'ich wuz a ebby-day 'currence wid 'em w'en dey wuz tired er wuk."

63. *The Current*, September 26, 1885.

64. "Sketches in Color," *Putnam's Magazine* 4 (December 1869): 742. Quote in original: "'kase I'se feared ole massa kill me."

65. Charles Frederick Stansbury, *The Lake of the Great Dismal* (New York: Albert & Charles Boni, 1925), 20.

66. John Patterson Green, *Recollections of the Inhabitants, Localities, Superstitions and Kuklux Outrages of the Carolinas* (n.p., 1880), 71–72. Quote in original: "as hard as a litewood not, an nuffin could hurt me." It was common practice for enslavers not to advertise for the return of a runaway until he or she had been gone for more than a month. Megan Kate Nelson, *Trembling Earth: A Cultural History of the Okefenokee Swamp* (Athens: University of Georgia Press, 2009), 25.

67. Kelly, "Runaway Jim," 123.

68. Guion Griffis Johnson, *Ante-bellum North Carolina: A Social History* (Chapel Hill: University of North Carolina Press, 1937), 515.

69. "In the Swamp," *The Liberator*, January 22, 1863.

70. Robert S. Starobin, *Industrial Slavery in the Old South* (New York: Oxford University Press, 1970), 84–85.

71. Thompson, *Flight to Freedom*, 142.

72. "Firewood," Virginia Department of Forestry, http://www.dof.virginia.gov/manage/firewood.htm (accessed May 6, 2020); "Different Types of Wood for Burning," https://www.southyorkshirefirewood.com/wood-burning-characteristics.html (accessed May 6, 2020); Diouf, *Slavery's Exiles*, 104.

73. Warner, *Authentic and Impartial Narrative*, 35.

74. James C. Scott, *The Art of Not Being Governed: An Anarchist History of Upland Southeast Asia* (New Haven, Conn.: Yale University Press, 2009), 190–95.

75. Hubert J. Davis, *The Great Dismal Swamp: Its History, Folklore and Science* (Richmond, Va.: Cavalier, 1962), 61; Jackson, "The Virginia Maroons," 145; Thompson, *Flight to Freedom*, 239–40.

76. "Recollections of Slavery," *The Emancipator*, September 13, 1838.

77. Eugene D. Genovese, *Roll Jordan Roll: The World the Slaves Made* (New York: Vintage, 1974), 599. See also "Life in the Swamp," *Lorain County News*, September 16, 1864.

78. Wm. Caswell to Col. Bryan, Sept. 4, 1781, in *The State Records of North Carolina*, ed. Walter Clark (Goldsboro: Nash Brothers, 1907), 22:592–93.

79. H. Cowles Atwater, *Incidents of a Southern Tour, or The South as Seen with Northern Eyes* (Boston: J. P. Magee, 1857), 50; "Life in the Swamp," *Lorain County News*, September 16, 1863, and "Life in the Swamp [concluded]," *Lorain County News*, September 23, 1863.

80. "Banditti Apprehended," *North-Carolina Free Press*, June 11, 1824.

81. *Weekly Raleigh Register*, June 6, 1823; Robert Arnold, *The Dismal Swamp and Lake Drummond: Early Recollections. Vivid Portrayal of Amusing Scenes* (Norfolk: Green, Burke, & Gregory, 1888), 7. Alexander Keeling was said to have owned a similar vest circa 1802. See Pickett, *Kunnoo Sperits*, 71–72.

82. See William Tynes Cowan, *The Slave in the Swamp: Disrupting the Plantation*

Narrative (London: Routledge, 2005), 55; and R. H. Taylor, "Slave Conspiracies in North Carolina," *North Carolina Historical Review* 5, no. 1 (January 1928): 25.

83. Sayers, *A Desolate Place*, 106.

84. Perdue, Barden, and Phillips, *Weevils in the Wheat*, 252; Still, *Still's Underground Railroad Record*, 424; Daisy Saunders interviewed in Golden, "'Through the Muck and Mire,'" 132.

85. Sayers, *Desolate Place*, 120–23, 126, 129, 141, 154; "Pompey's Secret," *Catholic World* 31, no. 4 (July 1880): 548; Henry Clapp, *The Pioneer, or, Leaves from an Editor's Portfolio* (Lynn, Mass.: J. B. Tolman, 1846), 77; F. Roy Johnson, *Tales from Old Carolina* (Murfreesboro, N.C.: Johnson, 1965), 162–63; Thompson, *Flight to Freedom*, 253; Michael Mullin, *Africa in America: Slave Acculturation and Resistance in the American South and the British Caribbean, 1736–1831* (Urbana: University of Illinois Press, 1992), 59.

86. Sayers, *A Desolate Place*, 145.

87. Sayers, 120–23, 126, 129, 141, 154–55. Sayers has dated multiple deep swamp structures to the early seventeenth century through optically stimulated luminescence (OSL) and other techniques.

88. Sayers, 121–22; Alexander Hunter, "Through the Dismal Swamp," *Potter's American Monthly* 17, no. 115 (July 1881): 13. See also "The Dismal Swamp," *New York Times*, n.d., in *Neenah (Wisc.) Daily Times*, February 17, 1892.

89. "Editorial Notes and Clippings," *DeBow's Review* 4, no. 4 (October 1867): 371; "In the Swamp," *The Liberator*, January 22, 1863; "The Dismal Swamp," *The Friend*, November 23, 1867.

90. *The Friend*, November 23, 1867; David Hunter Strother, "In the Dismal Swamp," *Harper's New Monthly Magazine* 13, no. 73 (June 1856): 453; Hunter, "Through the Dismal Swamp," 7.

91. "Life in the Swamp," *Lorain County News*, September 16, 1863, and "Life in the Swamp [concluded]," *Lorain County News*, September 23, 1863; *The Friend*, November 23, 1867; Belinda Hurmence, *We Lived in a Little Cabin in the Yard: Personal Accounts of Slavery in Virginia* (Winston-Salem, N.C.: John F. Blair, 2000), 16.

92. Sayers, *A Desolate Place*, 127–31.

93. Sayers, 118.

94. Sayers, 126–27.

95. Sayers, 121–22.

96. "Life in the Swamp," *Lorain County News*, September 16, 1864. Luckily for Abraham, Larinda was not within earshot when he made this statement.

97. Golden, "'Through the Muck and Mire,'" 37; Diouf, *Slavery's Exiles*, 144–45.

98. Johann David Schoepf, *Travels in the Confederation, 1783–1784*, trans. Alfred J. Morrison (Philadelphia, 1911), 100.

99. Jack Temple Kirby, *Poquosin: A Study of Rural Landscape and Society* (Chapel Hill: University of North Carolina Press, 1995), xii–xiii, 111–13.

100. Diouf, *Slavery's Exiles*, 143; Bland Simpson, *The Great Dismal: A Swamp Memoir* (Chapel Hill: University of North Carolina Press, 1990), 44–45; Jackson, "The Virginia Maroons," 145; Schoepf, *Travels in the Confederation*, 100; Smyth,

Tour in the United States of America, 238; "Pompey's Secret," 548; Atwater, *Incidents of a Southern Tour*, 48; Thomas H. Kearney, *Report on a Botanical Survey of the Dismal Swamp Region* (Washington, D.C.: Government Printing Office, 1901), 480.

101. Diouf, *Slavery's Exiles*, 143.

102. *The New Encyclopedia of Southern Culture: History*, ed. Charles Reagan Wilson (Chapel Hill: University of North Carolina Press, 2014), 3:89; Kearney, *Report on a Botanical Survey*, 467.

103. Pickett, *Kunnoo Sperits*, 70; Thompson, *Flight to Freedom*, 255.

104. Ruffin, "Observations," 519; Kearney, *Report on a Botanical Survey*, 478.

105. John Harding, ed., *Marsh, Meadow, Mountain: Natural Places of the Delaware Valley* (Philadelphia: Temple University Press, 2011), 63; "Making Aquatic Weeds Useful," *Development Digest* 15, no. 1 (January 1977): 64. See also B. S. DeForest, *Random Sketches and Wandering Thoughts* (Albany, NY: Avery Herrick, 1866), 109.

106. "The Dismal Swamp and Its Occupants," *Scientific American*, October 5, 1895; Frank A. Heywood, "The Game of the Dismal Swamp," *Southern States* 2 (November 1894): 520.

107. Frederick Street, "In the Dismal Swamp," *Frank Leslie's Popular Monthly* 55, no. 5 (March 1903): 530; Atwater, *Incidents of a Southern Tour*, 50; "Life in the Swamp," *Lorain County News*, September 16, 1863, and "Life in the Swamp [concluded]," *Lorain County News*, September 23, 1863; "The Dismal Swamp," *Frederick Douglass' Paper*, March 11, 1859; Schoepf, *Travels in the Confederation*, 100; Smyth, *A Tour in the United States*, 236–37; H. B. Frissell, *Dietary Studies of Negroes in Eastern Virginia* (Washington, D.C.: Government Printing Office, 1899), 10–11; "The Dismal Swamp," *Forest and Stream* 5, no. 23 (January 13, 1876); Chandra Manning, *Troubled Refuge: Struggling for Freedom in the Civil War* (New York: Knopf Doubleday, 2017), 61.

108. Alexander Hunter, "The Great Dismal Swamp," *Outing* 27, no. 1 (October 1895): 71. See also Hunter, "Through the Dismal Swamp," 8.

109. Edmund Ruffin, "Observations Made during an Excursion to the Dismal Swamp," *Farmer's Register* 4 (January 1837): 519.

110. Hunter, "Through the Dismal Swamp," 7.

111. Redpath, *The Roving Editor*, 292. Quote in original: "whar dar feet can't touch hard ground" and "knock dem over."

112. "Some Account of the Great Dismal Swamp," *Literary Magazine and American Register*, March 1805, 171; "The Dismal Swamp and Its Occupants," *Scientific American*, October 5, 1895, 220; Redpath, *The Roving Editor*, 291.

113. Redpath, *Roving Editor*, 291; "The Dismal Swamp and Its Occupants," *Scientific American*, October 5, 1895, 220; Janette Holley, "The Lake of the Dismal Swamp," *Watson's Jeffersonian Magazine* 1, no. 1 (January 1907): 116.

114. Thompson, *Flight to Freedom*, 254; Pearson, *The Poor White*, 84.

115. Sayers, *A Desolate Place*, 142; "The Copy-Book," *Southern Literary Messenger*, January 1838, 25; "The Dismal Swamp," *Frederick Douglass' Paper*, March 11, 1859; Rebecca Anne Peixotto, "Against the Map: Resistance Landscapes in the Great Dismal Swamp," PhD diss. (American University, 2017), 108–9.

116. See "In the Dismal Swamp," *Student's Journal* 26, no. 1 (January 1897): 15.

117. Redpath, *The Roving Editor*, 291.

118. Waverly Traylor, *The Great Dismal Swamp in Myth and Legend* (Pittsburgh: RoseDog, 2010), 31.

119. Ruffin, "Observations," 518.

120. Jedidiah Morse, *Geography Made Easy: Being an Abridgement of the American Geography* (Troy, N.Y.: Parker and Bliss, 1814), 202.

121. Alfred Trumbull, "Through the Dismal Swamp," *Frank Leslie's Popular Monthly* 11, no. 4 (April 1881): 409. This account is from 1881 but describes African American "woodmen and their wives and families" born and reared in the Dismal Swamp, a strong implication that at least the adults had once been maroons. See also Moses Grandy, *Narrative of the Life of Moses Grandy; Late a Slave in the United States of America* (London: G. Gilpin, 1843), 36–37; and Johnson, *Tales of Old Carolina*, 47–48.

122. John Habberton, "When Boys Were Men," *Winnipeg Tribune*, June 9, 1903; "200 Dollars Reward," *Edenton Gazette and North Carolina General Advertiser*, December 25, 1820; "Sketches in Color," *Putnam's Magazine*, December 1869, 742.

123. Hunter, "The Great Dismal Swamp," 71.

124. "The Dismal Swamp," *Forest and Stream* 5, no. 23 (January 13, 1876); Olmsted, *A Journey in the Seaboard Slave States*, 159–61; Clapp, *The Pioneer*, 76; Eaton, *Barn Doors and Byways*, 198; Walter Prichard Eaton, "The Real Dismal Swamp," *Harper's Monthly Magazine* 122, no. 727 (December 1910): 24, 26–27; "Life in the Swamp," *Lorain County News*, September 16, 1863; "Life in the Swamp [concluded]," *Lorain County News*, September 23, 1863.

125. Thompson, *Flight to Freedom*, 94–95.

126. "Life in the Swamp," *Lorain County News*, September 16, 1863; "Life in the Swamp [concluded]," *Lorain County News*, September 23, 1863; Thompson, *Flight to Freedom*, 94–95; C. D. Arfwedson, *United States and Canada, in 1832, 1833, and 1834* (London: Richard Bentley, 1834), 359; Olmsted, *A Journey in the Seaboard Slave States*, 159; Winslow, "The Dismal Swamp," 170.

127. M. Janson, "Voyages and Travels," in *Annual Review and History of Literature for 1807* (London, 1808), 6:44; *The Terrific Register, or, Record of Crimes, Judgments, Providences, and Calamities* (London, 1825), 2:130.

128. See Diouf, *Slavery's Exiles*, 119–20; and Jacob Stroyer, *My Life in the South* (Salem, Mass.: Observer Book and Job Print, 1890), 65.

129. David Hunter Strother, "In the Dismal Swamp," *Harper's Monthly* 13, no. 73 (June 1856): 452.

130. "Life in the Swamp," *Lorain County News*, September 16, 1863; "Life in the Swamp [concluded]," *Lorain County News*, September 23, 1863.

131. Atwater, *Incidents of a Southern Tour*, 50; "Eliphaz" to "Br. Stevens," February 8, 1848, in *Zion's Herald and Wesleyan Journal*, February 23, 1848. See also Diouf, *Slavery's Exiles*, 119–20.

132. Archaeologists have also found fragments of chert that was likely used as an

expedient replacement for gunflint. Although local, it certainly originated outside the swamp. Peixotto, "Against the Map," 122–23.

133. Randolph, *Sketches of Slave Life*, 17.

134. Sayers, *A Desolate Place*, 115; Peixotto, "Against the Map," 116–21.

135. "Banditti Apprehended," *North-Carolina Free Press*, June 11, 1824.

136. "Gunmaking," in *Foxfire 5: Iron-Making, Blacksmithing, Bear Hunting, Flintlock Rifles, and More*, ed. Eliot Wiggington (New York: Knopf Doubleday, 2010), 246; *Johnson's Universal Cyclopædia: A New Edition*, ed. Charles Kendall Adams (New York: D. Appleton, 1898), 7:276. The standard "recipe" for gunpowder produced from saltpeter was seventy-five parts saltpeter (potassium nitrate), fifteen parts charcoal, and ten parts sulfur. Sulfur, of course, would not have been readily available in deep swamp communities, but it was not absolutely necessary to produce explosive gunpowder (it served more as a stabilizer for the more volatile potassium nitrate).

137. Sayers, *A Desolate Place*, 137–40, 152–53; Karl Austin, "The Morass of Resistance during the Antebellum: Agents of Freedom in the Great Dismal Swamp," PhD diss. (American University, 2017). Very similar and better-documented fortified structures were features of other maroon communities, including those located in Surinam; Jamaica; and Savannah, Georgia. See Richard Price, *Maroon Societies: Rebel Slave Communities in the Americas* (Baltimore: Johns Hopkins University Press, 1996), 7.

138. Sayers, *A Desolate Place*, 139–40, 152, 185. See also "Eliphaz" to "Br. Stevens," February 8, 1848, in *Zion's Herald and Wesleyan Journal*, February 23, 1848.

139. "How Garry Got Bears," *Inter Ocean* (Chicago), December 8, 1901; Sayers, *A Desolate Place*, 169.

140. Sayers, *A Desolate Place*, 140.

141. Sayers, 135–39, 164–65.

142. Jackson, "The Virginia Maroons," 146–47.

143. "In the Swamp," *The Liberator*, January 22, 1863.

144. Perdue, Barden, and Phillips, *Weevils in the Wheat*, 252.

145. "In the Swamp," *The Liberator*, January 22, 1863; Janson, "Voyages and Travels," 44; *The Terrific Register, or, Record of Crimes, Judgments, Providences, and Calamities* (London, 1825), 2:130. See also Price, *Maroon Societies*, 6.

146. See Sayers, *A Desolate Place*, 164–65.

147. "In the Swamp," *The Liberator*, January 22, 1863; Strother, "In the Dismal Swamp," 452.

148. See "In the Swamp," *The Liberator*, January 22, 1863; Thompson, *Flight to Freedom*, 192–93; and Diouf, *Slavery's Exiles*, 134–36. Diouf describes the marronage of William Robinson, who sought shelter in a swamp south of the Dismal. To reach the maroon community of which he had heard rumors, he had to earn the trust of and be given directions by an enslaved elder on another labor camp, and answer the detailed questions of a sentry to confirm his identity. "It was necessary for him to be very cautious whom he admitted. . . . I finally convinced him that I was not a spy but an actual runaway." See Robinson, *From Log Cabin to the Pulpit*, 29–32.

149. Jackson, "The Virginia Maroons," 146; William C. Nell, *The Colored Patriots of the American Revolution* (Boston, 1855), 228; Strother, "In the Dismal Swamp," 452; *The Negro's Flight from American Slavery to British Freedom*, prefatory remarks by George Thompson (London: John Snow, 1849), 12–13; Pearson, *The Poor White*, 108. Scattered instances of Dismal Swamp maroons remaining alone for significant periods of time, even years, without encountering other maroons is sometimes offered as evidence that maroon *communities* were rare or did not exist at all. Two historians cite a man who had lived for many years in the swamp and claimed to have "never seen a woman. I had plenty of whisky and tobacco, but what I longed for was a real old plantation cornshucking." See Diouf, *Slavery's Exiles*, 218; and Simpson, *The Great Dismal*, 77. If a solitary maroon did not move about the swamp very widely, he indeed might not have encountered a maroon community, but it is also quite possible that community scouts did not, for whatever reason, deem him worthy or trustworthy enough to be approached and invited in. He may also have been concealing the truth from outsiders, even many years after the Civil War. Some people who had been maroons or were quite intimate with them disclaimed all knowledge of their existence when addressing certain outsiders decades later. Alexander Keeling, an African American man born in 1776, who lived in the swamp and served as minister to the maroons, told the suspect New Yorker Frank Taylor in 1881 that he had no firsthand knowledge of maroons. "Nevah seen 'em, no, sah. In dem times de niggahs nevah seen nuthin'." A woman born and raised near the Dismal in Nansemond County, Virginia, however, was able to get a fuller account of Alek's ministry to the maroons, even taking down in dictation one of his sermons he had memorized to deliver to the people of the swamp to whom he had been "friend, counsel, and protector." Frank H. Taylor, "Lost on Lake Drummond," *Potter's American Monthly* 17, no. 118 (October 1881): 336; LaSalle Corbell Pickett, "Four Famous American Apostles," *Washington Times*, April 25, 1897; Hunter, "The Great Dismal Swamp," 71. See also Simpson, *The Great Dismal*, 76–77; and Diouf, *Slavery's Exiles*, 218.

150. "In the Swamp," *The Liberator*, January 22, 1863.

151. Pearson, *The Poor White*, 110.

152. Redpath, *The Roving Editor*, 290; "In the Swamp," *The Liberator*, January 22, 1863.

153. Price, *Maroon Societies*, 16–17.

154. This was also the case in Cuba, Brazil, Surinam, and Jamaica. See Thompson, *Flight to Freedom*, 225–28; Sayers, *A Desolate Place*, 165, 169; and Price, *Maroon Societies*, 17.

155. "Dismal Swamp," *Southern Literary Messenger*, January, 1838, 25; William Kreutzer, *Notes and Observations Made during Four Years of Service with the Ninety-Eighth N.Y. Volunteers in the War of 1861* (Philadelphia, 1878), 168. Several projectile points were recovered in different historical contexts that point to reuse and modification of older tools for use in the scission community or communities. A modified Morrow Mountain Stemmed Type II point (archaic type, 5,000–3,500 BP) recovered by the GDSLS clearly demonstrates a historical reworking of one side of the original point into a knife or scraper. Sayers, *A Desolate Place*, 178, 204–7.

156. Sayers, *A Desolate Place*, 147.

157. "In the Dismal Swamp," *Frederick Douglass' Paper*, March 11, 1859; Sayers, *Desolate Place*, 136–37, 157–58.

158. Sayers, *A Desolate Place*, 142–47.

159. Thompson, *Flight to Freedom*, 222–23.

160. See *North-Carolina Free Press*, June 11, 1824; *National Gazette*, June 15, 1824; Kirby, *Poquosin*, 181.

161. "Dismal Swamp Canal," *Norfolk Virginian*, June 1, 1897.

162. "Weird Legends of the Dismal Swamp," *Raleigh News and Observer*, August 3, 1913.

163. Fred Hardesty, "The Great Dismal Swamp," *Raleigh News and Observer*, September 11, 1966.

164. "Winslow, Nathan," https://www.ncpedia.org/biography/winslow-nathan (accessed September 24, 2020). It is unlikely that Caleb Winslow, a white outsider, would have gained entry to a deep swamp community. However, his family's reputation as abolitionists may have gained him the trust of maroons. His grandfather had emancipated his family's slaves prior to his death in 1811. Although Caleb's father, Nathan, was disowned by the Society of Friends because of slave ownership, it is believed that he had bought enslaved people to keep them from being sold away from family. See "$50 Reward," *Edenton Gazette and North Carolina General Advertiser*, November 11, 1828, a runaway ad placed for an enslaved man named Dave who was suspected of having fled to Nathan Winslow's residence to be with his father, Spence, who lived there.

165. Caleb Winslow, "The Dismal Swamp: An Essay," 170, Caleb Winslow and Family Papers, 1712–1941, North Carolina State Archives, PC90.18.

166. Sayers, *A Desolate Place*, 115, 164–65.

167. Thompson, *Flight to Freedom*, 211–12; Sayers, *A Desolate Place*, 165–66.

168. See Sayers, *A Desolate Place*, 165–66.

169. See "Dismal Swamp on Display," *Rising Son*, December 22, 1906.

170. Golden, "'Through the Muck and Mire,'" 37.

171. Sayers, *A Desolate Place*, 166–68.

172. Cowan, *The Slave in the Swamp*, 61–62; Grey Gundaker, "Cast Out of the Garden: Scripturalization, Flowers, and Fallen Africa," in *Scripturalizing the Human: The Written as the Political*, ed. Vincent L. Wimbush (London: Routledge, 2015), 17.

173. James K. Bryant, *The 36th Infantry United States Colored Troops in the Civil War: A History and Roster* (Jefferson, N.C.: McFarland, 2012), 21–22. See also Cowan, *The Slave in the Swamp*, 151; Morris, "'Running Servants and All Others,'" 97–99; Diouf, *Slavery's Exiles*, 49, 59; Thompson, *Flight to Freedom*, 175; Strother, "In the Dismal Swamp," 9; and *Yankee Phalanx*, 21.

174. Blassingame, *The Slave Community*, 192–93.

175. "Sketches of the South No. III," *Parley's Magazine*, January 1, 1834, 71.

176. Interview with W. L. Bost, in *When I Was a Slave: Memoirs from the Slave Narrative Collection*, ed. Norman R. Yetman (Mineola: Dover, 2002), 17.

177. "Pompey's Secret," 549; *Richmond Enquirer*, August 26, 1831.

178. Larinda White said that she and her husband, Abraham Lester, attended "regular prayer meetings on Thursday evening, at different camps in the swamp." See "Life in the Swamp [continued]," *Lorain County News*, September 23, 1864.

179. Cassandra Pybus, "'One Militant Saint': The Much Traveled Life of Mary Perth," *Journal of Colonialism and Colonial History* 9, no. 3 (Winter 2008), https://muse.jhu.edu/article/255267; "Letter from the Rev. Mr. Clarke," July 29, 1796, in *Evangelical Magazine* 4 (July 1796): 460–63.

180. Bryant, *The 36th Infantry*, 24.

181. Redpath, *The Roving Editor*, 293. Quote in original: "Many's been de 'zortation I have 'sperienced, dat desounded t'rough de trees, an we would almos' 'spect de judgement day was comin', dar would be such loud nibrations, as de preacher called dem. . . . I b'lieve God is no inspector of persons, an' he knows his childer, and kin hear dem just as quick in de Juniper Swamp as in de great churches."

182. "A Centenarian Slave Preacher," *Suffolk Herald*, n.d., in *The Times*, December 20, 1881; Arnold, *The Dismal Swamp*, 23–25; David Hunter Strother, "The Dismal Swamp," *Harper's New Monthly Magazine*, September 1856, 454. Alexander Keeling's name appears in the record many different ways, including as Alexander, Alek, Aleck, and Alick.

183. Strother, "The Dismal Swamp," 455; "Editor's Drawer," *Harper's New Monthly Magazine* 29, no. 169 (June 1864): 141.

184. See Peixotto, "Against the Map," 111–15.

185. Pickett, *Kunnoo Sperits*, 75. Quote in original: "Gord-er-moughty."

186. Arnold, *The Dismal Swamp*, 23–25. Jacob Keeling, however, continued to enslave people. These included men named Nat, Max, and Anthony, whom he sometimes hired out to the Dismal Swamp Company. See Nevius, *City of Refuge*, 85.

187. Pickett, *Kunnoo Sperits*, 71. Quotes in original: "praher-book 'Piskerpaleyun thoo en thoo"; "Alexander 'low . . . dat his 'ligeon was mo' perteckshun ter 'im fum de daid an fum de libin', fum de wileen de tame, fum cunjur erf um p'izen dan de whole er Col. Willis Ridick's merlishy [militia] wuz."

188. Pickett, 74.

189. "A Centenarian Slave Preacher," *Suffolk Herald*, n.d., in *The Times*, December 20, 1881; Arnold, *The Dismal Swamp*, 23–25.

190. Arnold, *The Dismal Swamp*, 23–25.

191. "Life in the Swamp," *Lorain County News*, September 16, 1863.

192. Byrd, *The Westover Manuscripts*, 17.

193. Personal email correspondence with Daniel Sayers, November 29, 2020.

194. See "Great Dismal Swamp National Wildlife Refuge and Nansemond National Wildlife Refuge Final Comprehensive Conservation Plan, July 2006," https://www.fws.gov/uploadedFiles/Region_5/NWRS/South_Zone/Great_Dismal_Swamp_Complex/Great_Dismal_Swamp/FinalCCP_GDS.pdf (accessed September 25, 2020).

195. "How Garry Got Bears," *Inter Ocean*, December 8, 1901.

196. Sayers, *A Desolate Place*, 161–64; Thompson, *Flight to Freedom*, 200.

197. Peixotto, "Against the Map," 151–53; Rebecca Anne Peixotto, "Glass in the Landscape of the Great Dismal Swamp," MA thesis (American University, 2013), 8–9, 59.

198. The "Cross Canal" archaeological site is located adjacent to the Cross Canal approximately one mile into the swamp from the Nansemond Scarp (the canal's origin). See Sayers, *A Desolate Place*, 24.

199. "The Dismal Swamp," *Poultney Journal*, January 13, 1933; Stansbury, *The Lake of the Great Dismal*, 25.

200. Sayers, *A Desolate Place*, 123, 147, 163.

201. These skills, of course, were often the inheritance of their African ancestors, or had been honed as skilled craftsmen on slave labor camps. See Thompson, *Flight to Freedom*, 256; and Sayers, *A Desolate Place*, 166.

202. Holley, "The Lake of the Dismal Swamp," 116; "The Dismal Swamp and Its Occupants," *Scientific American* 73, no. 14 (October 5, 1895); Redpath, *The Roving Editor*, 291; Aitchison and Parker Account Book, 1763–1804, Accession #12992, Special Collections, University of Virginia Library, 51.

203. "How Garry Got Bears," *Inter Ocean*, December 8, 1901; "Capturing Contraband Whiskey," *Dakota Farmer's Leader*, December 4, 1908.

204. Sayers, *A Desolate Place*, 33–34, 162. Sayers points out that "Diasporans finally had immanent, palpable, and actualized control over their creative efforts, the products of those efforts, and the kinds of labor they did and for whom they labored. This is a very poignant signal that swamp Diasporans grasped the basics of their conditions in the external world and that transforming the nature of the creative labor was a central element of their praxis."

205. Kirby, *Poquosin*, 13.

206. Kirby, 13.

207. Simpson, *The Great Dismal*, 105.

208. Edmund Ruffin, *Agricultural, Geological, and Descriptive Sketches of Lower North Carolina, and the Similar Adjacent Lands* (Raleigh: Institution for the Deaf & Dumb & Blind, 1861), 206, 209; Simpson, *The Great Dismal*, 112; Traylor, *The Great Dismal Swamp in Myth and Legend*, 333.

209. Curtis J. Badger, *A Natural History of Quiet Waters: Swamps and Wetlands of the Mid-Atlantic Coast* (Charlottesville: University of Virginia Press, 2007), 126; Simpson, *The Great Dismal*, 114.

210. Thomas C. Parramore, Peter C. Stewart, and Tommy L. Bogger, *Norfolk: The First Four Centuries* (Charlottesville: University of Virginia Press, 1994), 145.

211. Sayers, *A Desolate Place*, 91.

212. "Statement of Mr. W. B. Brooks of Baltimore," in *Lake Drummond Canal, VA and NC* (Washington, D.C.: Government Printing Office, 1922), 2; Diouf, *Slavery's Exiles*, 212. See also Grandy, *Narrative*, 37–38.

213. *The North American Tourist* (New York: A. T. Goodrich, 1839), 442–43; Street, "In the Dismal Swamp," 530; Grandy, *Narrative*, 37–38; Diouf, *Slavery's Exiles*, 212; Simpson, *The Great Dismal*, 46–47; Strother, "The Dismal Swamp," 451; Nevius, *City of Refuge*, 69.

214. Simpson, *The Great Dismal*, 46–47; Sayers, *A Desolate Place*, 192.

215. Simpson, *The Great Dismal*, 46–47.

216. William Henry Stewart, *History of Norfolk County, Virginia, and Representative Citizens* (Chicago: Biographical Publishing, 1902), 407.

217. *The North American Tourist*, 442.

218. Ruffin, "Observations," 518. See also *The New American Cyclopaedia: A Popular Dictionary of General Knowledge*, ed. George Ripley and Charles A. Dana (New York: D. Appleton, 1867), 6:505.

219. See, for example, *North-Carolina Star*, August 21, 1812; "Eliphaz" to "Br. Stevens," February 8, 1848, in *Zion's Herald and Wesleyan Journal*, February 23, 1848; *North Star*, March 31, 1848; "The Dismal Swamp," *Forest and Stream* 5, no. 23 (January 13, 1876); Street, "In the Dismal Swamp," 530; and Grandy, *Narrative*, 25–45.

220. Grandy, *Narrative*, iv, 25–26.

221. Olmsted, *A Journey in the Seaboard Slave States*, 155–56.

222. Olmsted, 153–55.

223. Stewart, *History of Norfolk County*, 160. See also Kirby, *Poquosin*, 168; and Nevius, *City of Refuge*, 11. Nevius points out that "unfreedom for slaves did not equate to absolute mastery by enslavers."

224. See, for example, *North-Carolina Star*, August 21, 1812; "Eliphaz" to "Br. Stevens," February 8, 1848, in *Zion's Herald and Wesleyan Journal*, February 23, 1848; *North Star*, March 31, 1848; "The Dismal Swamp," *Forest and Stream* 5, no. 23 (January 13, 1876); Street, "In the Dismal Swamp," 530; and Grandy, *Narrative*, 25–45.

225. *The North-Carolina Star*, August 21, 1812.

226. Strother, "The Dismal Swamp," 452; Redpath, *The Roving Editor*, 290.

227. Sayers, *A Desolate Place*, 85.

228. Olmsted, *A Journey in the Seaboard Slave States*, 160.

229. Sayers, *A Desolate Place*, 130–31.

230. Nevius, *City of Refuge*, 74–76; Stewart, *History of Norfolk County*, 407. The usage was not because of an accent or grammatical error but rather intentional. One DSC manager wrote about his fears of laborers being drawn away by other employers: "They will *get* all the good shingle *gitters* from us" (emphasis added). See Leaming, *Hidden Americans*, 281.

231. The task numbers would vary depending on if they were producing thirty-two-, twenty-two-, or twenty-inch shingles, fence rails, or barrel staves. See Stewart, *History of Norfolk County*, 407.

232. Olmsted, *A Journey in the Seaboard Slave States*, 153–54.

233. Ruffin, "Observations," 518.

234. Leaming, *Hidden Americans*, 281.

235. Street, "In the Dismal Swamp," 530; "The Dismal Swamp," *Frederick Douglass' Paper*, March 11, 1859; Strother, "In the Dismal Swamp," 451; Leaming, *Hidden Americans*, 281.

236. "The Dismal Swamp," *Greensboro (N.C.) Times*, October 1, 1857.

237. "The Dismal Swamp," *Greensboro Times*, October 1, 1857; Strother, "In the Dismal Swamp," 451; Winslow, "The Dismal Swamp," 170.

238. Frederick L. Olmsted, "The South, #13," *New York Daily Times*, April 23, 1853;

Street, "In the Dismal Swamp," 530; Redpath, *The Roving Editor*, 243; Olmsted, *A Journey in the Seaboard Slave States*, 153–54; Redpath, *The Roving Editor*, 243; Johnson, *Tales from Old Carolina*, 160; "Life in the Swamp [continued]," *Lorain County News*, September 23, 1864.

239. Stewart, *History of Norfolk County*, 407.

240. Stewart, 407.

241. Edward Austin Johnson, *A School History of the Negro Race* (Chicago: W. B. Conkey, 1895), 94–95; Dismal Swamp Land Company Records, October 1860 and August 1860, cited in Edward Maris-Wolf, "Between Slavery and Freedom: African Americans in the Great Dismal Swamp, 1763–1863," MA thesis (College of William and Mary, 2002), 104.

242. Nevius, *City of Refuge*, 69.

243. "The Dismal Swamp," *Greensboro Times*, October 1, 1857.

244. Hunter, "The Great Dismal Swamp," 71.

245. "How Garry Got Bears," *Inter Ocean*, December 8, 1901.

246. Stewart, *History of Norfolk County*, 407.

247. Olmsted, *A Journey in the Seaboard Slave States*, 160.

248. See Sayers, *A Desolate Place*, 182–88; and Diouf, *Slavery's Exiles*, 151–52.

249. Sayers, *A Desolate Place*, 176–77.

250. "How Garry Got Bears," *Inter Ocean*, December 8, 1901.

251. Pickett, *Kunnoo Sperits*, 72; "A Centenarian Slave Preacher," *Suffolk Herald*, n.d., in *The Times*, December 20, 1881; Arnold, *The Dismal Swamp*, 23–25; Strother, "The Dismal Swamp," 454.

252. "The Dismal Swamp," *Forest and Stream* 5, no. 23 (January 13, 1876); "Life in the Swamp," *Lorain County News*, September 16, 1863.

253. Sayers, *A Desolate Place*, 183–88.

254. Sayers, 203–4.

255. Sayers, 204–5.

256. Strother, "In the Dismal Swamp," 452; "How Garry Got Bears," *Inter Ocean*, December 8, 1901.

257. Olmsted, *A Journey in the Seaboard Slave States*, 159; Strother, "In the Dismal Swamp," 451.

258. Strother, "In the Dismal Swamp," 451.

259. "The Dismal Swamp," *Greensboro Times*, October 1, 1857.

260. Sayers, *A Desolate Place*, 129–30, 138–39.

261. Sayers, 130–31, 138, 202.

262. Hunter, "The Great Dismal Swamp," 71; Sayers, *A Desolate Place*, 101.

263. Arnold, *The Dismal Swamp*, 24–25.

CHAPTER FIVE

1. Russel B. Nye, "Freedom Road: Nat Turner," *Centennial Review of Arts & Science* 1, no. 3 (Summer 1957): 251–53.

2. Herbert Aptheker, *Nat Turner's Slave Rebellion: Including the 1831 "Confessions"* (New York: Humanities, 1966), 61. See also Lydia Juliette Plath, "Not One Black

Was Spared That Fell into Their Hands: North Carolina's Reaction to the Nat Turner Rebellion," MA thesis (University of Warwick, 2006).

3. Higginson, "Nat Turner's Insurrection," *The Atlantic*, August 1861," 60; Stephen Weeks, "The Slave Insurrection in Virginia, 1831," in *The Nat Turner Rebellion: The Historical Event and the Modern Controversy* (New York: Harper and Row, 1971), 74; F. Roy Johnson, *Tales from Old Carolina* (Murfreesboro, N.C.: Johnson, 1965), 159.

4. Johnson, *Tales from Old Carolina*, 159.

5. Kerry Walters, *American Slave Revolts and Conspiracies: A Reference Guide* (New York: ABC-CLIO, 2015), 124.

6. Herbert Aptheker, *American Negro Slave Revolts* (New York: Columbia University Press, 1943), 152.

7. "Nat Turner's Insurrection," *The Liberator*, August 2, 1831.

8. C. D. Arfwedson, *United States and Canada, in 1832, 1833, and 1834* (London: Richard Bentley, 1834), 359; Samuel Warner, *Authentic and Impartial Narrative of the Tragical Scene* (New York: Warner and West, 1831), 12.

9. Aptheker, *American Negro Slave Revolts*, 307–8; Johnson, *Tales from Old Carolina*, 159; Hugo Prosper Leaming, *Hidden Americans: The Maroons of Virginia and the Carolinas* (New York: Garland, 1995), 260; *Weekly Raleigh Register*, September 29, 1831; *New York Gazette*, n.d., in *The Liberator*, September 17, 1831; "The South," *Niles Weekly Register* (Baltimore), September 17, 1831; Daniel O. Sayers, *A Desolate Place for a Defiant People: The Archaeology of Maroons, Indigenous Americans, and Enslaved Laborers in the Great Dismal Swamp* (Gainesville: University Press of Florida, 2014), 104.

10. Aptheker, *American Negro Slave Revolts*, 307–8.

11. "The Great Dismal Swamp," *Cincinnati Commercial*, n.d., in *Wayne County (Pa.) Herald*, November 11, 1869.

12. *Index to the Executive Documents of the House of Representatives for the Second Session of the Forty-Fifth Congress, 1877–'78* (Washington, D.C.: Government Printing Office, 1878), 10:80.

13. Willis Augustus Hodges, *Free Man of Color: The Autobiography of Willis Augustus Hodges*, ed. Willard B. Gatewood (Knoxville: University of Tennessee Press, 1982), xxvii, 25; Ira Berlin, *Slaves without Masters: The Free Negro in the Antebellum South* (New York: Pantheon, 1974), 188–89.

14. Hodges, *Free Man of Color*, 63–68; Isaac S. Harrell, "Gates County to 1860," in *Historical Papers of the Trinity College Historical Society* (Durham, N.C.: Seeman, 1916), 65, 71.

15. Henry Clapp, *The Pioneer, or, Leaves from an Editor's Portfolio* (Lynn, Mass.: J. B. Tolman, 1846), 77–78. See also "A Pleasant Gathering," *The Liberator*, June 22, 1855.

16. I have chosen in this book to not fully reproduce racial epithets as found in source material. This usage should in no way effect my analysis or the reader's clear understanding of the quoted material.

17. Frederick Law Olmsted, *A Journey in the Seaboard Slave States* (New York: Dix and Edwards, 1856), 159–60; Robert Arnold, *The Dismal Swamp and Lake*

NOTES TO PAGES 140–42

Drummond: Early Recollections. Vivid Portrayal of Amusing Scenes (Norfolk: Green, Burke, & Gregory, 1888), 7; Isabella Mayo, "The Roots of Honor," in *The Family Friend* (London: S. W. Partridge, 1895), 179; Francis William Newman, *Character of the United States of America* (Manchester: Union and Emancipation Society's Depot, 1863), 6.

18. *Elizabethtown Phenix*, n.d., in *The Freeman's Journal*, February 5, 1839.

19. "Ranaway," *Phoenix*, December 31, 1838, in Sylviane A. Diouf, *Slavery's Exiles: The Story of the American Maroons* (New York: New York University Press, 2014), 228.

20. "The Bloodhound Myth," *Louisville Courier-Journal*, n.d., in *Kincaid (Kans.) Kronicle*, May 28, 1887. Actual bloodhounds, contrary to abolitionist propaganda, were rare in Virginia and North Carolina.

21. Olmsted, *A Journey in the Seaboard Slave States*, 159–60. See also "Recollections of Slavery," *The Emancipator*, August 23, 1838.

22. "Eliphaz" to "Br. Stevens," February 8, 1848, in *Zion's Herald and Wesleyan Journal*, February 23, 1848.

23. Clapp, *The Pioneer*, 76–78.

24. Olmsted, *A Journey in the Seaboard Slave States*, 159–60; "Foreign Correspondence," *Little's Living Age* 18, no. 216 (July 1846): 287.

25. C. H. Peterson, "Some Unexpected Catches," *Hunter-Trader-Trapper* 22, no. 3 (June 1911): 41.

26. Winslow, "The Dismal Swamp," 170; John Boyle O'Reilly, *Athletics and Manly Sport* (Boston: Pilot, 1890), 352.

27. See *Alexandria Gazette and Virginia Advertiser*, September 23, 1856; "Eliphaz" to "Br. Stevens," February 8, 1848, in *Zion's Herald and Wesleyan Journal*, February 23, 1848; John Hamilton Howard, *In the Shadow of the Pines* (New York: Easton and Mains, 1906), 83, 86; John Habberton, "When Boys Were Men," *Winnipeg Tribune*, June 9, 1903.

28. Aptheker, *American Negro Slave Revolts*, 301; Kathryn Elise Benjamin Golden, "'Through the Muck and Mire': Marronage, Representation, and Memory in the Great Dismal Swamp," PhD diss. (University of California, Berkeley, 2018), 72; Sally E. Hadden, *Slave Patrols: Law and Violence in Virginia and the Carolinas* (Cambridge, Mass.: Harvard University Press, 2001), 46–47.

29. Moses Grandy, *Narrative of the Life of Moses Grandy; Late a Slave in the United States of America* (London: G. Gilpin, 1843), 56–57.

30. "Eliphaz" to "Br. Stevens," February 8, 1848, in *Zion's Herald and Wesleyan Journal*, February 23, 1848.

31. John Henderson Russell, *The Free Negro in Virginia, 1619–1895* (Baltimore: Johns Hopkins University Press, 1913), 172; Hodges, *Free Man of Color*, 68.

32. Hodges, *Free Man of Color*, 25.

33. Hodges, 27.

34. Hodges, 42. Instead, Hodges left his employment in the swamp and moved to New York, where he became an active abolitionist and editor of the antislavery newspaper *Ram's Horn*.

35. Hodges, 57–59; Russell, *The Free Negro in Virginia*, 173.

36. "A Resolution Addressed to the Governor of This State," *Laws of the State of North Carolina, Passed by the General Assembly at the Session of 1846–47* (Raleigh: Thomas J. Lemay, 1847), 249; "Legislature of Virginia," *Richmond Enquirer*, February 12, 1847; "Slaves in the Dismal Swamp," *Natchez (Miss.) Courier*, March 10, 1847. See also "Serendipity in Misfiled Docs," https://swampscapes.wordpress.com/?s =serendipity (accessed January 13, 2021).

37. "An Act to Provide for the Apprehension of Runaway Slaves in the Great Dismal Swamp and for Other Purposes," *Laws of the State of North Carolina . . . 1846–47*, 109–10.

38. "An Act to Provide for the Apprehension of Runaway Slaves," 109–13. See Raymond Parker Fouts, *Registration of Slaves to Work in the Great Dismal Swamp, Gates County, North Carolina, 1847–1861* (Cocoa, Fla.: GenRec, 1995).

39. "Runaways," in *The Laws of North-Carolina, Passed by the General Assembly at the Session of 1848–49* (Raleigh: Thos. J. Lemay, 1849), 213–15.

40. Olmsted, *A Journey in the Seaboard Slave States*, 141.

41. William Tynes Cowan, *The Slave in the Swamp: Disrupting the Plantation Narrative* (London: Routledge, 2005), 45; M. Janson, "Voyages and Travels," in *Annual Review and History of Literature for 1807* (London, 1808), 6:44.

42. "An Act to Provide for the Apprehension of Runaway Slaves in the Great Dismal Swamp and for Other Purposes," *Laws of the State of North Carolina . . . 1846–47*, 109–10.

43. "The Insurrection," *Vermont Mercury*, September 9, 1831.

44. "An Act to Provide for the Apprehension of Runaway Slaves in the Great Dismal Swamp and for Other Purposes," *Laws of the State of North Carolina . . . 1846–47*, 109–13.

45. Golden, "'Through the Muck and Mire,'" 74; J. M. McKim, "The Slave's Ultima Ratio," *The Liberator*, February 5, 1858.

46. Cowan, *The Slave in the Swamp*, 60.

47. Harriet Beecher Stowe, *Dred: A Tale of the Great Dismal Swamp* (London: Sampson Low, Son, 1856), 210.

48. See Guion Griffis Johnson, *Ante-bellum North Carolina: A Social History* (Chapel Hill: University of North Carolina Press, 1937), 515.

49. "The Chincapinites," *The Liberator*, December 4, 1863.

50. Harriet Jacobs, *Incidents in the Life of a Slave Girl* (Boston: Harriet Jacobs, 1861), 171–72.

51. J. M. McKim, "The Slave's Ultima Ratio," *The Liberator*, February 5, 1858. See also Damian Alan Pargas, *Slavery and Forced Migration in the Antebellum South* (New York: Cambridge University Press, 2015), 77–78.

52. See *The Negro in Virginia* (New York: Hastings House, 1940), 172; L. Maria Child, "Letter XI," December 9, 1841, in *Letters from New York* (New York: C. S. Francis, 1852), 73; "Miscellany," *Rural Repository*, May 4, 1844, 150; and "Life in the Swamp [continued]," *Lorain County (Ohio) News*, September 23, 1864.

53. *The Laws of North Carolina, Enacted in the Year 1822* (Raleigh: Bell & Lawrence, 1823), 28–29.

54. See "Life in the Swamp," *Lorain County News*, September 23, 1863; J. M. McKim, "The Slave's Ultima Ratio," *The Liberator*, February 5, 1858; and Atwater, *Incidents of a Southern Tour*, 50.

55. J. M. McKim, "The Slave's Ultima Ratio," *The Liberator*, February 5, 1858.

56. Diouf, *Slavery's Exiles*, 308–9.

57. Cowan, *The Slave in the Swamp*, 37. See Winthrop D. Jordan, *Tumult and Silence at Second Creek: An Inquiry into a Civil War Slave Conspiracy* (Baton Rouge: Louisiana State University Press, 1993).

58. See Edmund Ruffin, "Observations Made during an Excursion to the Dismal Swamp," *Farmer's Register* 4 (January 1837): 513–21.

59. David F. Allmendinger Jr., "The Early Career of Edmund Ruffin, 1810–1840," *Virginia Magazine of History and Biography* 93, no. 2 (April 1985): 128.

60. Ruffin, "Observations," 518–19.

61. "Fidelity of Slaves to Their Masters," *DeBow's Review* 30, no. 1 (January 1861): 119.

62. Former Dismal Swamp maroon Charlie remembered "Ole Man Fisher" as a fellow maroon and his personal spiritual leader while in the Dismal. See James Redpath, *The Roving Editor, or, Talks with Slaves in the Southern States* (New York: A. B. Burdick, 1859), 293.

63. Megan Kate Nelson, "Hidden Away in the Woods and Swamps: Slavery, Fugitive Slaves, and Swamplands in the Southeastern Borderlands, 1739–1845," in *"We Shall Independent Be": African American Place Making and the Struggle to Claim Space in the United States*, ed. Angela David Nieves and Leslie M. Alexander (Boulder: University Press of Colorado, 2008), 267; M. Allewaert, "Swamp Sublime: Ecologies of Resistance in the American Plantation Zone," *PMLA* 123, no. 2 (March 2008): 350–53.

64. Ryan A. Quintana, *Making a Slave State: Political Development in Early South Carolina* (Chapel Hill: University of North Carolina Press, 2018), 1; "Census; District; Georgetown," *Camden (N.Y.) Gazette*, March 8, 1821.

65. Quintana, *Making a Slave State*, 7.

66. See John W. Blassingame, *The Slave Community: Plantation Life in the Antebellum South* (New York: Oxford University Press, 1979), 139; and James C. Scott, *Domination and the Arts of Resistance: Hidden Transcripts* (New Haven, Conn.: Yale University Press, 1992).

67. Blassingame, *The Slave Community*, 139.

68. Cowan, *The Slave in the Swamp*, 1, 12–16.

69. Cowan, 3, 6–7.

70. "Extracts from the Rev. Mr. May's Sermon on Slavery in the United States," *The Liberator*, July 2, 1831; "The Dismal Swamp," *The Liberator*, January 5, 1849. See also "The Union," *Vermont Telegraph*, n.d., in *The Liberator*, June 24, 1842.

71. "Insurrection in Virginia," *The Liberator*, September 3, 1831; "Further Particulars," *The Liberator*, September 17, 1831.

72. Frederick Douglass, "Enmity of Man to Man," *North Star*, n.d., in *The Liberator*, August 2, 1850.

73. Frederick Douglass, "Inhumanity of Slavery: Extract from a Lecture on Slavery, at Rochester, December 8, 1850," in *My Bondage and My Freedom* (New York: Miller, Orton, 1855), 435–36.

74. "Slaves in the Dismal Swamp," *Zion's Herald*, n.d., in *Anti-slavery Bugle*, April 21, 1849.

75. Bessie Graham, *Bookman's Manual: A Guide to Literature* (New York: R. R. Bowker, 1921), 143.

76. Georgann Eubanks, *Literary Trails of Eastern North Carolina: A Guidebook* (Chapel Hill: University of North Carolina Press, 2013), 246; "Worcester County (South Division) Anti-slavery Society," *The Liberator*, January 26, 1844.

77. "New and Original Panorama," *The Liberator*, May 10, 1850.

78. Daphne Brooks, *Bodies in Dissent: Spectacular Performances of Race and Freedom, 1850–1910* (Durham, N.C.: Duke University Press, 2006), 104.

79. "Fifteenth Annual Meeting of the American Anti-slavery Society," *The Liberator*, May 18, 1849.

80. Frederick Douglass, "The Heroic Slave," in *Autographs for Freedom* (Boston: John P. Jewett, 1853), 192–94.

81. In fact, he apparently even plagiarized portions of his Dismal Swamp section from an 1848 issue of *Scientific American*. See Geoffrey Sanborn, "'People Will Pay to Hear the Drama': Plagiarism in *Clotel*," *African American Review* 45, no. 1/2 (Spring/Summer 2012): 65–82; "The Dismal Swamp," *Scientific American* 3, no. 44 (July 22, 1848): 350.

82. William Wells Brown, *Clotel, or, The President's Daughter: A Narrative of Slave Life in the United States* (London: Partridge & Oakey, 1853), 212–13.

83. Robert S. Levine, introduction to Harriet Beecher Stove, *Dred: A Tale of the Dismal Swamp* (Chapel Hill: University of North Carolina Press, 2000), xxx. See also Cowan, *The Slave in the Swamp*, 3.

84. Levine, introduction to Stowe, *Dred*, xvii.

85. See "A Letter from Suffolk, VA: The Dismal Swamp," *Philadelphia Inquirer*, November 19, 1862.

86. See "$30 Reward," *Old North State*, August 4, 1849; "$40 Reward," *Old North State*, October 13, 1849; "$75 Reward," *Old North State*, August 21, 1852; "$50 Reward," *Spirit of the Age*, March 15, 1854; "$20 Reward," *Democratic Pioneer*, January 5, 1858.

87. "Killed by Runaway Slaves," *Wilmington Journal*, n.d., in *The Baltimore Sun*, August 16, 1856; Aptheker, "Maroons within the Present Limits of the United States," *Journal of Negro History* 24, no. 2 (April 1939): 163; Diouf, *Slavery's Exiles*, 144.

88. Edmund Jackson, "The Virginia Maroons," in *The Liberty Bell* (Boston: Prentiss and Sawyer, 1852), 149.

89. Redpath, *The Roving Editor*, 300.

90. Redpath, 2.

91. See Redpath, 288–95.

92. Redpath, 302.

93. Redpath, 305.

94. Redpath, 306.

95. Richard J. Hinton, *John Brown and His Men* (New York: Funk and Wagnalls, 1894), 66; Ralph Keeler, "Owen Brown's Escape from Harper's Ferry," *Atlantic Monthly* 33, no. 197 (March 1874): 343.

96. David S. Reynolds, *John Brown, Abolitionist: The Man Who Killed Slavery, Sparked the Civil War, and Seeded Civil Rights* (New York: Vintage, 2006), 106.

97. Thomas Wentworth Higginson, "Kansas and John Brown," *Atlantic Monthly* 79, no. 375 (May 1897): 673. See also Martha Schoolman, *Abolitionist Geographies* (Minneapolis: University of Minnesota Press, 2014), 183–84.

98. Reynolds, *John Brown*, 106–9.

99. See Keeler, "Owen Brown's Escape," 343; "The Haytians and John Brown," *New York Times*, August 8, 1860.

100. Keeler, "Owen Brown's Escape," 343; "The Haytians and John Brown," *New York Times*, August 8, 1860.

101. See Hodges, *Free Man of Color*, 78n8; Richard Lowe, "Willis Augustus Hodges: 'We Are Now Coming to New Things," in *The Human Tradition in the Civil War and Reconstruction*, ed. Steven E. Woodworth (Wilmington, Del.: SR Books, 2000), 222; Philip J. Schwartz, *Migrants against Slavery: Virginians and the Nation* (Charlottesville: University of Virginia Press, 2001), 70; and Daegan Miller, *This Radical Land: A Natural History of American Dissent* (Chicago: University of Chicago Press, 2018), 66–67.

102. Linwood Morings Boone, *The Chronological History of the Roanoke Missionary Baptist Association and Its Founders from 1866–1966* (Bloomington, Ind.: AuthorHouse, 2012), 1:45; Jack Salzman, David L. Smith, and Cornel West, eds., *Encyclopedia of African-American Culture and History* (New York: Macmillan, 1996), 3:1288.

103. Keeler, "Owen Brown's Escape," 343.

104. "A Significant Letter," *Portsmouth Transcript*, n.d., in *Daily Exchange*, December 8, 1859.

105. See "The Negro Insurrection in 1831," *New York Daily Herald*, October 19, 1859; "Harpers Ferry and Its Lesson," *The Liberator*, November 18, 1859.

106. John Brown Jr. to Fabre Geffard, April 16, 1860, in *Moniteur Haïtien*, n.d., reprinted in *Freemont Weekly Journal*, August 17, 1860.

107. "Harpers Ferry and Its Lesson," *The Liberator*, November 18, 1859.

108. "Harpers Ferry and Its Lesson."

109. Reynolds, *John Brown*, 422.

110. See Edmund Ruffin, *Anticipations of the Future, to Serve as Lessons for the Present Time* (Richmond: J. W. Randolph, 1860), 69–73.

111. Edmund Ruffin, *Agricultural, Geological, and Descriptive Sketches of Lower North Carolina, and the Similar Adjacent Lands* (Raleigh: Institution for the Deaf & Dumb & Blind, 1861), 204.

112. Cassandra Newby-Alexander, *An African American History of the Civil War in Hampton Roads* (Charleston, S.C.: History Press, 2010), 24–26.

113. S. G. Howe to J. M. Forbes, August 19, 1861, in *Letters and Recollections of John Murray Forbes*, ed. Sarah Forbes Hughes (Boston: Houghton, Mifflin, 1900), 238.

114. Newby-Alexander, *An African American History of the Civil War in Hampton Roads*, 28–29.

115. Winslow, "The Dismal Swamp," 172.

116. "Negroes Taking Refuge at Fort Monroe," *Frank Leslie's Illustrated Newspaper*, June 8, 1861.

117. J. B. Magruder to George Deas, August 9, 1861, in *The War of the Rebellion: A Compilation of the Official Records of the Union and Confederate Armies*, ser. 2, vol. 1 (Washington, D.C.: Government Printing Office, 1894), 764.

118. Marion Blackburn, "Letter from Virginia," *Archaeology* (July–August 2015), https://www.archaeology.org/issues/184-1507/letter-from/3339-letter-from-virginia -contraband-camp.

119. Edwin W. Stone, *Rhode Island in the Rebellion* (Providence: George H. Whit- ney, 1864), 351.

120. Jack Temple Kirby, *Poquosin: A Study of Rural Landscape and Society* (Chapel Hill: University of North Carolina Press, 1995), 198–99.

121. Kirby, 183–84; David J. Eicher, *The Longest Night: A Military History of the Civil War* (New York: Simon and Schuster, 2002), 201.

122. Kirby, *Pocquosin*, 184; Eicher, *The Longest Night*, 201–2.

123. L. C. Bateman, "Escape from Slavery through the Dismal Swamp: The Ex- perience of John Nichols, a Lewiston Citizen," in *A Distant War Comes Home: Maine in the Civil War Era*, ed. Donald A. Beattie, Rodney Cole, and Charles Waugh (Lanham, Md.: Down East, 196), 199–200.

124. Bateman, 200–201.

125. David Cecelski, "Escape through the Dismal Swamp," https://davidcecelski .com/2019/10/14/escape-through-the-dismal-swamp/ (accessed November 20, 2020).

126. S. Millett Thompson, *Thirteenth Regiment of New Hampshire Volunteer Infan- try in the War of the Rebellion, 1861–1865* (New York: Houghton, Mifflin, 1888), vi, 119.

127. D. J. Evans to Mr. Editor (*The Citizen*), November 20, 1863, reprinted in "3rd Regiment Cavalry, NY Volunteers Civil War Newspaper Clippings," New York State Division of Military and Naval Affairs, https://dmna.ny.gov/historic /reghist/civil/cavalry/3rdCav/3rdCavCWN.htm (accessed August 4, 2020).

128. "During War Times," *National Tribune*, October 4, 1900.

129. Bryant, *The 36th Infantry*, 18.

130. Pearson, *The Poor White*, 215–16.

131. Edward A. Wild to George H. Johnson, December 28, 1863, in *The War of the Rebellion: A Compilation of the Official Records of the Union and Confederate Armies*, ser. 1, vol. 29 (Washington, D.C.: Government Printing Office, 1890), 913.

132. "Paul Wiggins," Descriptive Rolls 36th Regiment, U.S. Colored Troops, U.S. Colored Troops Formed in North Carolina, http://www.ncgenweb.us/ncusct/cod36f .htm (accessed July 16, 2020); "Life in the Swamp," *Lorain County News*, Septem- ber 16, 1863; "Life in the Swamp [concluded]," *Lorain County News*, September 23, 1863.

133. Bryant, *The 36th Infantry*, 20.

134. "Life in the Swamp," *Lorain County News*, September 16, 1863; "Life in the Swamp [concluded]," *Lorain County News*, September 23, 1863.

135. "Life in the Swamp," *Lorain County News*, September 16, 1863; "Life in the Swamp [concluded]," *Lorain County News*, September 23, 1863; Bateman, "Escape from Slavery," 199–200; David Silkenat, *Driven from Home: North Carolina's Civil War Refugee Crisis* (Athens: University of Georgia Press, 2016), 18; Charles Grandy, interview by David Hoggard, 1937, *Born in Slavery: Slave Narratives from the Federal Writer's Project, 1936–1938*, Library of Congress, https://www.encyclopediavirginia.org/_Interview_of _Mr_Charles_Grandy_1937 (accessed March 4, 2013); James K. Bryant, *The 36th Infantry United States Colored Troops in the Civil War: A History and Roster* (Jefferson, N.C.: McFarland, 2012), 32–33; "During War Times," *National Tribune*, October 4, 1900.

136. B. S. DeForest, *Random Sketches and Wandering Thoughts* (Albany, NY: Avery Herrick, 1866), 109–10; Chandra Manning, *Troubled Refuge: Struggling for Freedom in the Civil War* (New York: Knopf Doubleday, 2017), 61; *The Yates Phalanx: Proceedings of the Annual Reunion* (Farmer City, Ill.: Republican Job Printing, 1889), 21.

137. *The Yates Phalanx*, 21.

138. Bryant, *The 36th Infantry*, 18; Edward A. Wild to George H. Johnson, December 28, 1863, in *The War of the Rebellion*, ser. 1, vol. 29, 913.

139. Stone, *Rhode Island in the Rebellion*, 351–52.

140. Thompson, *Thirteenth Regiment*, 618.

141. Bryant, *The 36th Infantry*, 10.

142. Bryant, 18; Edward A. Wild to George H. Johnson, December 28, 1863, in *The War of the Rebellion*, ser. 1, vol. 29, 913.

143. Bryant, *The 36th Infantry*, 10.

144. T. Seymour to J. W. Turner, March 25, 1864, in *The War of the Rebellion: A Compilation of the Official Records of the Union and Confederate Armies*, ser. 1, vol. 35 (Washington, D.C.: Government Printing Office, 1891), 288–90; Bryant, *The 36th Infantry*, 32.

145. "Guerillas Termed Pirates," *Boston Globe*, December 12, 1913; John G. Barrett, *The Civil War in North Carolina* (Chapel Hill: University of North Carolina Press, 1963), 178.

146. Butler declared that Wild had done "his work with great thoroughness." Patricia Catherine Click, *Time Full of Trial: The Roanoke Island Freedmen's Colony, 1862–1867* (Chapel Hill: University of North Carolina Press, 2001), 65; Barrett, *Civil War in North Carolina*, 177; Edward A. Wild to George H. Johnson, December 28, 1863, in *War of the Rebellion*, ser. 1, vol. 2, 913, 915.

147. Newby-Alexander, *An African American History of the Civil War in Hampton Roads*, 59–71.

148. "During War Times," *National Tribune*, October 4, 1900.

149. Matthew J. Graham, *The Ninth Regiment, New York Volunteers (Hawkins' Zouaves)* (New York: E. P. Cody, 1900), 214–16; *Operations on the Atlantic Coast, 1861–1865, Virginia, 1862, 1864, Vicksburg* (Boston: Military Historical Society of Massachusetts, 1912), 81.

150. Warren Scott Boyce, *Economic and Social History of Chowan County, North Carolina, 1880–1915* (New York: Columbia University Press, 1917), 244; Graham, *The Ninth Regiment*, 216, 240–41.

151. A. E. Burnside to E. M. Stanton, March 21, 1862, in *The War of the Rebellion: A Compilation of the Official Records of the Union and Confederate Armies*, ser. 2, vol. 1 (Washington, D.C.: Government Printing Office, 1894), 812.

152. Manning, *Troubled Refuge*, 61.

153. Charles Frederick Stansbury, *The Lake of the Great Dismal* (New York: Albert & Charles Boni, 1925), 45–46.

154. Boone, *The Chronological History*, 45; Lowe, "Willis Augustus Hodges," 222; Schwartz, *Migrants against Slavery*, 70; "Obituaries: Alice Walton," *Virginia Pilot*, March 9, 2010, https://www.legacy.com/obituaries/pilotonline/obituary.aspx?n=alice -walton&pid=140507067 (accessed October 28, 2020); B. D. White, "Gleanings in the History of Princess Anne County," in *Economic and Social Survey of Princess Anne County*, ed. E. E. Ferebee and J. Pendleton Wilson (Charlottesville: University of Virginia Press, 1924), 11.

155. *Norfolk Virginian*, December 7, 1878. See also White, "Gleanings," 11.

156. Lowe, "Willis Augustus Hodges," 218. See also Brent Tarter, "The Remarkable Hodges Family of Princess Anne County and Norfolk," *Uncommonwealth: Voices from the Library of Virginia*, https://uncommonwealth.virginiamemory.com /blog/2019/03/06/the-hodges-family/ (accessed July 9, 2020); Boone, *The Chronological History*, 45.

157. Hodges, *Free Man of Color*, 57–59.

158. Silkenat, *Driven from Home*, 18; Vincent Colyer, *Report of the Services Rendered by the Freed People to the United States Army, in North Carolina* (New York: Vincent Colyer, 1864), 17–22. The swamp in which Kinnegy marooned was somewhere in eastern North Carolina north of Goldsboro. How far north is not clear, although historian David Silkenat places Kinnegy in the Great Dismal Swamp.

159. "A Letter from Suffolk, Va.—The Dismal Swamp," *Philadelphia Inquirer*, November 19, 1862.

160. "An Adventure in the Dismal Swamp," *Cosmopolitan* 1, no. 2 (April 1886): 99–102. Quote in original: "'nuff fur dis business."

161. Kirby, *Poquosin*, 185. See also Frederick Phisterer, ed., *New York in the War of the Rebellion, 1861 to 1865* (Albany, N.Y.: Weed, Parsons, 1890), 170, 210, 211.

162. Richard Benbury Creecy, *Grandfather's Tales of North Carolina History* (Raleigh: Edwards & Broughton, 1901), 235–36.

163. George Haven Putnam, *Memories of My Youth, 1844–1865* (New York: G. P. Putnam's Sons, 1914), 427.

164. "The War in the Carolina Swamps," *Richmond Examiner*, n.d., in *Fayetteville Weekly Observer*, January 18, 1864.

165. Creecy, *Grandfather's Tales*, 234; Jesse F. Pugh, *Three Hundred Years along the Pasquotank: A Biographical History of Camden County* (Durham, N.C.: Seeman, 1957), 162.

166. Edward A. Wild to George H. Johnson, December 28, 1863, in *War of the Rebellion*, ser. 1, vol. 29, 915; Kirby, *Poquosin*, 184–85.

167. Pugh, *Three Hundred Years*, 162; Putnam, *Memories*, 427.

168. L. J. Johnson to Cousin, August 22, 1863, in *North Carolina Civil War Documentary*, ed. W. Buck Yearns and John Gilchrist Barrett (Chapel Hill: University of North Carolina Press, 1980), 48; Johnson, *Tales from Old Carolina*, 235.

169. Richard Dillard, *Civil War in Chowan County, North Carolina* (n.p., 1916), 14.

170. Brenda Chambers McKean, *Blood and War at My Doorstep* (Bloomington, Ind.: Xlibris, 2011), 408.

171. "For the Register," *Raleigh Register*, October 25, 1862.

172. Thomas C. Parramore, *Cradle of the Colony: The History of Chowan County and Edenton, North Carolina* (Edenton, NC: Edenton Chamber of Commerce, 1967), 75; Earl J. Hess, *Lee's Tar Heels: The Pettigrew-Kirkland-MacRae Brigade* (Chapel Hill: University of North Carolina Press, 2002), 340; "For the Register," *Raleigh Register*, October 25, 1862.

173. Phil Rubio, "Civil War Reenactments and Other Myths," in *Race Traitor*, ed. Noel Ignatiev and John Garvey (New York: Routledge, 1996), 187.

174. Creecy, *Grandfather's Tales*, 234–36.

175. "The War in the Carolina Swamps," *Fayetteville Weekly Observer*, January 18, 1864.

176. "Guerillas Termed Pirates," *Boston Globe*, December 12, 1913.

177. "Old Times in Betsy," *Weekly Economist*, August 31, 1900.

178. Edward Alfred Pollard, *Southern History of the War: The Third Year of the War* (New York: Charles B. Richardson, 1865), 172. See also Putnam, *Memories*, 427.

179. Pollard, *Southern History*, 171.

180. Herbert Aptheker, *To Be Free: Studies in American Negro History* (New York: International, 1968), 30.

181. J. H. Duncan to Joseph Finegan, January 21, 1865, *The War of the Rebellion: A Compilation of the Official Records of the Union and Confederate Armies*, series 1, vol. 46 (Washington, D.C.: Government Printing Office, 1895), 1144–45.

182. Quoted in Andrew F. Smith, "Did Hunger Defeat the Confederacy?," *North and South* 13, no. 1 (May 2011): 45.

183. Joseph Wheelan, *Their Last Full Measure: The Final Days of the Civil War* (Philadelphia: Da Capo, 2015), 59.

184. "Confederate Emancipation," in William L. Barney, *The Oxford Encyclopedia of the Civil War* (New York: Oxford University Press, 2011), 84.

185. "Jeff Davis Fighting for Negro Equality," *Chicago Tribune*, November 4, 1864.

186. "Sketches in Color," *Putnam's Magazine* 4, no. 24 (December 1869): 742. Quote in original: "heered de news, dat de n— all b'longed ter darselves now."

187. Arnold, *The Dismal Swamp*, 39.

188. "$40 Reward," *Old North State*, October 13, 1849.

189. Bateman, "Escape from Slavery," 201.

190. Details regarding Abraham Lester and family are drawn from "Life in the Swamp," *Lorain County News*, September 16, 1863, and "Life in the Swamp [concluded]," *Lorain County News*, September 23, 1863.

EPILOGUE

1. John Habberton, "When Boys Were Men," *Winnipeg Tribune*, June 9, 1903.

2. "The Dismal Swamp," *Neenah (Wisc.) Daily Times*, April 19, 1900; F. Roy Johnson, *Tales from Old Carolina* (Murfreesboro, N.C.: Johnson, 1965), 160. See also "The Dismal Swamp," *New York Times*, n.d., in *Neenah Daily Times*, April 19, 1900.

3. Frank H. Taylor, "Tide-Water Virginia," *The Independent*, January 22, 1891.

4. Sayers, *A Desolate Place*, 25.

5. "The Dismal Swamp," *New York Times*, n.d., in *Neenah Daily Times*, April 19, 1900.

6. "A Veteran on His Travels," *Richmond Dispatch*, May 13, 1876; "Old Mule Aleck," *Suffolk News-Herald*, May 12, 1937. See also "1880; Census Place: Sleepy Hole, Nansemond, Virginia; Roll: 1379; Page: 139C; and Enumeration District: 056," ancestry.com (accessed December 4, 2020).

7. "1870; Census Place: Portsmouth Jefferson Ward, Norfolk, Virginia; Roll: M593_1667; Page: 433A; Family History Library Film: 553166" and "1880; Census Place: Portsmouth, Norfolk, Virginia; Roll: 1382; Page: 521A; Enumeration District: 076," ancestry.com (accessed December 4, 2020).

8. See "Excerpts of the Speeches by Willis A. Hodges at the Constitutional Convention Held in Richmond, Virginia, 1867–68," in Hodges, *Free Man of Color: The Autobiography of Willis Augustus Hodges*, ed. Willard B. Gatewood (Knoxville: University of Tennessee Press, 1982), 83–86; *Danville Register*, September 3, 1883.

9. "1900; Census Place: Pantego, Beaufort, North Carolina; Page: 21; Enumeration District: 0006; FHL microfilm: 1241182," ancestry.com (accessed December 4, 2020); "How Garry Got Bears," *Inter Ocean* (Chicago), December 8, 1901. Quote in original: "de oldes' swamuh in de wul'."

10. Robert Arnold, *The Dismal Swamp and Lake Drummond: Early Recollections. Vivid Portrayal of Amusing Scenes* (Norfolk: Green, Burke, & Gregory, 1888), 38–39. Quote in original: "I staid dar 'til de war was ober. I cum out and hab been lookin' 'bout dis place to see if I node anybody, but dey all gone ded, an nobody nose me. I tell you, boss, when you git in de desart ef nobody ses nuffin, de runaway ketchers can't kotch you. I am berry ole now, and my home folks are all ded an gone an I no nobody."

INDEX

Aaron (Great Dismal Swamp Maroon), v, 79
abolitionist movement, 153
abolitionists, 7, 94, 98, 99, 152, 153, 155–56, 158, 160, 161, 162, 165, 167, 177, 179, 219n164, 225n34; and support of GDS maroons locally, 101; writings on GDS maroons, 1, 77, 94, 98, 101, 117, 139, 147, 155–56, 158
Abram (Great Dismal Swamp Maroon), v, 140
Ackiss, Harper, 83–85
acorns, 111, 126
Adventurers to Drain the Dismal Swamp. *See* Dismal Swamp Company
Africans, 14, 19, 23, 26, 31, 45, 46, 48, 56, 58, 69, 121, 193n62
Albemarle Assembly, 31
Albemarle County, 24, 30, 48, 80
Albemarle Sound, 2, 13, 20, 21, 24, 26, 28, 37, 38, 42, 58, 75, 82, 127, 164
alligators, 3, 51, 76, 112, 137, 148, 151
American Anti-Slavery Society, 155
American Revolution, 65, 67, 72, 75, 94, 166, 203n20; maroons' involvement in, 15, 71
Anglicans, 13, 32, 33–35
Angola Peter (Great Dismal Swamp Maroon), v, 47, 56–57
Anne, Queen, 34
Anticipations of the Future, to Serve as Lesson for the Present Time (Ruffin), 162
Aptheker, Herbert, 7, 8
Arnold, Robert, 180
arrowheads, 114, 117, 125
Ashanti, 120
Atlantic Coastal Plain, 20
Atlantic Ocean, 2, 20, 24, 35

Atlantic white cedar, 22, 124, 190n6
Atlantic world, 4, 13
axe heads, 125

Bacon's Rebellion, 30, 46
Baker Farm, 167
bald cypress, 22, 190n6
bamboo, 51
banjo, 59, 136
Baptists, 101
Barbados Company, 27
barrel staves, 127, 144, 222n231
baskets, 126
Bath (N.C.), 37
Bath County, 35
Battle of Bull Run, 163
Battle of Gettysburg, 170
Battle of South Mills, 164
Batts, Nathaniel, 26–29, 192n38
Batz, Nathaniel. *See* Batts, Nathaniel
Bay River (Native Americans), 22
beans, 111
bears, 3, 17, 52, 72, 107, 112, 126, 146, 151, 156, 177, 179
Beaufort County, North Carolina, 143
beavers, 112
bees, 104, 111, 125
Berkeley, John, 27
Berkeley, William, 27, 28, 29
Bertie County (N.C.), 39, 79, 80
Big Charles (Great Dismal Swamp Maroon), v, 79
black gum, 22, 111
Black Pioneers, 69
Blackwater mercenaries, 3
Black Water (Va.), 83, 85, 101
Blake, or, the Huts of America (Delany), 77
Blassingame, John, 104, 121, 150
Blount, Richard, 104